IMAGES
of America

Richland Township and Richlandtown Borough

On the Cover: Edwin C. Fritz had a bakery and retail store on Hellertown Avenue in Quakertown. His rural customers were served by horse-drawn delivery wagon in 1914, when this photograph was taken. By the 1940s, Fritz delivered baked goods to country folks early in the morning from his motorized van. In this image, a female customer has climbed into the wagon to make her selection. (FFIM.)

IMAGES
of America

RICHLAND TOWNSHIP AND RICHLANDTOWN BOROUGH

Robert L. Leight and
Thomas R. Moll

ARCADIA
PUBLISHING

ISBN 978-0-7385-7405-9

Published by Arcadia Publishing
Charleston, South Carolina

Printed in the United States of America

Library of Congress Control Number: 2010932478

For all general information, please contact Arcadia Publishing:
Telephone 843-853-2070
Fax 843-853-0044
E-mail sales@arcadiapublishing.com
For customer service and orders:
Toll-Free 1-888-313-2665

Visit us on the Internet at www.arcadiapublishing.com

This work is dedicated to Mary, my wife of 51 years, and the Leight family, who have lived in Richland Township since 1919.

—Robert L. Leight

To my aunt Jane, who taught at Richland Elementary School many years and has always supported my interest in history.

—Thomas R. Moll

Contents

ACKNOWLEDGMENTS

The following individuals were kind in providing images and information: Rachel Adamczyk (RA), Lisa Andrejko, Stella Bauman (SB), Bob Beck, Larry Benner, Alice Bishop, Rachel Demchick, Kathy Fedorocsko and Dale Henninger (KFDH), Elda Fox (EF), Harold Freed, Ray Fulmer, Joe Geib, Scott Godshalk, Bill Harr (BH), Bob Heitz, Lynn Hillegass (LH), Curt Hinkle (CH), George Jester, John E. Kandel (JEK), Kristen Kiehstaller (KK), Robert Leight (RL), Gerald Meyers (GM), Jocelyn and Michael Meyers, Thomas Moll (TM), Ivan Moyer (IM), Mary Musselman (MM), Leonard Musselman (LM), Arlene and Leon Refsnider (ALR), Helen Refsnider (HR), Marvin Refsnider (MR), Lyle Rosenberger (LR), Calvin Ruth (CR), Ellen and Jeffrey Schroy (JLS), Jack Schick, Steve Sechriest, Mahlon Shelly, Steven Smith (SS), pastor Sue Sosnin, Leslie Staffeld, Victor Stevens, Donna Stutzman (DS), Venanzio Poccia, Diane Wassmer (DW), David Wismer, and Lester K. Wismer (LKW). Some images were photographed by Flora Fellman and provided by Ivan Moyer (FFIM), photographed by Walter Beam and provided by Richland Historical Society (RHWB), and photographed by Ray Fulmer and provided by Robert Leight (RFRL).

These institutions were generous in contributing images: QNB (QNB), Quakertown Christian School (QCS), Phoebe Healthcare Center, Quakertown Community School District (QCSD), Richland Feed Company (RFC), Richlandtown Fire Company (RFC), Richland Historical Society (RHS), Richland Library Company (RLC), Richland Township (RT), Richlandtown Borough (RB), Richland Township Fire and Rescue RTFR), St. John's Evangelical Lutheran Church (SJL), St. John's United Church of Christ (UCC), and United Mennonite Church (UMM).

INTRODUCTION

Richland Township and Richlandtown Borough are municipalities in northern Bucks County. Bucks County was one of three original counties laid out by William Penn in 1682. Because the region that includes Richland Township was poorly drained, it was commonly called the "Great Swamp". However, when Welsh, English, and German pioneers settled in the area, they found that European farming techniques could produce fertile soil. The region came to be called "Rich Land," and the township was incorporated as "Richland Township" in 1734. The original township contained about 14,000 acres. Richlandtown Borough is located in the eastern section of the township. It was incorporated as a separate municipality in 1890.

The area located along the Lehigh River to the north of Richland Township was also being settled during the middle years of the 18th century, and a turnpike to Bethlehem passed through the township. The village of Quakertown grew up between the meetinghouse and the Red Lion Inn. It became the religious and commercial center of the township.

Members of the Society of Friends were the dominant group in the township during the 18th century. They faced an ethical dilemma during the Revolutionary War. As pacificists, their philosophy caused most of them to avoid taking a stand about independence. However, several members took oaths of allegiance to the Revolutionary cause and were dismissed from the meeting. They were reinstated after the conclusion of the war. The Liberty Bell is reputed to have been hidden behind one of the homes in colonial Quakertown. The stone house along present West Broad Street is called "Liberty Hall." The Richland Library Company was chartered in 1788, one of the first of its kind in Pennsylvania.

German ethnic groups were migrating into Pennsylvania about the same time as the incorporation of Richland Township. They were primarily from Protestant dissenting sects. German Reformed and Lutherans worshipped in churches, while Mennonites worshipped in homes or plain meetinghouses similar to the Quakers. Tensions between the ethnic Germans and Quakers broke out in 1799 when John Fries led a "rebellion" against the imposition of a property tax. One of the events of Fries Rebellion was a confrontation between the German-speaking group led by Fries and the ethnic British assessors who were setting a value on homes in order to assess the hated house tax. Several of the assessors were roughed up at the Red Lion Inn. Fries was found guilty of treason for later confrontations in Bethlehem and was sentenced to be hanged in a gallows in front of the Red Lion. Fortunately for him, Fries was pardoned at almost the last minute by Pres. John Adams.

An ethical concern of the early 19th century was slavery. Quakers took leadership in establishing an *Underground Railroad* to aid escaped slaves to freedom in Canada. Richard Moore, a potter and leader of the Quakers at the Richland Friends' Meeting recorded the number of escaped slaves who passed through his home and pottery. He helped at least 600 slaves on their way to freedom.

With the passage of the Free School Act in 1834, a network of elementary schools was established throughout the township in the villages and within walking distance of rural children. During the early 19th century, the ethnic Germans tended to live in the rural areas of the township. Eastern Pennsylvania was a bilingual region. Especially on the farms, "Pennsylvania Dutch" was a common vernacular language, although schools were conducted in English.

A railroad that ran through Richland Township to the Lehigh Valley was completed in 1855, and Quakertown was incorporated as a borough in the same year. The railroad station was about a mile from the original Quakertown. The section around the railroad station had its own post office (Richland Centre), and Richland Centre became a busy hub of commercial and industrial activity. In 1874, Richland Centre was incorporated as part of Quakertown, although the post office continued in Richland Centre for several decades. The railroad also had a station at the village of Shelly, and stores and factories were in operation there after the Civil War.

When Quakertown became a separate municipality, the remainder of Richland Township was primarily rural, although several villages such as Richlandtown and Rich Hill had their own post offices and stores. During the 19th century, a network of dirt roads was laid out as farm families built impressive stone homes and large barns and other outbuildings. Most 19th-century farms could be considered to be general farms, as farm families produced most of their foodstuffs on the premises. The main cash crop was dairy products. Farmers took their milk to creameries to be processed for retail sale.

With a post office, inn, public school, stores, and several factories, Richlandtown petitioned to have the borough form of government, becoming an autonomous borough in 1890. Within the decade, the new borough was linked with Quakertown by both railroad and trolley service. There was hourly trolley service to Quakertown. The Quakertown and Eastern Railroad was completed to the Delaware River to the east. Manufactured products could be sent from Richlandtown to the east and on the New York or to Quakertown and then to Philadelphia or the Lehigh Valley.

Farm families were large, and often produced a surplus of labor beyond what was needed on family farms. By 1880, many farm children, both male and female, left school after the eighth grade to work in factories in Richlandtown, Quakertown, neighboring boroughs, or at Bethlehem Steel. Large brick factories in Richlandtown and Quakertown produced shoes, cigars, clothing, harnesses, and other manufactured products.

During the first two decades of the 20th century, train service to Philadelphia and its suburbs brought city tourists to Richland to enjoy rural life. People would take the train to the station in Quakertown or Shelly and be picked up by a farm family. During a week of vacation, the city folks could enjoy the fresh air and fine food from farm kitchens. Train or trolley service could work the other way. Rural families could enjoy an excursion by rail to amusement parks such as Willow Grove.

Tohickon Creek, as the only substantial waterway in the township, was a local recreational site. A dam allowed boating and swimming near the bridge on Richlandtown Pike. During the winter, ice was harvested from the Tohickon for iceboxes in kitchens before refrigerators were in common use.

By the 1920s, the automobile began to challenge horse-drawn and rail transportation. Farmers favored all-weather roads in order to get their products to consumers and train stations. It became a priority of state government to macadamize secondary roads in the country. During the first few decades of the 20th century, telephones and rural mail delivery began to link rural farms to the towns. During the 1920s and 1930s, enrollment in secondary schooling increased. Richlandtown even had its own high school, although enrollment was not sufficient to justify its small program, which was terminated in 1927, about the same time that trolley service between Quakertown and Richlandtown ended. After 1929, bus service had replaced the trolley between Richlandtown and Quakertown.

A major development of the Depression years was the construction of a federal highway through the township to relieve traffic on the Bethlehem Pike. U.S. Route 309 entered the township close to Rich Hill in the south, cut through farms to the west and south of Quakertown, and ran close to Shelly Station on its way to Lehigh County and the coal regions. Gas stations, restaurants, and stores soon filled in along the highway. The section of Route 309 near Quakertown was named

West End Boulevard. Three restaurants became well known: Trainer's Restaurant, Benetz Inn, and Meyers' Family Restaurant.

The Depression hit hard, as farmers had a difficult time protecting their farms from sheriff sale. When the United States entered the Second World War, farms and factories ramped up to full production in the war effort. Farms in the township diversified to produce vegetables, such as tomatoes for Campbell's Soup Company, poultry, and swine.

After the conclusion of World War II, there was an exodus from the city to once-rural areas. At first, newly constructed ranch houses filled in between the farm lanes on secondary roads. Children from these homes were part of the postwar baby boom. Later zoning in Richland Township directed development into planned areas of industrial parks, commercial properties along Route 309, and into housing developments, which consumed many of the farms in the township. Mainly because of housing developments, population in the township more than doubled during the 40 years from 1970 to 2000. Census records show the following growth of population: 1970, 4,089; 1980, 6,286, 1990, 8,560, and 2,000, 9,920.

The short history above was a narrative "snapshot" of the development of a community over 300 years. The pages that follow will feature some actual snapshots of selected events. The vintage photographs that follow will recall a way of life that is far different than the Richland Township and Richlandtown of today.

One

Early Richland

This chapter describes early Richland from 1710 to 1855. Those dates bookmark important events in the history of the township. The first permanent European settlers came in 1710. And the year 1855 has a dual importance: the railroad was completed through the township in 1855 and the main village, Quakertown, became a separate government unit, a borough.

The early history of Richland is intertwined with the religious life of the Quakers. Peter Lester is credited with being the earliest settler, and the first religious meetings were held in his home. By 1729, a lot was purchased for a permanent meetinghouse at the present location of the Friend's meeting. A petition for township status was granted to Richland by Bucks County in 1734.

A trail from Philadelphia to Bethlehem passed close to the meetinghouse as did another from Milford to Newtown, then the county seat. The settlement around them became known as Quakertown. Walter McCoole built a tavern at the intersection of the two roads. Later the Liberty Bell is reported to have been hidden close by. An episode in Fries Rebellion took place in and around the Red Lion Inn. By 1803, there was a Quakertown post office.

Perhaps the most respected individual in Richland Township during the decades from 1820 to his death in 1874 was a Quaker, Richard Moore. Moore had two major careers. At first, he was a teacher. He then purchased a thriving pottery and had a fine house built next to it. His major importance was as the conscience of the community, as his home and pottery were stations on the Underground Railroad helping escaped slaves find freedom.

When an actual railroad connected Richland Township with Philadelphia and the Lehigh Valley in 1855, it marked the end of an era and the beginning of another. Quakertown, Richland Centre, and Richlandtown became residential and commercial centers; Richland Township became known for its fine farms.

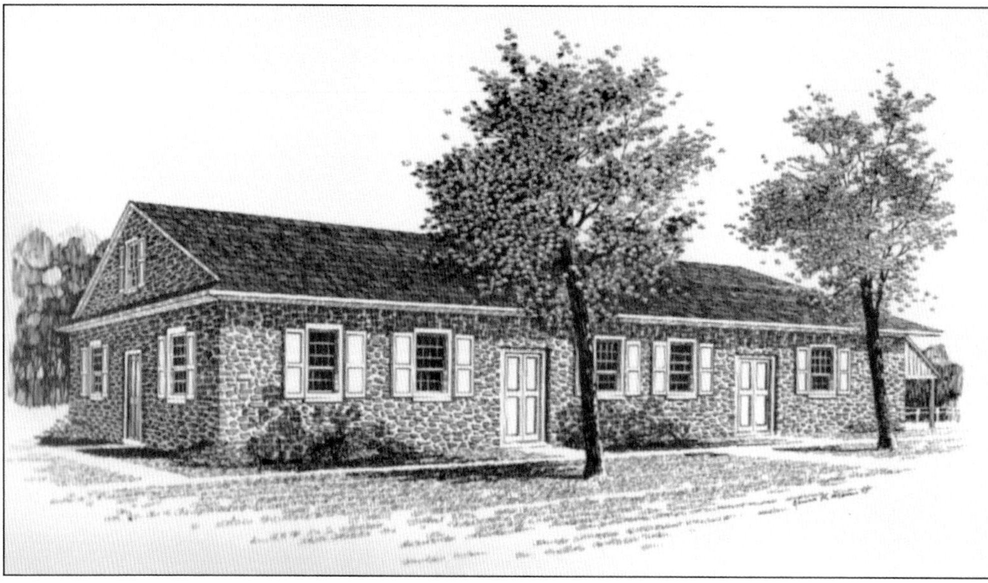

The first meetinghouse erected by the Friends in Richland Township was located at what is now the intersection of Station Road and Old Bethlehem Pike. Due to problems with securing clear title to the land, a new site was selected for a meetinghouse further north. The second meetinghouse was constructed about 1730 on 10 acres donated by Morris Morris at what is now Main Street in Quakertown. This is an artist's rendering (above) of the Friends meetinghouse erected in 1795. It was constructed of stone. In 1862, the Friends sold 4 acres of their property in order to finance the construction of a larger meetinghouse (below). This meetinghouse still serves the Friends in Quakertown. (Above, QNB; below, TM.)

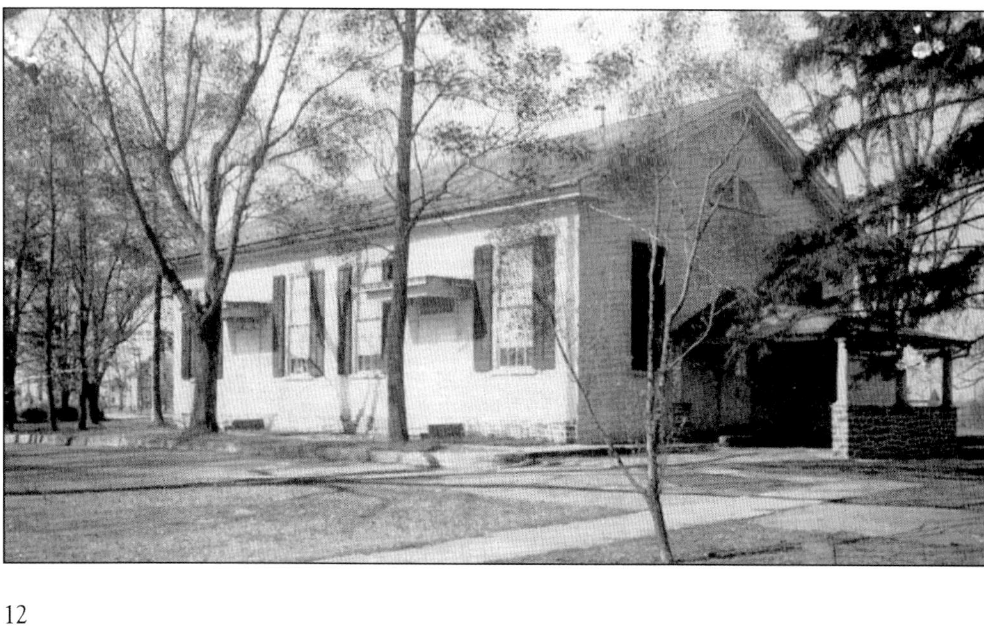

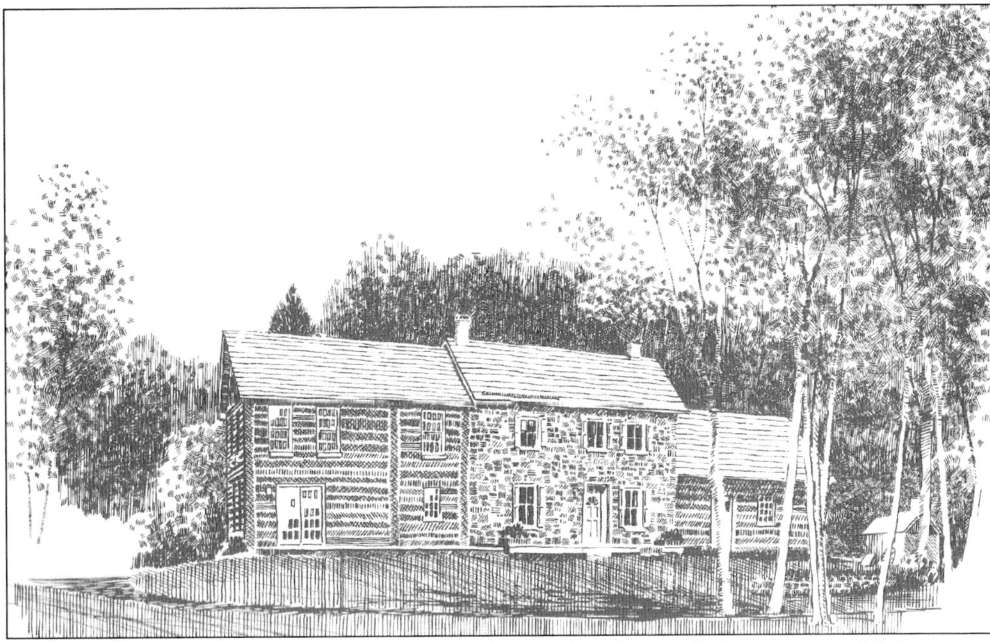

Hugh Foulke was a pioneer settler in Richland Township. He settled on a tract of 313 acres on the west side of the road to Durham, now known as California Road. Hugh Foulke divided his land between his sons Theophilus and Samuel in 1756; Samuel received the home above. When Samuel died in 1797, the house passed to his son John. The Foulke home, as depicted in the above sketch, was built in three distinct sections. At the time of the Direct Tax of 1798, the central stone section of the house had already been constructed. The longevity of the residence is a testament to how well it was built and maintained throughout its life, as seen in the photograph below. (Above, QNB; below, RT.)

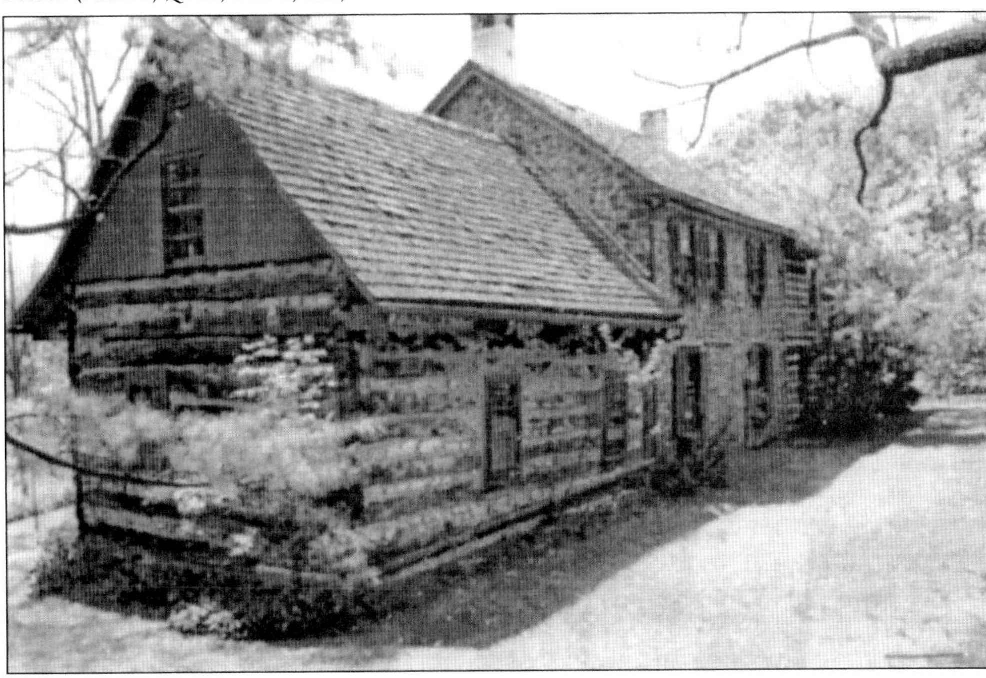

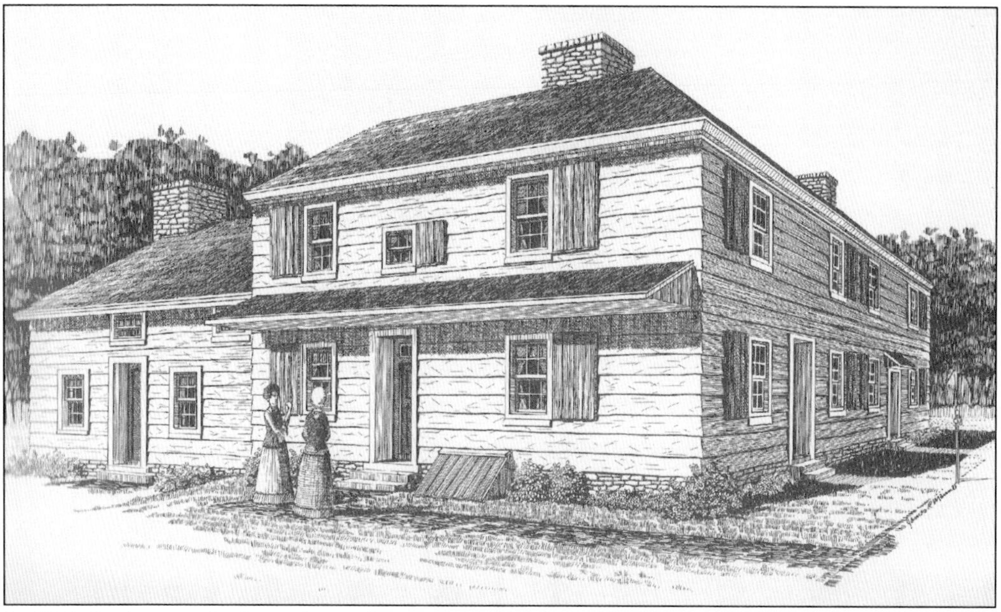

In 1799, this house, which was located on present West Broad Street, was the home of Squire Griffith. Cephas Childs, one of the assessors challenged by John Fries, had taken refuge in the house during the confrontation at the Red Lion Inn. Fries took Childs to the inn, where Childs was verbally abused by the crowd. The house was later the home of civic leader Joseph Lancaster. (QNB.)

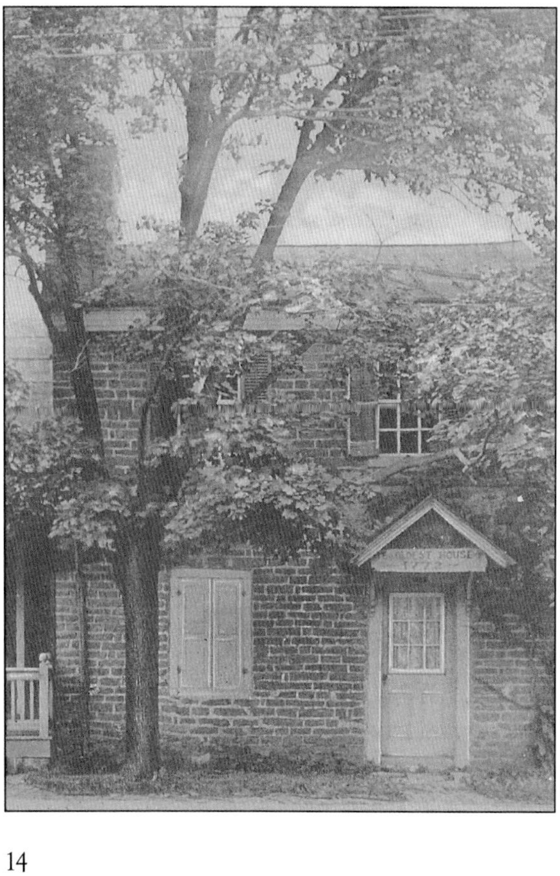

Called Liberty Hall, this edifice on what is now West Broad Street in Quakertown was once owned by John Foulke. The building dates to 1772. The Liberty Bell was hidden under a stack of hay behind this building on the night of September 23, 1777. A wagon carried the bell up the Old Bethlehem Pike from Philadelphia to a hiding place in Allentown. (TM.)

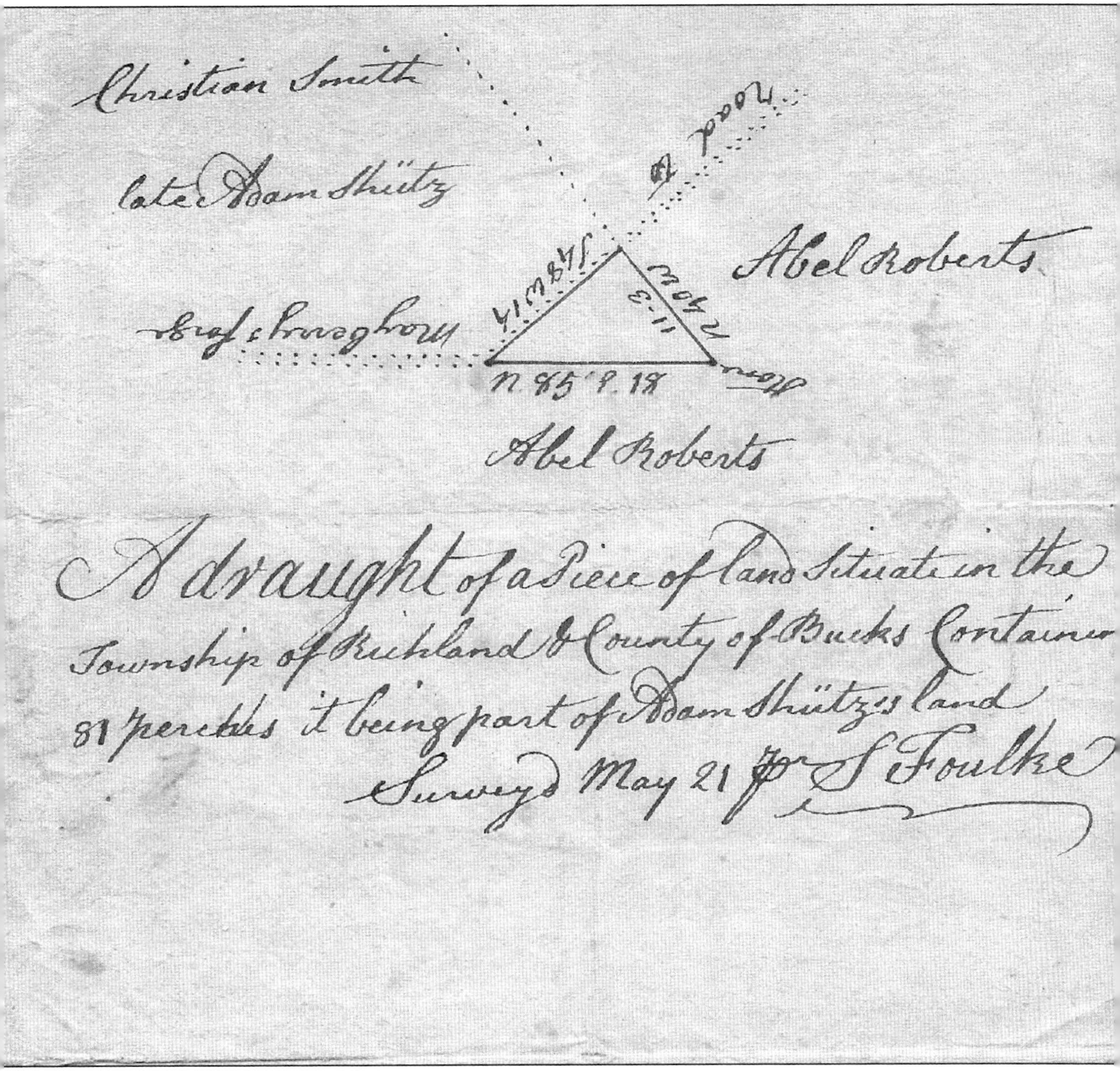

Samuel Foulke, who was born in 1718, was active in the early development of Richland. He was elected clerk of the Richland Monthly Meeting in 1742 and held the post until 1779. Foulke was elected to the provincial assembly, where he served from 1761 to 1768. He was justice of the peace for many years in Richland Township and was responsible for writing many early wills, deeds, and other legal documents. He is credited with drafting an early map of Richland in 1767, on which the contemporary landholders are identified, and he completed the above survey for a small plot of land in Richland sold by Adam Shuetz. In Foulke's time, it was common to include with the deed a draft of the tract being sold, so he must have done a lively business. Samuel Foulke died in Richland in 1797. (RLC.)

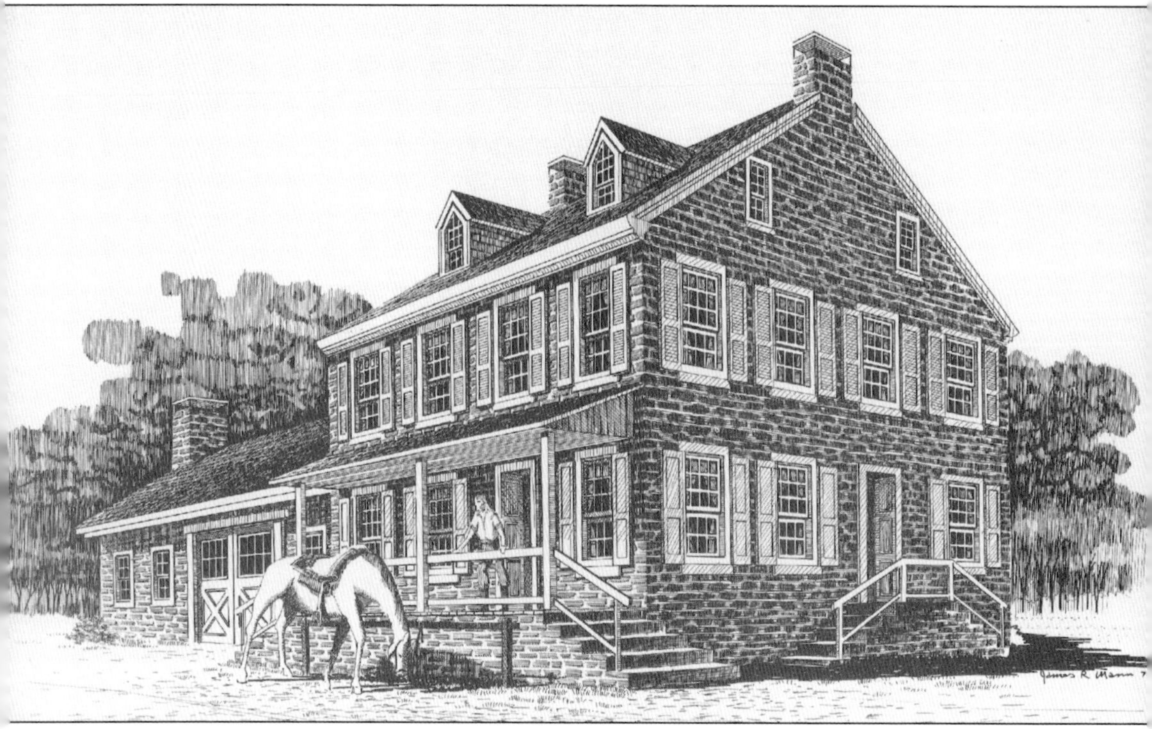

This sketch depicts the inn now known as McCoole's tavern in 1799, when it was the scene of important events in Fries' Rebellion. On March 6, 1799, John Fries of Milford Township led a group of about 100 men to the tavern. They threatened and manhandled two officials who had been attempting to assess properties in Milford Township earlier in the day. Although there were threats of violence, Fries was a moderating influence and helped to defuse the situation. The next day, Fries led a larger force to the Sun Inn in Bethlehem, where he negotiated the release of two prisoners who were being held by federal marshals. News of these incidents reached Philadelphia, and a federal army was dispatched. Fries was captured near Rich Hill. According to eyewitness reports, residents of Richland Township were harassed by the federal troops. (QNB.)

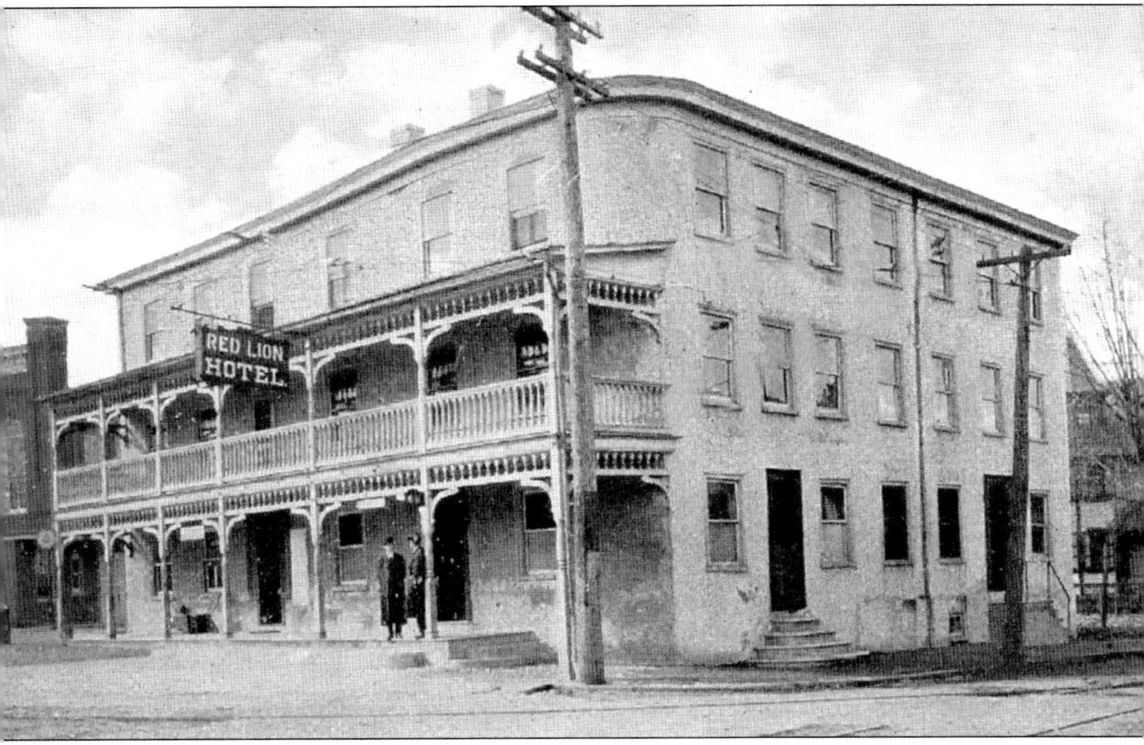

The Red Lion Inn has been remodeled several times during the last two centuries. By the 20th century, a full third story and two-story porch had been added to the edifice. In 1800, however, the area in front of the inn had been selected as a spot for a gallows. After leading the protest against the "window tax," John Fries and two associates, Frederick Heany and John Getman, were tried for treason. They were convicted and sentenced to be hanged. Fries was imprisoned until the sentence could be carried out. While in prison, Fries wrote to Pres. John Adams to "save him from an ignominious death, and to rescue a large, and hitherto happy family, from misery and ruin." Fortunately for Fries and his friends, President Adams pardoned them just 48 hours before the sentence was to be carried out. (TM.)

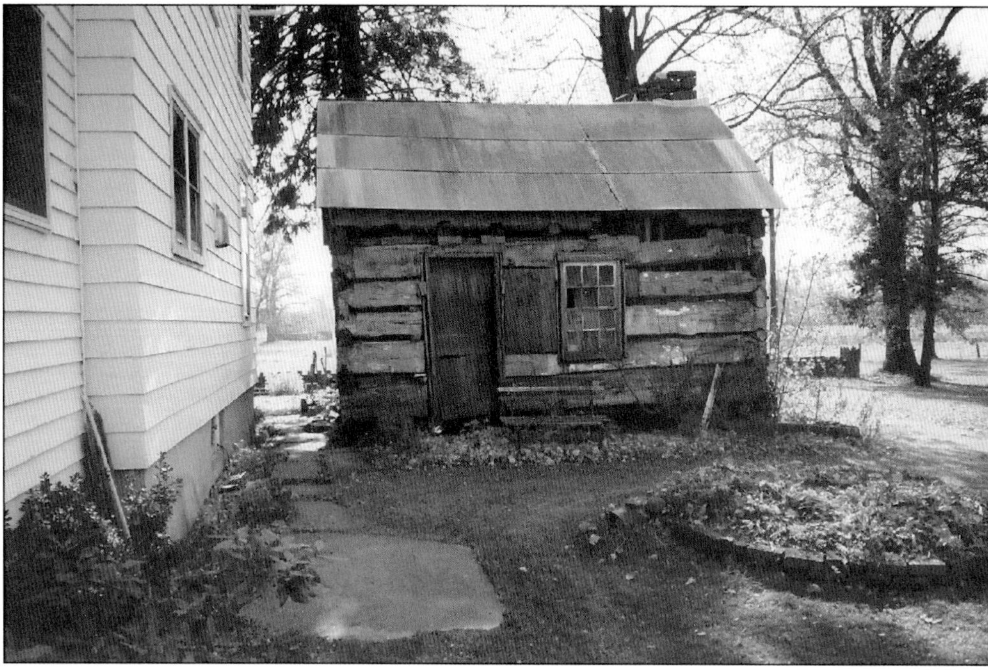

This small log dwelling is one of the few extant examples of the type of home the earliest settlers would have constructed. The structure is a single room with a stone fireplace and chimney at one end. There is a small loft. The logs are of chestnut, and the house has a few windows and a single door. It still stands on Erie Road. (CR.)

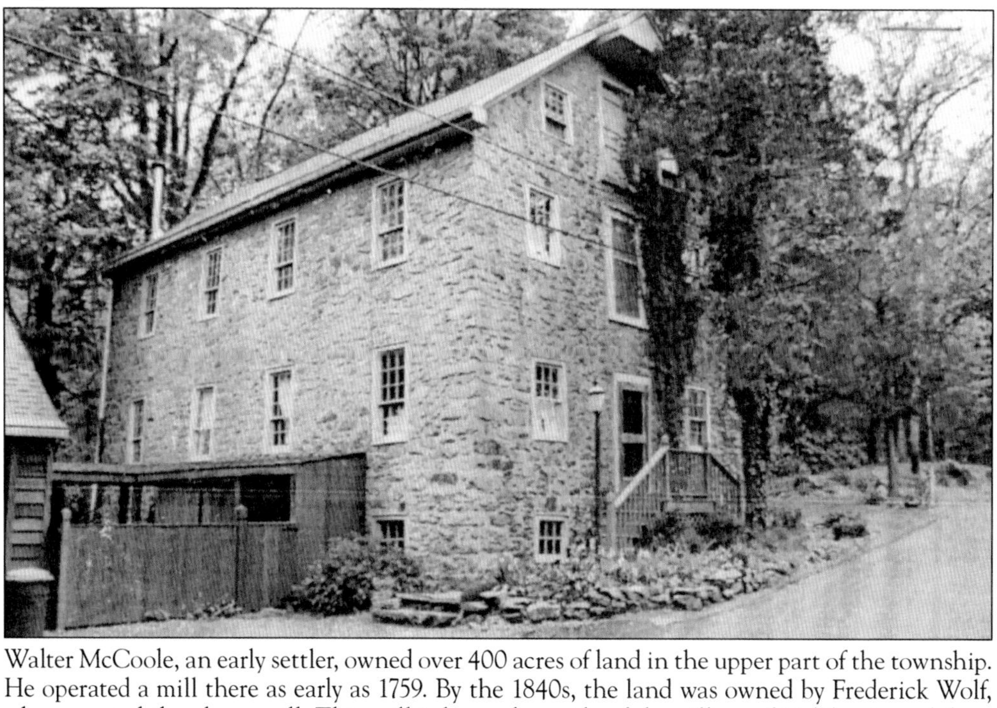

Walter McCoole, an early settler, owned over 400 acres of land in the upper part of the township. He operated a mill there as early as 1759. By the 1840s, the land was owned by Frederick Wolf, who operated the above mill. This mill is located outside of the village of California and drew its power from the Tohickon Creek. (RT.)

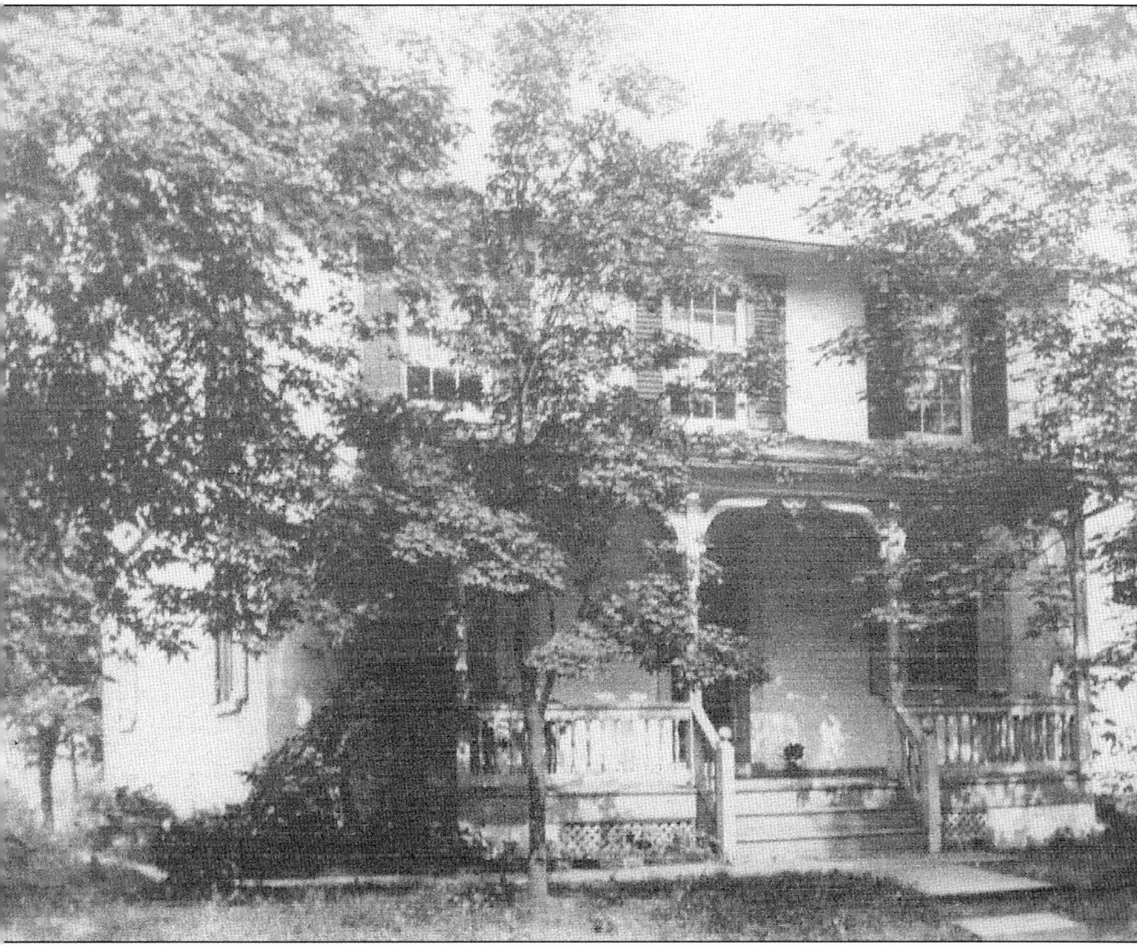

The early settlers of Richland valued knowledge, and in 1788 some of them resolved to organize the Richland Library Company. For a subscription of 20 shillings, a person could own a share of reading stock in the library, which allowed the subscriber borrowing privileges and the ability to propose titles for acquisition. By 1790, one hundred thirty-one books had been purchased for the collection. The stockholders secured a charter from the Commonwealth of Pennsylvania in 1795. During the early years, the library had no permanent home; books were housed with the librarian or in rented rooms. In 1911, Susan Foulke made her house (above) available to the library. The library still utilizes this building on Main Street, Quakertown, and operates as a corporate entity under the terms of its original charter. It is one of the oldest libraries in the state and continues to serve the public. (RLC.)

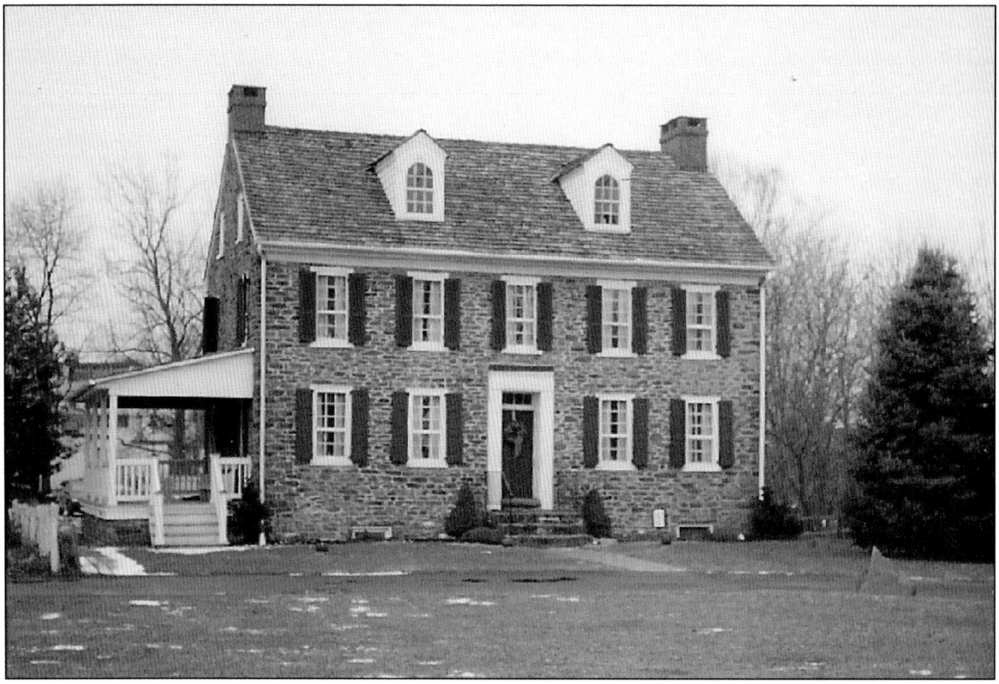

Edward Foulke built this stone house in 1812 and was elected the first burgess of Quakertown in 1854. The home stood on the road to Trumbauersville, several hundred feet west of the Richland meetinghouse. When Route 309 was constructed through Richland, the house was left close to the highway. When development threatened to raze the structure, local citizens raised $40,000 to move the entire house to Quakertown. (RL.)

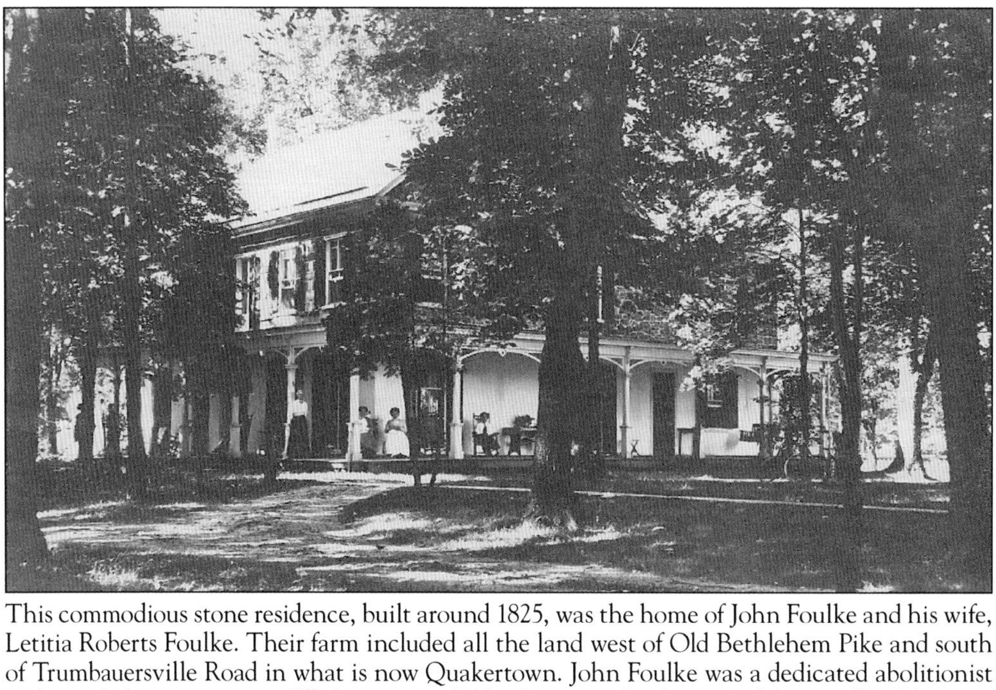

This commodious stone residence, built around 1825, was the home of John Foulke and his wife, Letitia Roberts Foulke. Their farm included all the land west of Old Bethlehem Pike and south of Trumbauersville Road in what is now Quakertown. John Foulke was a dedicated abolitionist and traveled many times to Washington to lobby Congress for the end of slavery. (RLC.)

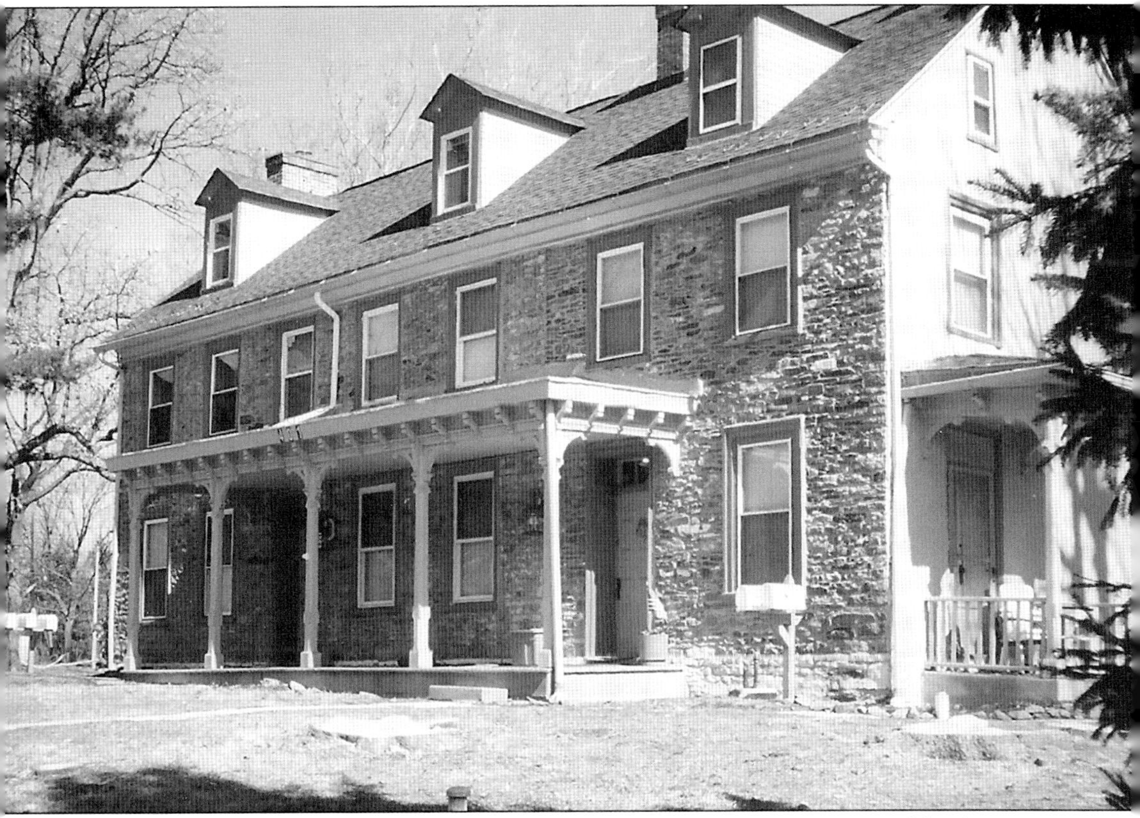

This large stone residence was once the home of Richard Moore, who came to Richland in 1818 as a teacher. He married Sarah Foulke in 1819. Moore taught for seven years and then acquired a tract of land south of Quakertown upon which he conducted a pottery. He built the above home in 1834. Moore was active in the anti-slavery movement, and the house served as a station on the Underground Railroad. After helping a large number of fugitive slaves, Moore began to keep a record of the slaves he helped and documented that well over 600 slaves passed through Richland Township on their way to freedom. Runaway slaves were hidden in the barn, under straw, during the day. They were smuggled from the property in the pottery wagon. The house was enlarged for Richard's son Jackson Moore, and the pottery operated until about 1880. (RL.)

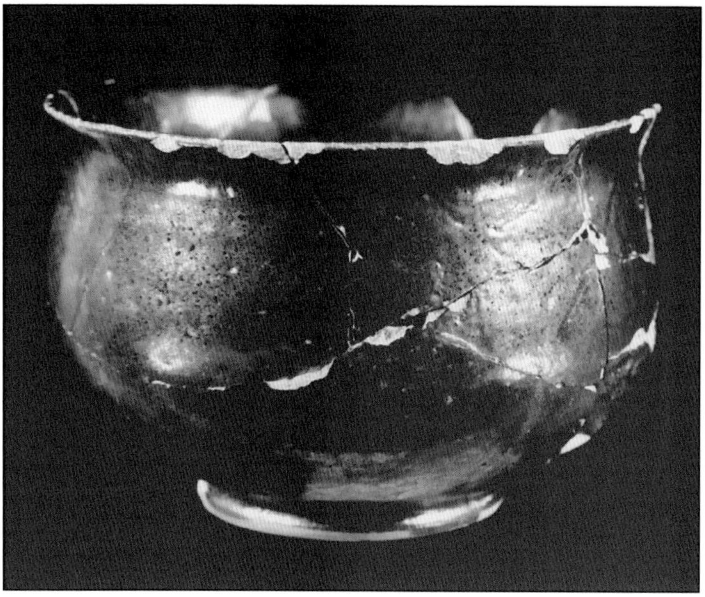

This porringer was excavated from the Penrose-Moore Pottery by Prof. Lyle Rosenberger and his students from the historic preservation program at Bucks County Community College. Pottery manufactured in the facility was typical of the product of potteries in the early 1800s. Richard Moore purchased the pottery about 1828. By 1850, it was one of the largest industries in Richland Township. (LR.)

This is a redware dish excavated from the site of the Moore pottery behind the Richard Moore house. It is displayed by the Quakertown Historical Society in the Burgess Foulke House on Main Street. Copies of the original dish were made as souvenirs for the 150th anniversary of the incorporation of Quakertown. Although the former Moore property is now within Quakertown, it was in Richland Township during his lifetime. (LR.)

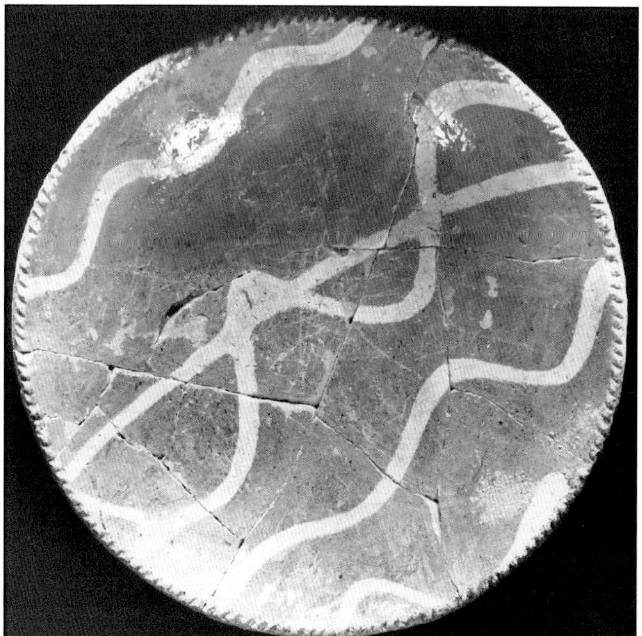

Two

RICHLANDTOWN

Early Richlandtown grew up around a church and an inn. Lutheran and German Reformed congregations constructed the union church building in 1808. By 1812, an inn, first called the Spread Eagle, had begun operation. There was a U.S. Post Office as early as 1839. Population in the village and the area around it grew sufficiently that a new brick two-room schoolhouse was constructed in 1855.

Like many of the villages in Upper Bucks County in the period after the Civil War, the community grew and attracted manufacturing and commercial enterprises as well as homes. By 1890 a group within the village petitioned to incorporate Richlandtown as a borough. Henry Freed was elected as the first chief burgess and, along with his brothers, had established the town's major industry, a shoe factory. By the time of its incorporation, Richlandtown was virtually self-sufficient. Within the borough were shoe and cigar factories, butchers, doctors, blacksmiths, feed dealers, and a creamery.

Important to the new borough was its connections to markets such as Philadelphia and the Lehigh Valley. During the 1890s Richlandtown was linked with Quakertown by trolley and railroad. Telephones were in use as early as 1905, and the church was electrified by 1913.

Early in the 20th century, the Richlandtown Volunteer Fire Company began service. A new four-room borough school was built in 1909. In addition to the fire company, Richlandtown has had many community associations, including the Richlandtown Playground Association, Lions Club, and Boy and Girl Scouts. The Playground Association sponsored local baseball and basketball teams. It purchased 13 acres in 1941 and in 1950 decided to build a hall. The hall was named for Charles Benner, a sailor who had lost his life in the Second World War. Community life in Richlandtown has centered around its churches, the fire company, Benner Hall, and youth organizations such as the Scouts.

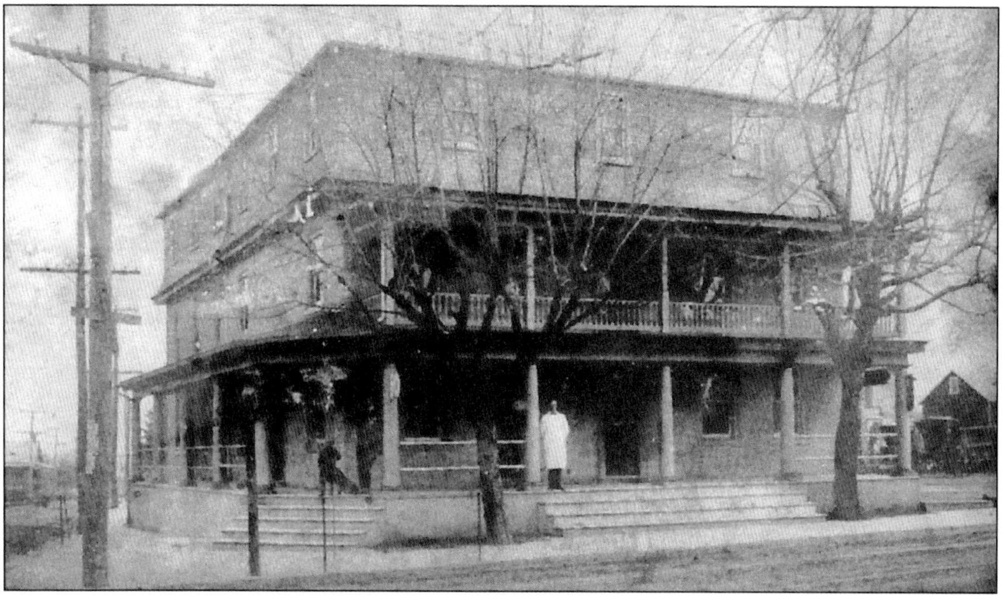

There was an inn called the Spread Eagle in what is now Richlandtown as early as 1812. Various owners conducted the establishment during the 19th century. Frank Weller, who owned it about 1907, changed the exterior to stucco and added a third story (above). The inn was given the name Eagle Hotel in 1936 (below) and renamed Richlandtown Inn in 1983. The present bar actually dates to 1904. The stone building behind the hotel was constructed in 1897 and was originally a carriage house and livery stable. During the 20th century, it was used for meetings and shows. It is presently Carriage House Apartments. (Above, RB; below, LH.)

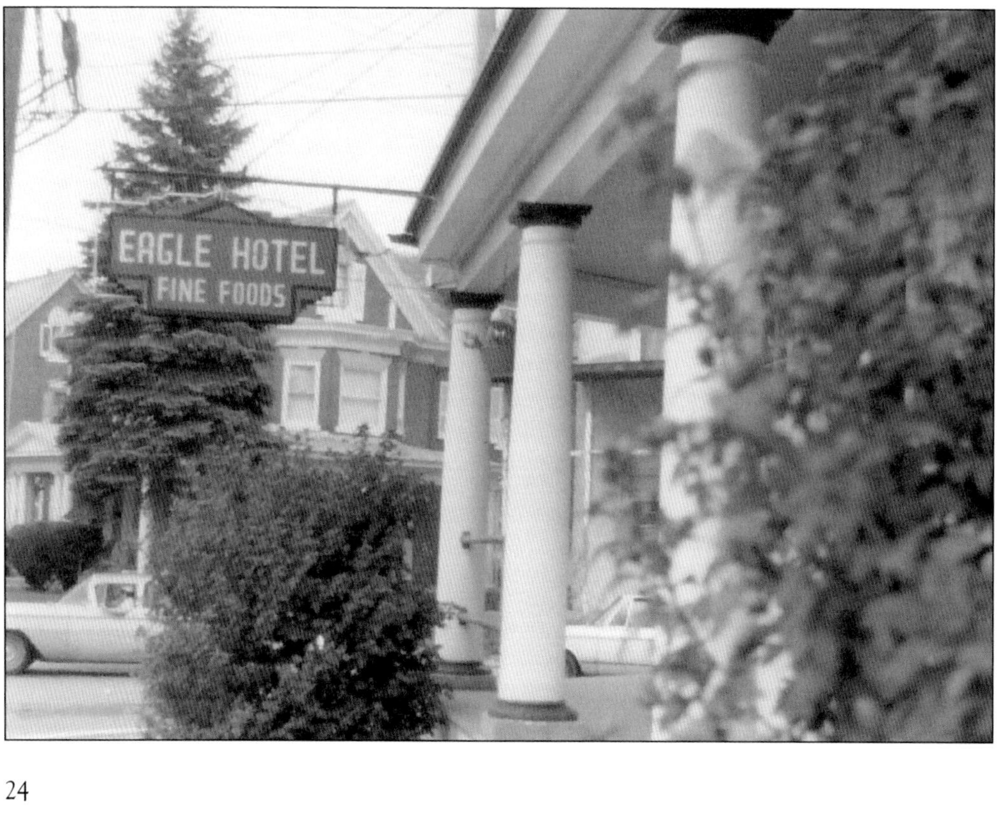

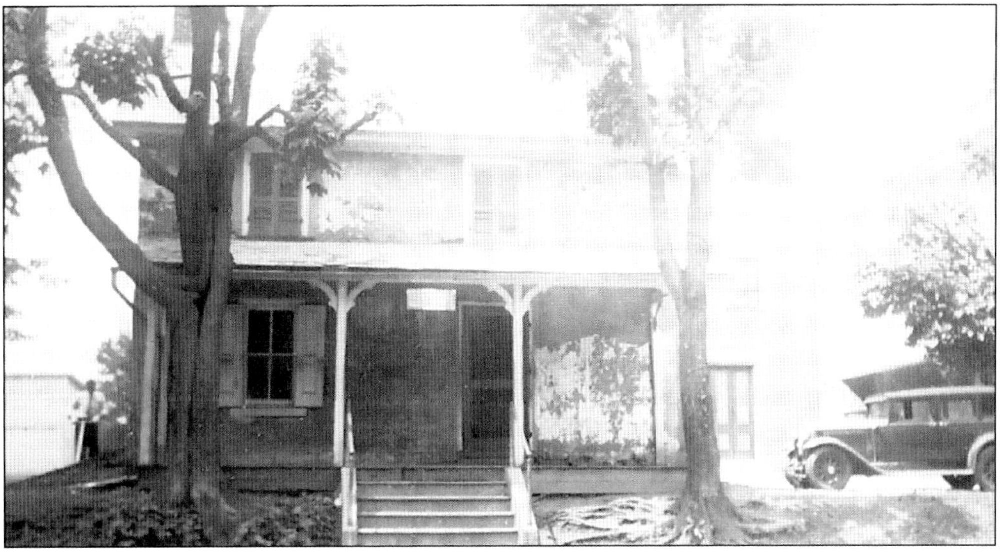

The first post office was established in 1828, with John Matts as postmaster. The post office name, and therefore the name of the village, was changed to Richlandtown in 1839. The second postmaster was Christian Snyder, who was followed in the post by Charles Diehl, Amandus Kemmerer, Lewis Benner, Charles Fellman, Wayne Gabel, Milton Weaver, Jacob Benner, and James Shelly. In 1914, the post office moved to this building at 16 North Main Street when John E. Freed was postmaster. The photograph above shows the post office in the 1940s. This post office was still in use when the photograph below was taken in 1989. The original porch and steps were removed; the building had been plastered, and the facade was remodeled. (HR.)

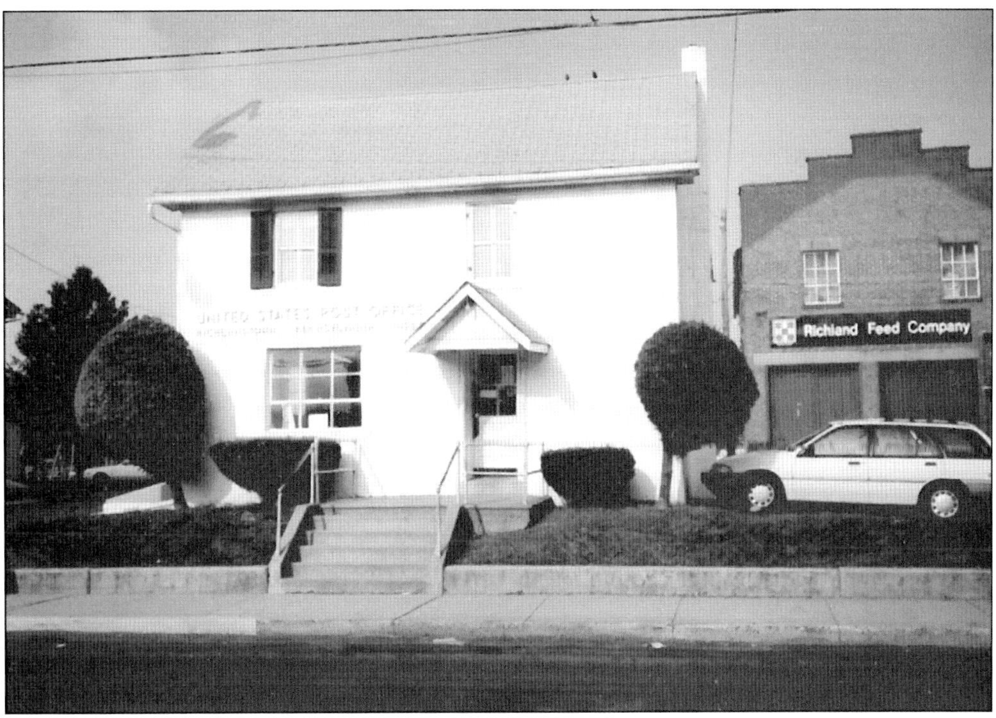

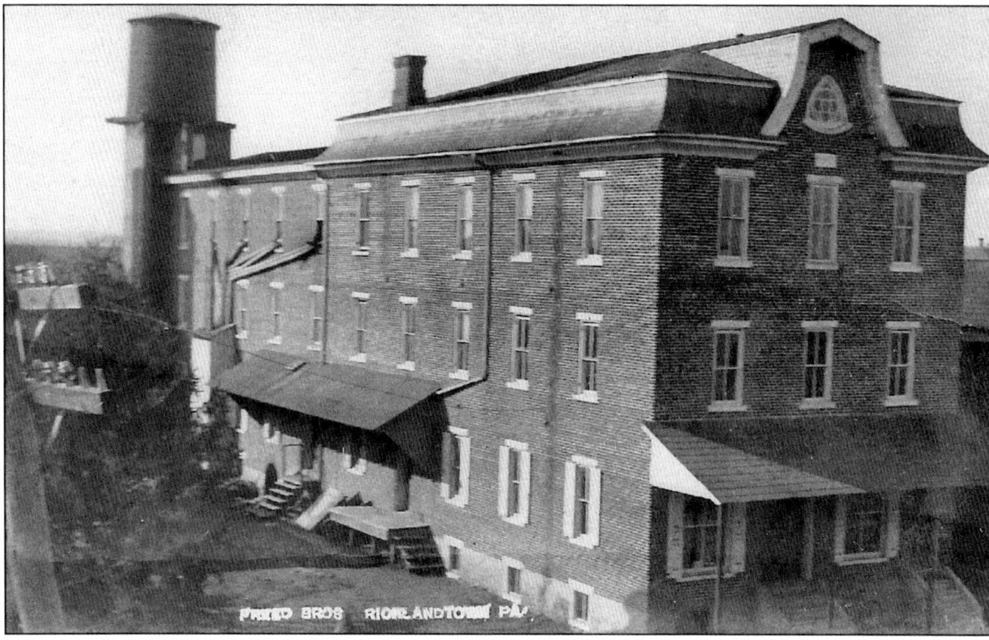

Henry W. Freed commenced his shoemaking business in 1851 and produced footwear for 22 years. In 1861, his brothers William D. Freed and Charles E. Freed began to manufacture shoes in Richland Township. In 1874, the three brothers formed a partnership called Freed Brothers and built a three-story factory on Main Street (above). By around 1900, they employed over 150 workers, who could turn out 800 pairs of shoes per day. By 1902, Harvey Freed, son of William Freed, had been admitted to the business as a full partner. In the early 20th century, the company advertised "hand-made boots and shoes" and promised to fill orders promptly (below). The business operated until 1943. (Both, JLS.)

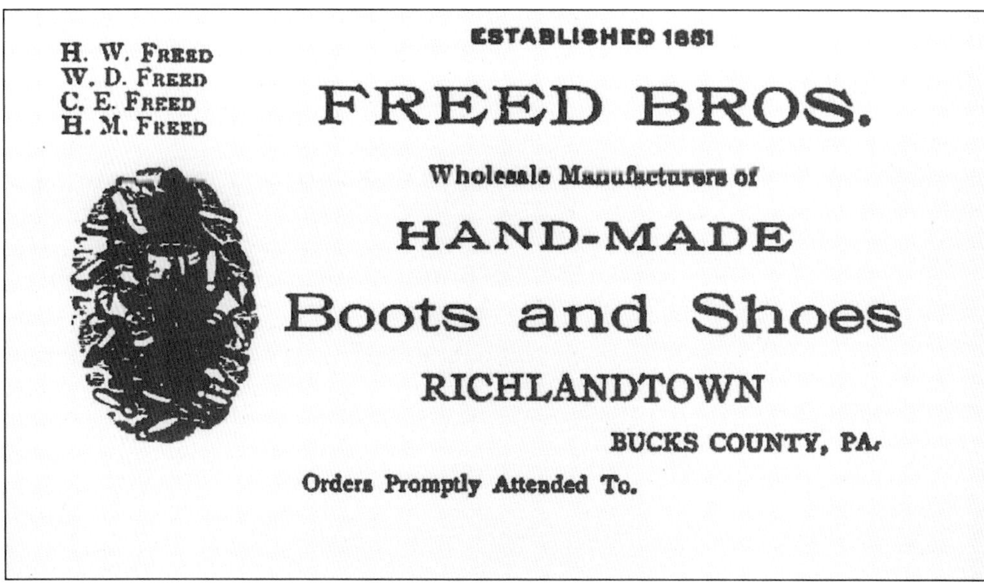
H. W. FREED
W. D. FREED
C. E. FREED
H. M. FREED

ESTABLISHED 1851

FREED BROS.

Wholesale Manufacturers of

HAND-MADE

Boots and Shoes

RICHLANDTOWN

BUCKS COUNTY, PA.

Orders Promptly Attended To.

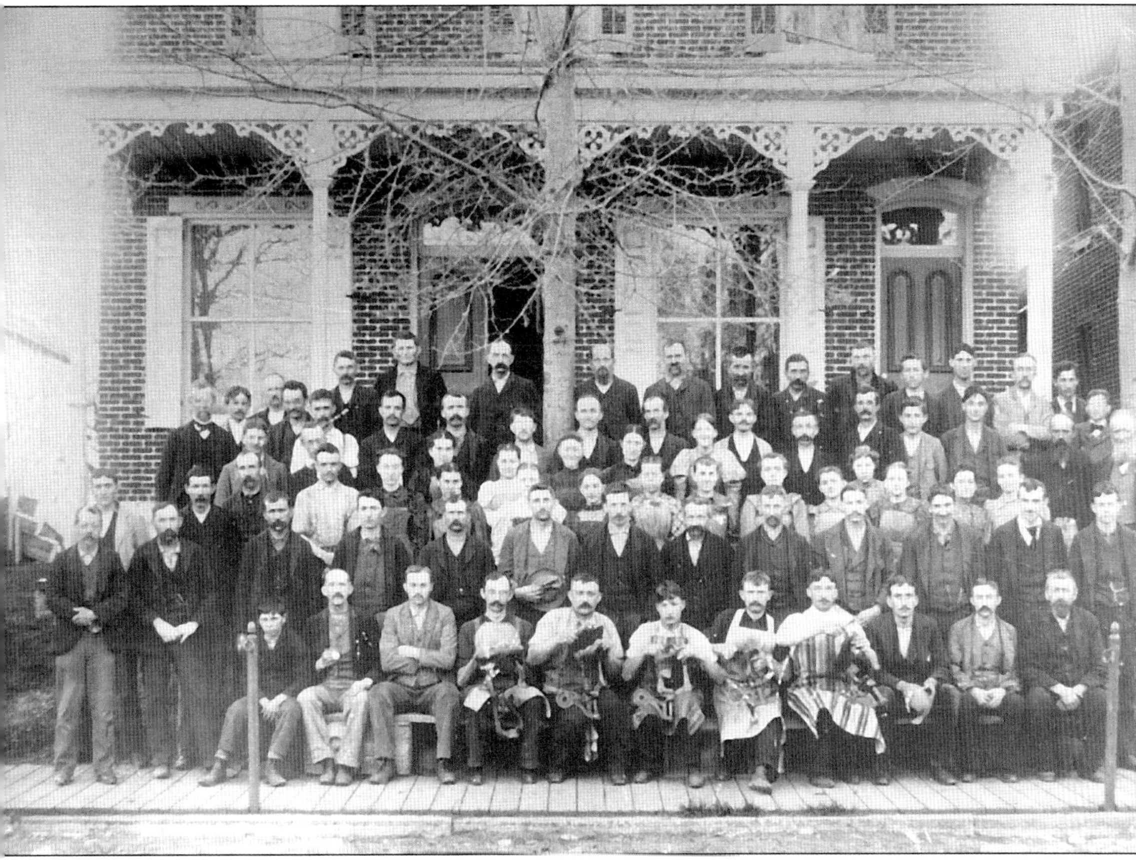

Henry W. Freed, the bearded gentleman on the right in the third row, posed with the employees of the Freed Brothers Shoe Factory in 1891. At the time of the photograph, the following people were in the employ of the company: Ambrose Benner, Lewis Taylor, Charles Taylor, Milton Maugle, John Younkin, Charles Rapp, Agnes Rapp, Andrew Judd, Charles Frankenfield, Mary Frankenfield, Norman Refsnider, Martin Stoneback, Harry Stoneback, Frank Sacks, Hattie Hoffert, Sallie Hoffert, Calvin Hoffert, Maggie Heller, Elmer Althouse, Colin Neamand, Charles Ahlum, Aaron Ahlum, Philip Bleam, Anthony Amey, Hezekiah Althouse, George Reinert, William Walp, Milton Ruth, Ezra Mills, Mary Sterner, Carson Shell, Zackarias George, Charles Freed, John Freed, William Freed Jr., and William Freed Sr. The business endured for 50 years after this picture was taken and evolved to meet changing tastes. By the early 20th century, the enterprise was producing shoes, boots, and "athletic shoes." (JLS.)

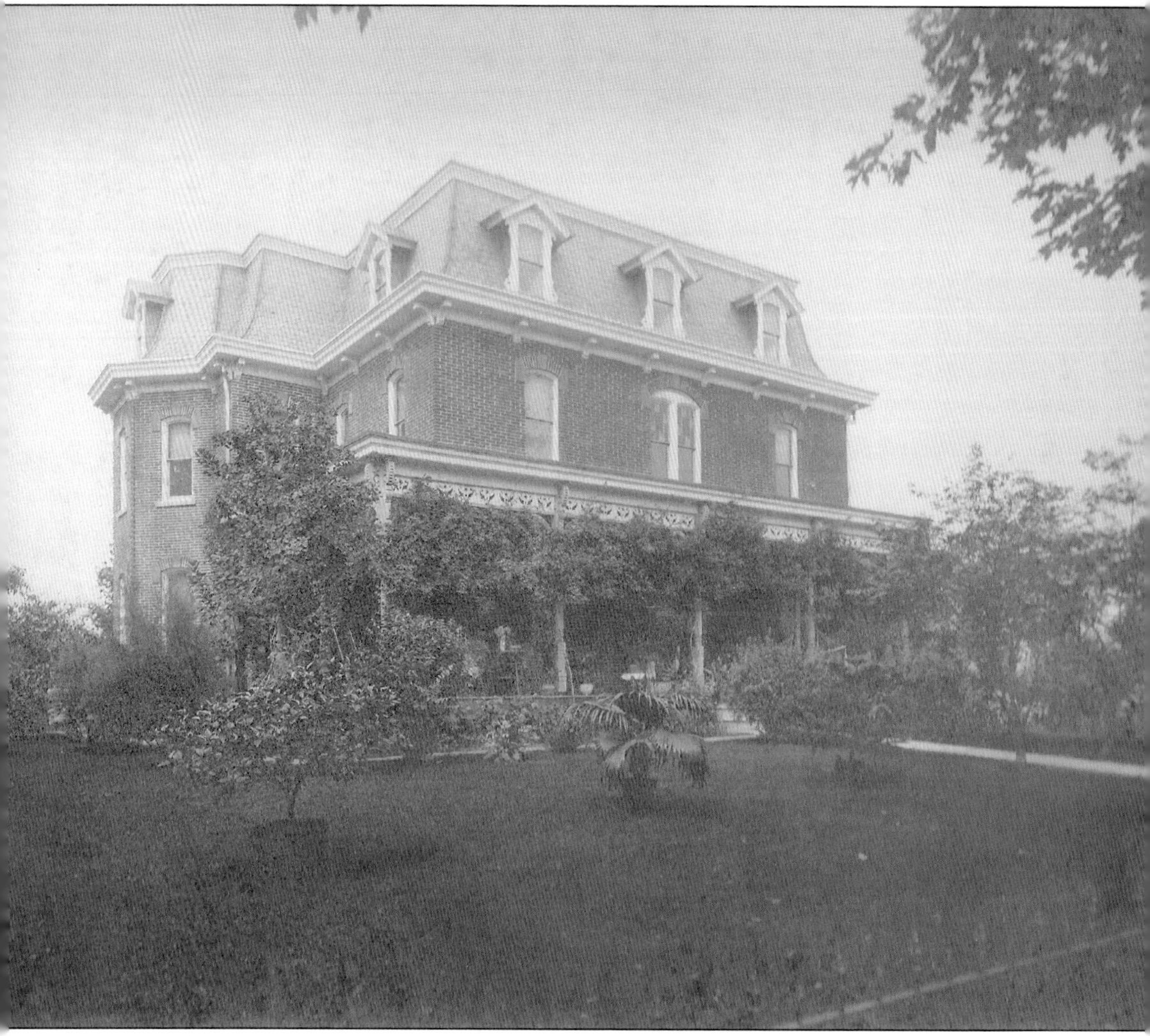

This brick home on Main Street was the home of Henry W. Freed, one of the partners of the Freed Shoe Factory. Henry Freed was a prominent leader in the borough of Richlandtown. He served as the first chief burgess (mayor) and also on the borough council. He was also the organist and choir director of the Richlandtown church for 50 years. The home was purchased by the Lutheran congregation in 1929. Half of the residence was used as a parsonage, and the other half was rented. After May 1953, the entire house served as a parsonage. The barn behind the home was torn down, and the material was used to construct a garage. Later the front porch was removed. In the late 1950s, a large number of maple trees were removed from the property to make way for West Union Street and First Avenue. The house continued to serve as a parsonage for many years. (ALR.)

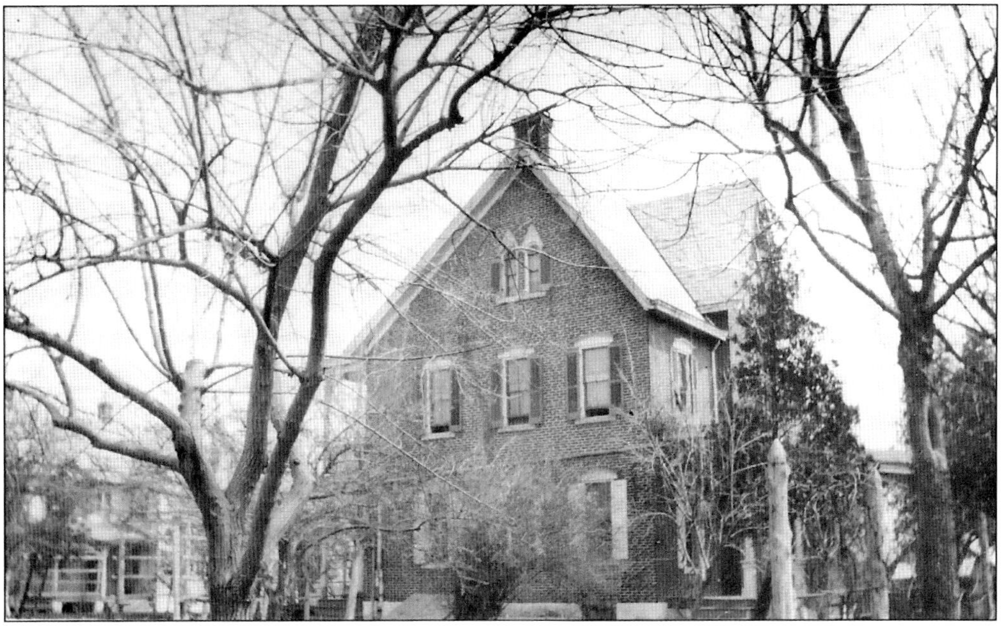

William D. Freed built this home about 1864. Freed owned 20 acres on the northwest corner of Cherry and Main Streets in Richlandtown, and the tract upon which the house was built is believed to be part of the Freed family farm. There were several outbuildings on the property. At one time, there was a shop next to the home. Pictured below is a small building thought to be a cookhouse. The larger building is a barn. William Freed learned the shoemaker's trade as a young man. He pursued shoemaking and farming until he partnered with his brother Charles to manufacture shoes. (Both, DW.)

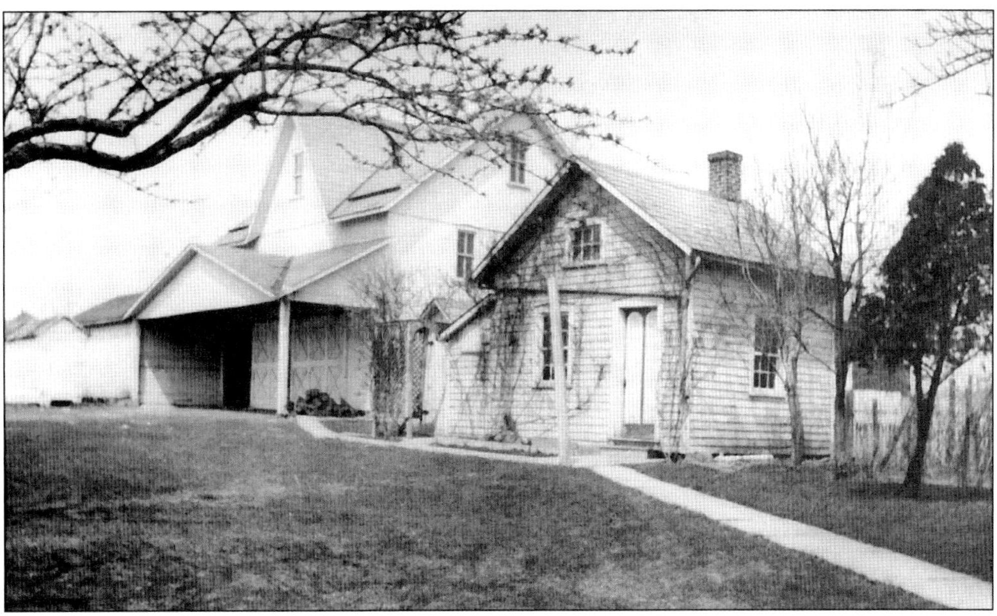

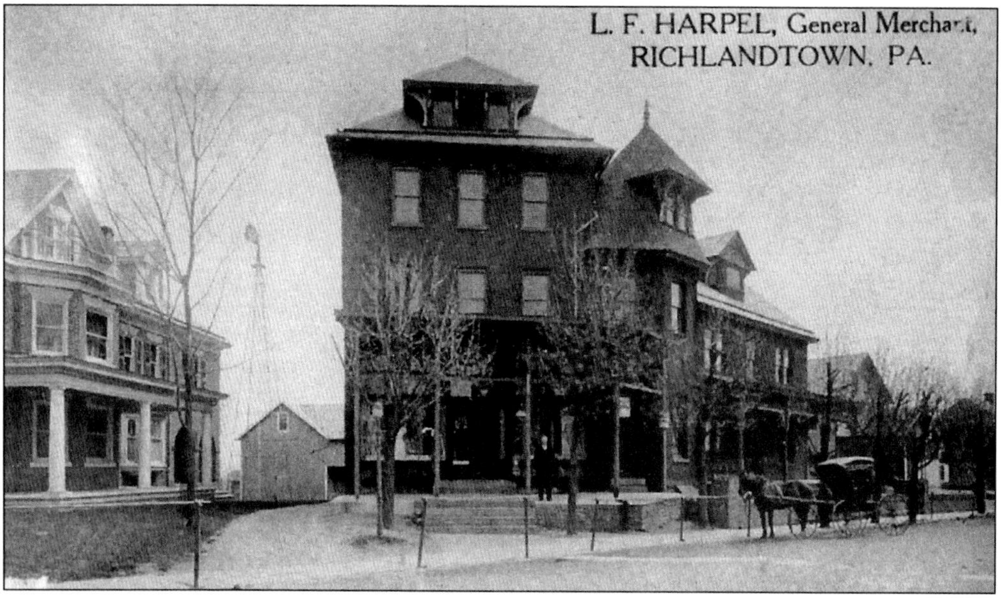

This distinctive building at the corner of Main and Union Streets housed a dry goods store operated by Charles Fellman. The store passed to James Shelly and was later run by Leidy F. Harpel. Winfield and Sevilla Keller purchased the building in 1948 and ran their own general store there until 1961. Since then various businesses have utilized the structure. (RB.)

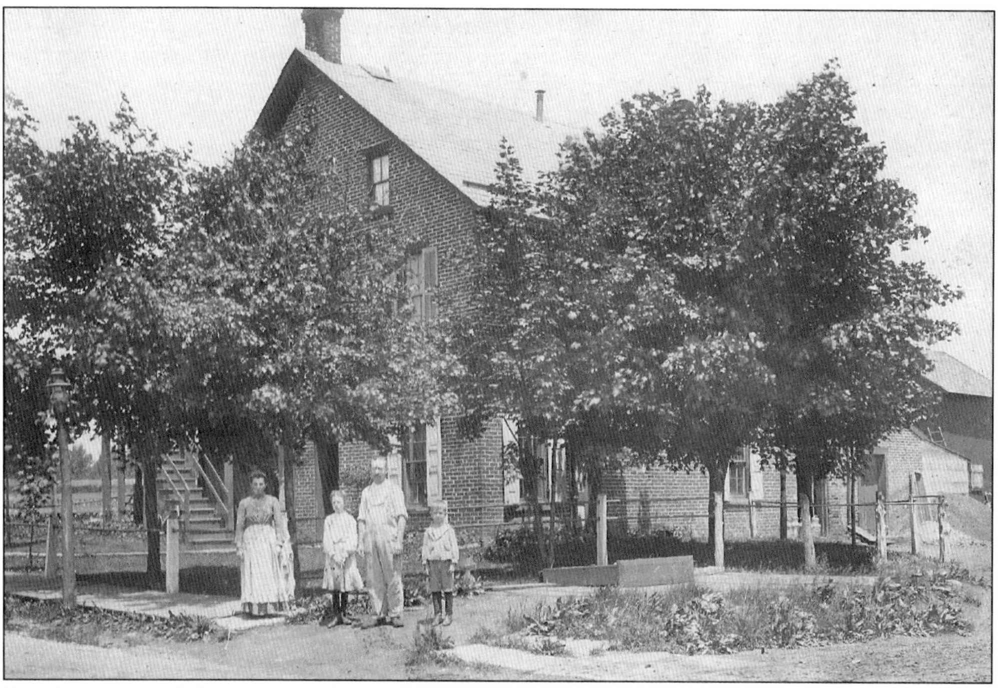

Charles and Ida Schroy pose in front of the Richlandtown Creamery with their children Mamie and James. The creamery was located on Union Street and was owned by James Shelly. Shelly was an enterprising gentleman; he was director of the Quakertown and Eastern Railroad, president of Merchant's National Bank of Quakertown, and served for 14 years as postmaster of Richlandtown. (JLS.)

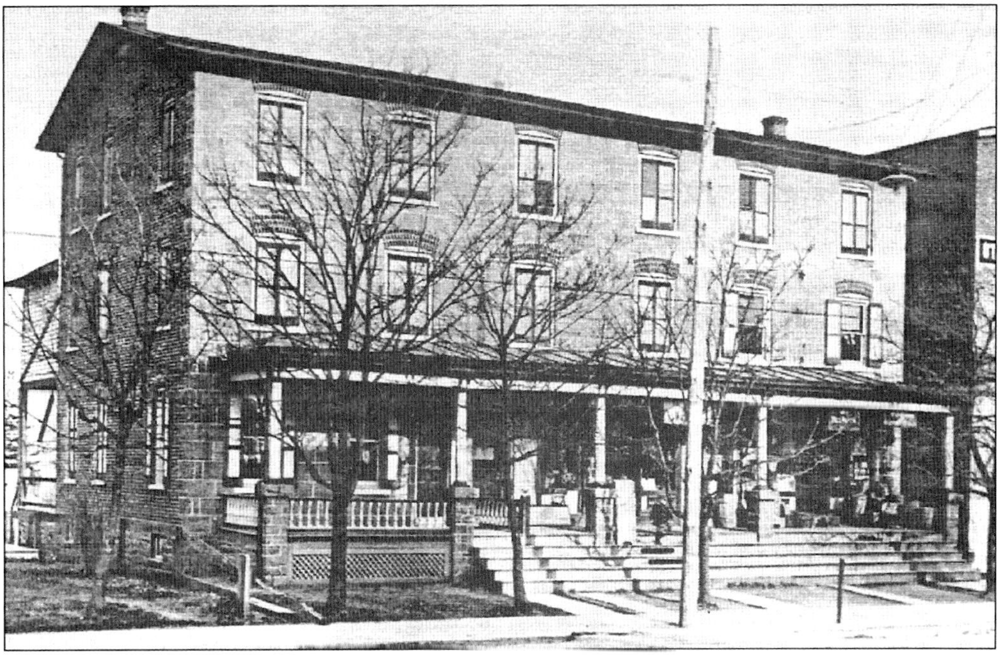

A grocery store and ice cream parlor was operated by Henry Ziegenfuss in this building for 51 years, beginning in 1902. Oysters were available, and the staff shucked them while the customer waited. During the 1920s, a child sent to the store during the Christmas holiday would be presented with an orange. (RB.)

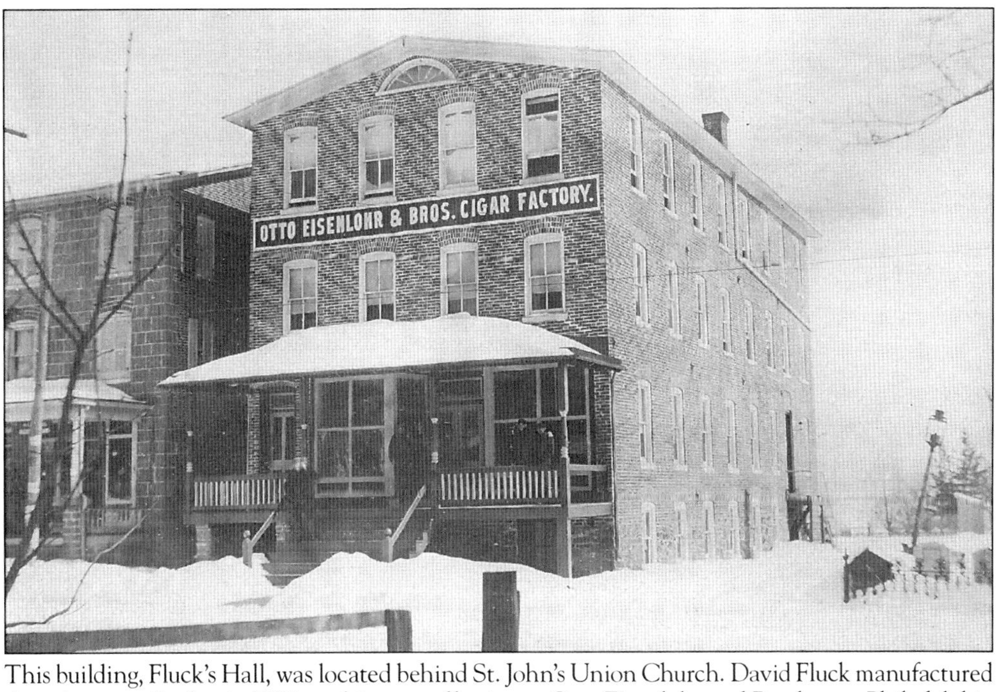

This building, Fluck's Hall, was located behind St. John's Union Church. David Fluck manufactured shoes here until a fire in 1897 put him out of business. Otto Eisenlohr and Brothers, a Philadelphia firm, then used the building to manufacture cigars. In 1919, the factory employed 138 men, 123 women, and had an office staff of two. (RHS.)

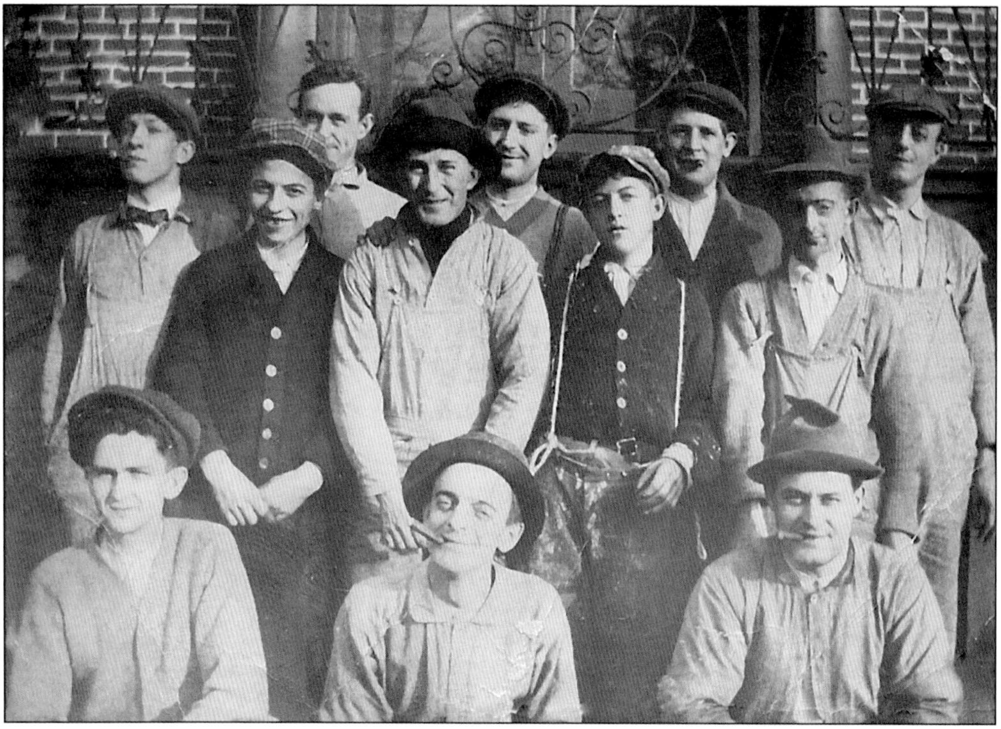

Two groups of workers from the Otto Eisenlohr factory take a break from their work and pose for these photographs about 1910. Cigar making was a labor-intensive industry, and hundreds of area residents were employed to make and pack the product. The cigars were handmade, and cigar rollers were highly skilled workers who had to turn out hundreds of identical cigars per day. Two workers in the foreground above are enjoying the fruits of their labor. Cigar factories employed both men and women as cigar rollers (below). Rollers had to work quickly and efficiently to produce cigars that would sell for as much as 5¢ each. (Both, RHS.)

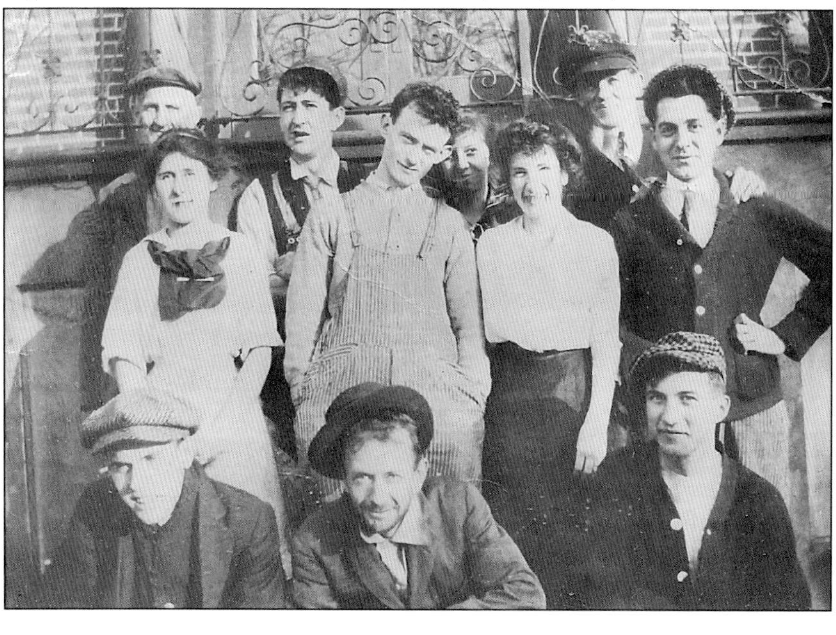

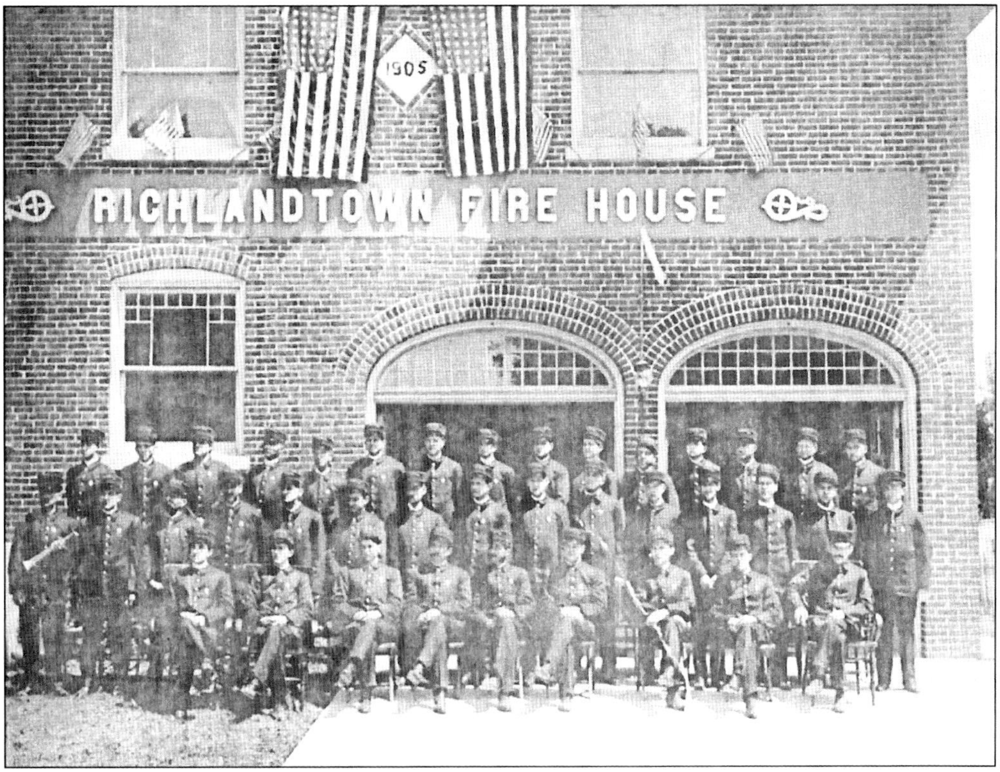

The Richlandtown Fire Company was organized on November 16, 1905, with 18 active members and 25 honorary members. Robert Kline was elected president. Shortly thereafter, the company erected a firehouse on Main Street (above). A chemical engine hook and ladder truck was purchased by Richlandtown Borough for $1,285 in 1905 and given to the fire company. The firehouse is pictured with two early pieces of firefighting equipment (below). In September 1907, the company responded to its first call when the barns belonging to Anthony Amey and Leidy Ahlum were destroyed by a blaze. (Both, RB.)

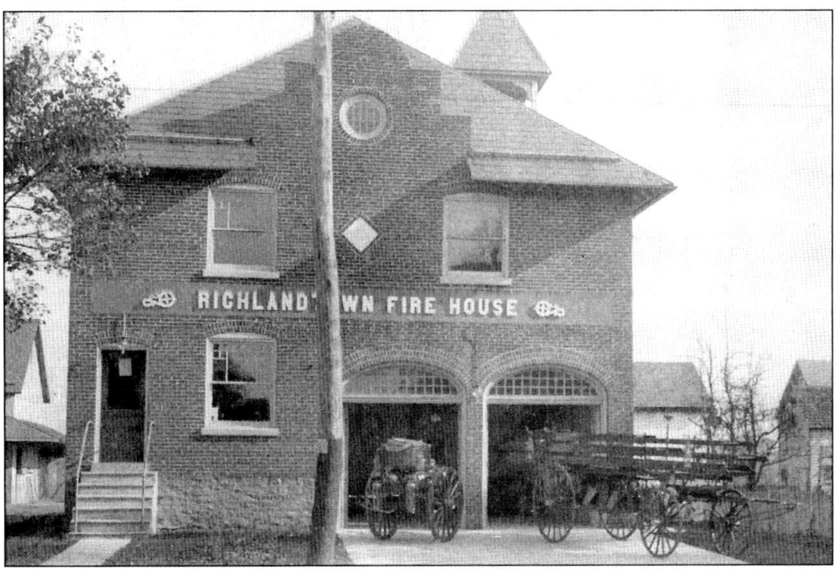

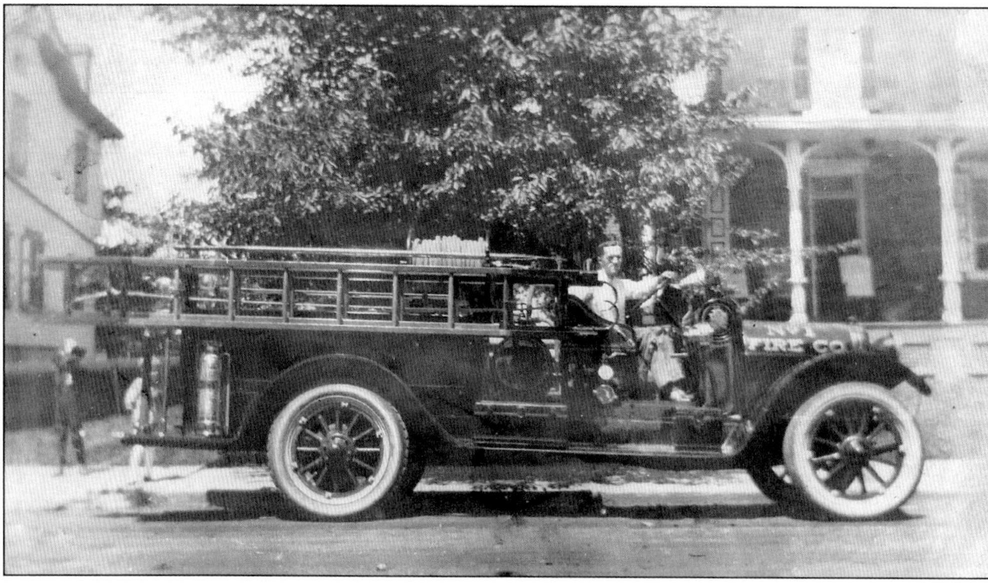

The above vehicle is the Reo Pumper Truck that was purchased by the Richlandtown Fire Company in 1921. The vehicle arrived at the firehouse a few days before the local firefighters could be instructed on its use. Before the instructor arrived there was a fire at the Wismer Pants Factory on Main Street. The new truck could not be used, and the three-story frame structure was completely destroyed. During the 1920s and 1930s, the fire company modernized. In 1923, a fire alarm system was installed. It was purchased by the ladies auxiliary and the system was tested every Monday evening at 7:00 p.m. Below is the 1937 Chevy fire truck that served the company for many years. (Above, RB; below, CH.)

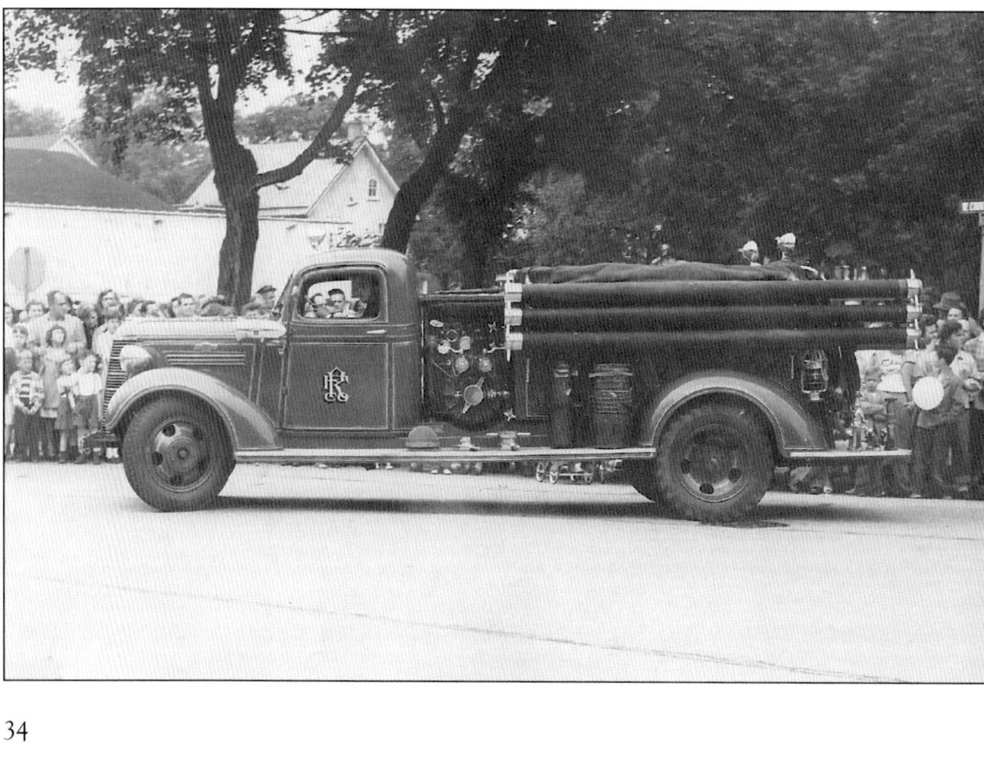

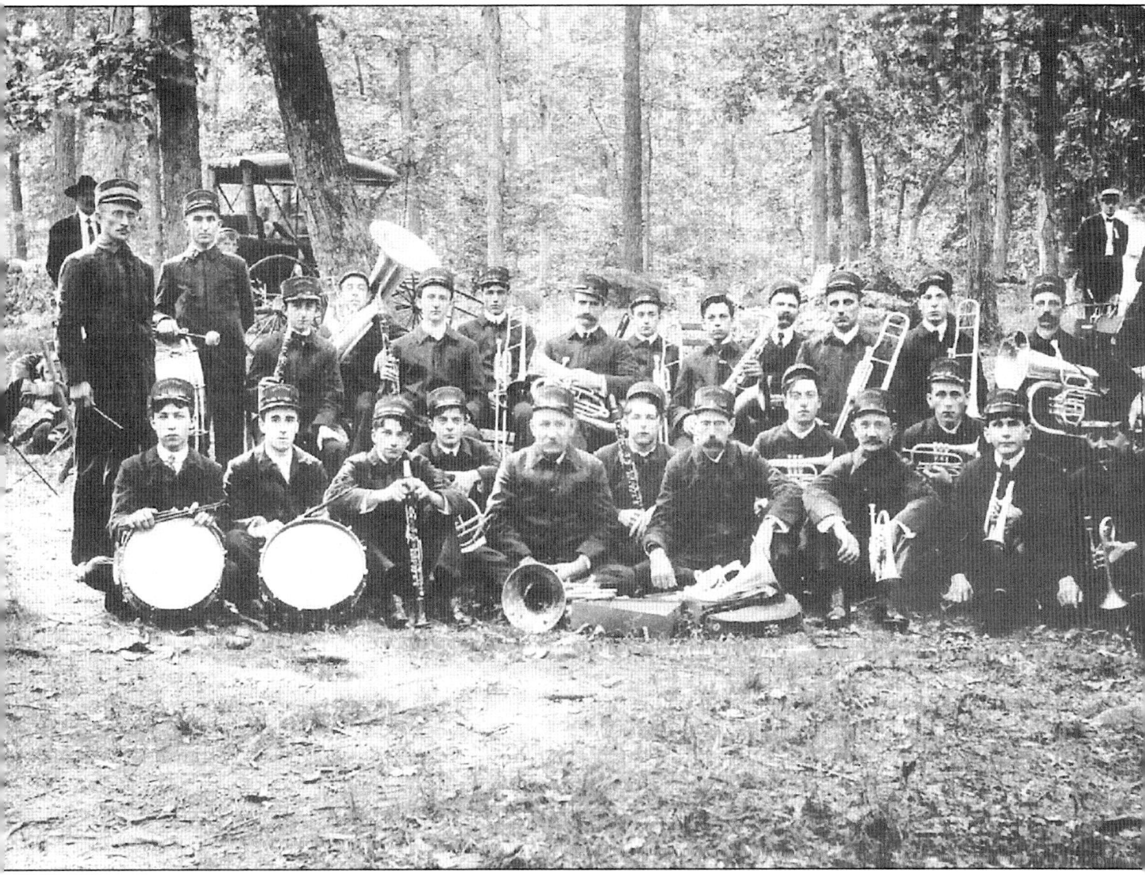

The Keystone Band was organized on July 22, 1901, by residents of Richlandtown. At the time, the band numbered 23 members, who paid a 25¢ per month fee. The above picture was taken on July 7, 1906. From left to right are (first row) Milton Heller, Hardy Frankenfield, James Rapp, Norman Benner, Milton Stoneback, William Sames, Philip Bleam, unidentified, Harvey Price, Erwin Erney, William Erney, and Norman Refsnider; (second row) Harvey Freed, Henry Heller, Allen Stoneback, unidentified, Herbert Weiland, Charles Althouse, John Horne, unidentified, John Erney, Harry Bartholomew, Preston Hillegas, Frank Schaffer, and unidentified. (RB.)

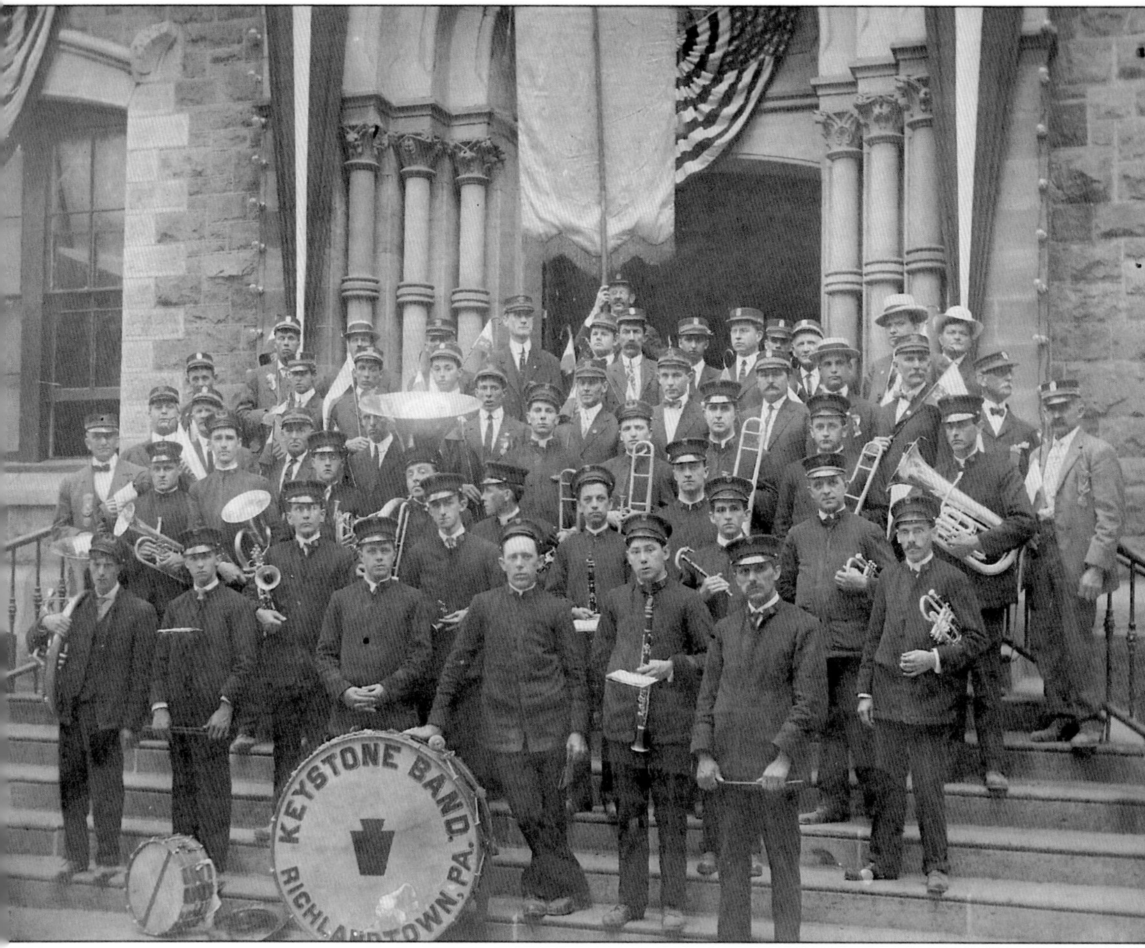

The first leader of the Keystone Band was Harvey M. Freed, who served from 1901 until 1916. He was succeeded by William H. Benner, Harvey Price, and Clarence Benner. In its heyday, the Keystone Band had nearly 50 members. This photograph was taken about 1918. From left to right are (first row) unidentified, Milton Heller, Ed Hess, Milton Schick, Charles Taylor, and unidentified; (second row) William Erney, Allen Stoneback, Harry Bartholomew, Oswald Hendricks, and unidentified; (third row), Robert Reichenbach, Frank Ahlum, Howard Erney, Herbert Wieland, Erwin Erney, and Clarence Benner; (fourth row), unidentified, Otto Mease, unidentified, John Erney, and five unidentified. Everyone else is unidentified. Paul Scheetz, a member of the Keystone Band in the 1920s and 1930s, was able to identify some members of the band in this photograph in 2002. He was the oldest surviving member of the Keystone Band and died in 2004 at 101 years of age. (RHS.)

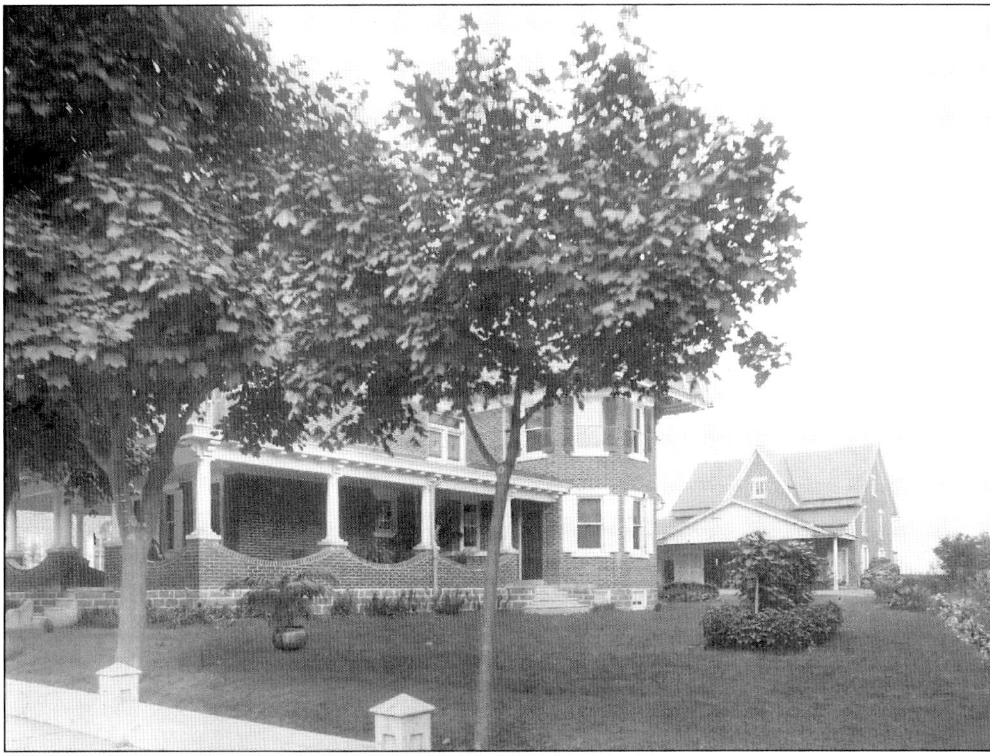

Harvey M. Freed, son of William Freed and a partner in Freed Brothers Shoe Factory, was born in 1870. He married neighbor Alice Biehn in 1895, and they lived in this handsome home on Main Street, where they raised a large family. In the 1940s, the fine old place was converted into a nursing facility by a Mrs. Potts, who operated it as the Potts Convalescent Home. (KK.)

The first known owner of this sulky was Thomas Hillpot of Tinicum, who used it to come to Quakertown to court his future wife. Later the sulky was given to Samuel T. Hillpot, Thomas's son. Samuel Hillpot lived on Richlandtown Pike. He became the agent of Richland Grange and the proprietor of the store in the Grange Hall. (RHWB.)

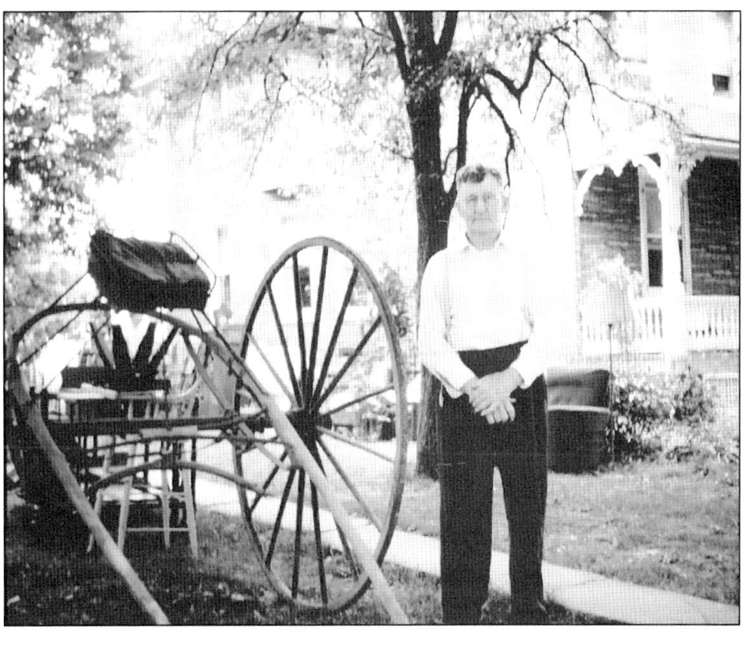

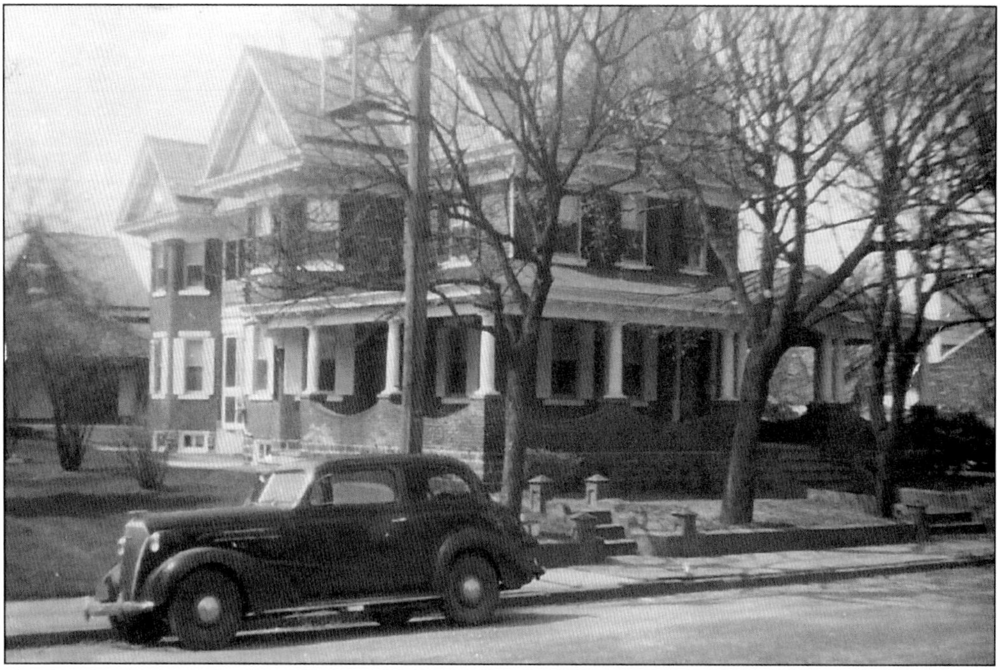

As the Potts Convalescent Home, the Harvey Freed house retained its original look (above). Ownership of the property passed to John and Olive Zohlman in the 1950s; they operated the facility as Zohlman Nursing Home. Various modifications were made to the house in the 1950s, as shown by the picture below. Several wings were added in the 1960s and 1970s, raising capacity to 169 beds. Sadly, the original mansion was demolished and replaced with dining, therapy, and lounge areas. The facility is now operated by Phoebe Ministries as Phoebe Richland Healthcare Center. (Above, RHS; below, KK.)

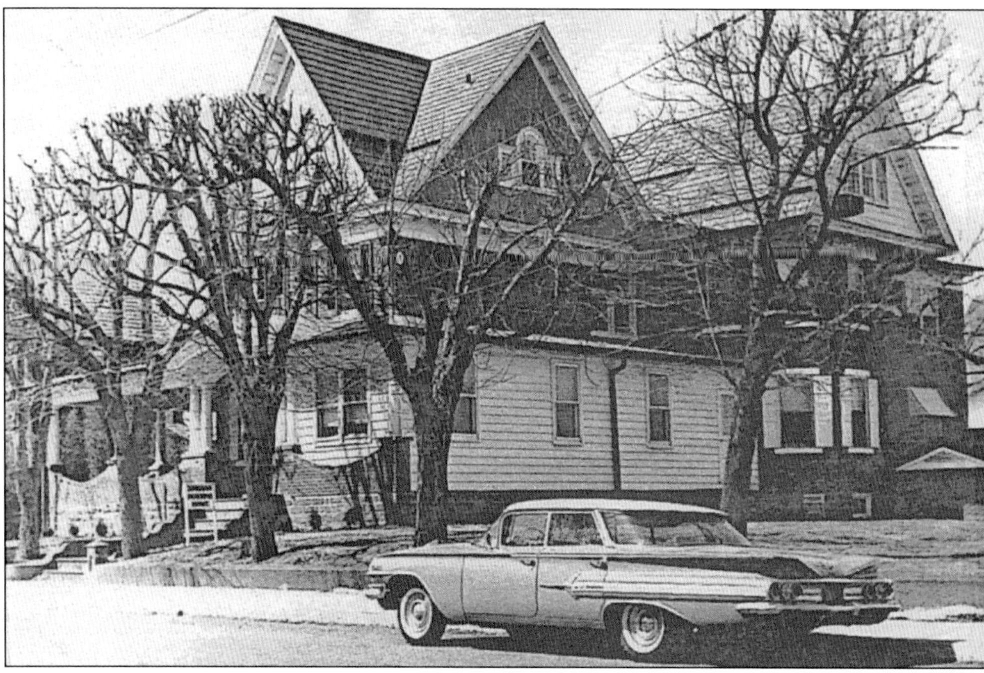

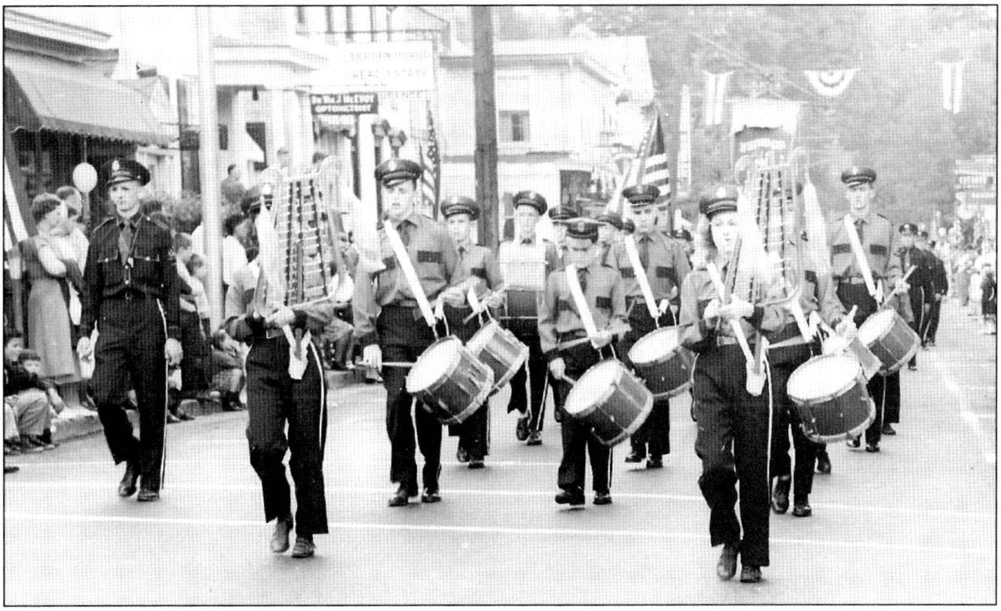

After World War II, the Richlandtown Fire Company sponsored a drum and bugle corps, which succeeded the Keystone Band as the outlet for local musical talent. The corps is seen above marching in a parade. It had 40 members and utilized the old Richlandtown School, built in 1855, as a practice hall. A class was started for majorettes, who marched in parades with the corps (below). Participation in the band dwindled in the late 1950s, and a motion was made to disband the organization in 1959, but no formal action was ever taken. In the 1960s, the funds of the corps were transferred to the Richlandtown Fire Company, and the drums were donated to Quakertown Junior High School. (Both, RB.)

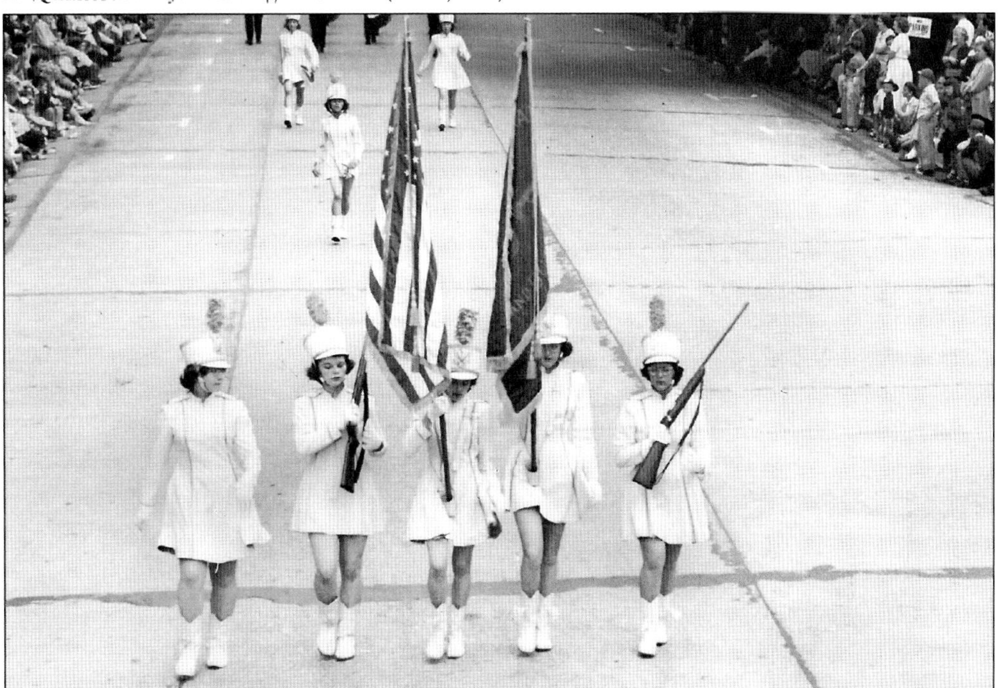

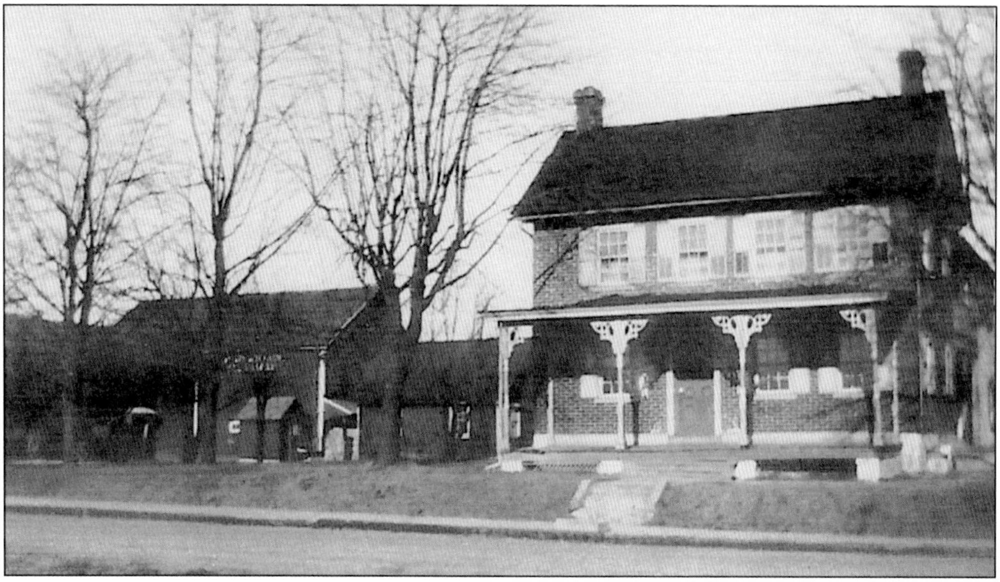

The John C. Hinkle family lived in this house on Main Street in Richlandtown. Hinkle began an ice delivery service in 1908, when he was 20 years old. When he first started the business, he secured use of the California Ice Dam and built a storage barn there to hold the ice. In the 1930s, Hinkle expanded his business to include coal. (CH.)

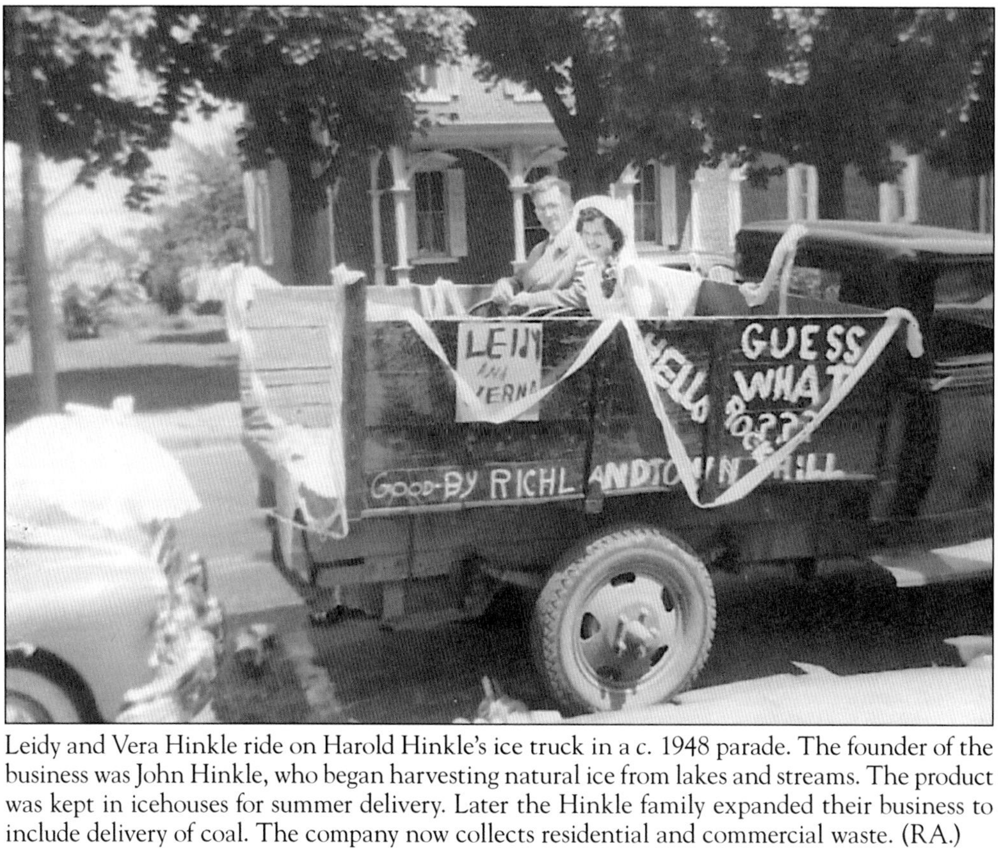

Leidy and Vera Hinkle ride on Harold Hinkle's ice truck in a c. 1948 parade. The founder of the business was John Hinkle, who began harvesting natural ice from lakes and streams. The product was kept in icehouses for summer delivery. Later the Hinkle family expanded their business to include delivery of coal. The company now collects residential and commercial waste. (RA.)

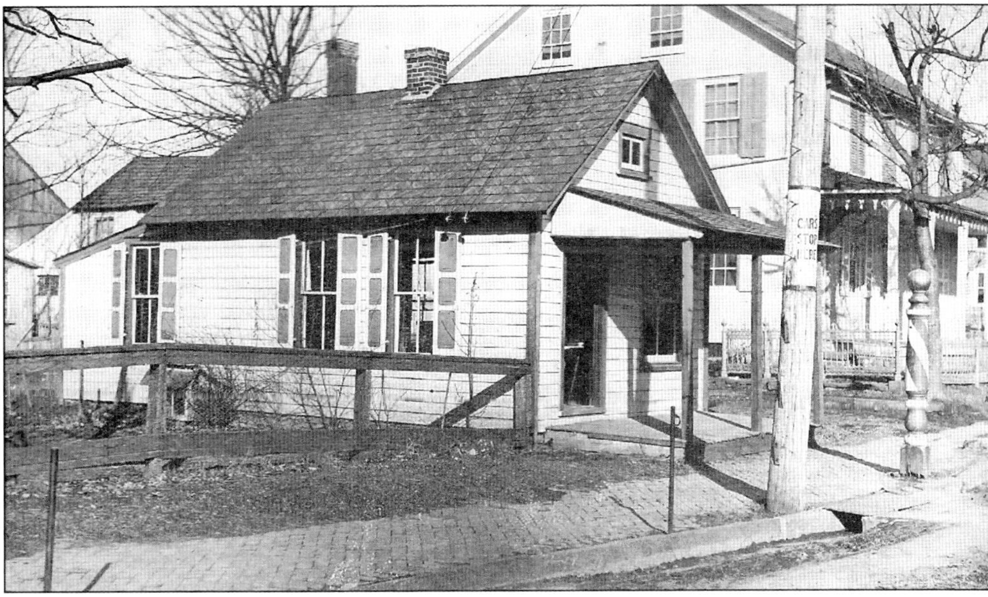

A striped pole on the sidewalk identified the Kandel barbershop on Main Street. John Kandel came to Richlandtown from Philadelphia in 1920 and opened his shop in this building. The barbershop was operated by three generations of the Kandel family—John, his son Peter, and his grandson John E. Kandel. (JEK.)

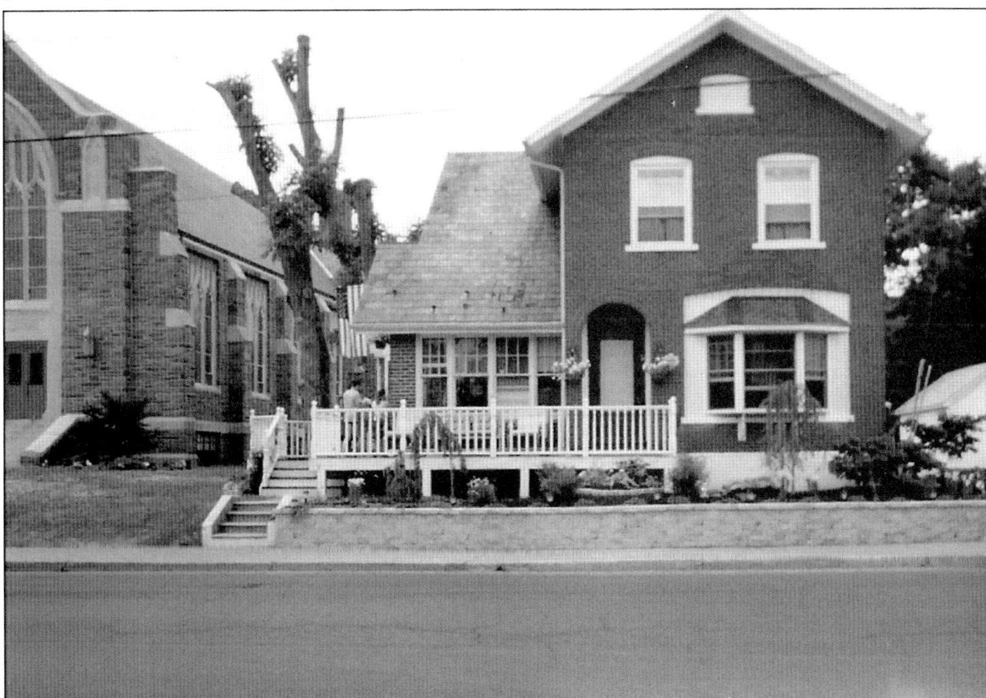

By 1927, the old Kandel barbershop was abandoned and a new structure built. The above building served the Kandel family as both living quarters and place of business. John Kandel sold some of his property to St. John's Lutheran congregation, who purchased the land so that they could build their own sanctuary. The church can be seen on the left. (JEK.)

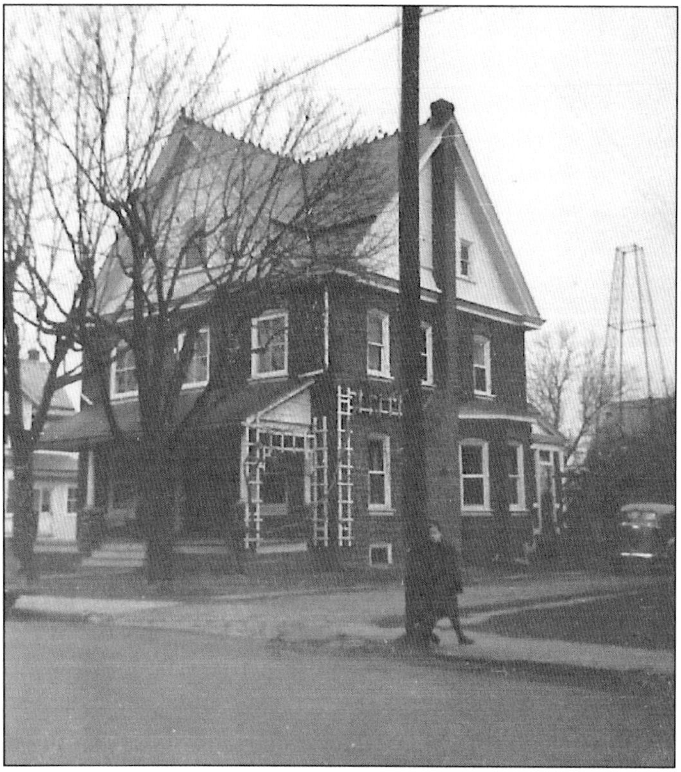

Walter Smith was the doctor in Richlandtown from 1935 until 1980. His office was located in his home next to the firehouse. Dr. Smith saw duty as a physician in the army during World War II. When he returned to private practice, he was also a school physician. This photograph, taken in the early 1940s, shows Paul Smith, the oldest child of Walter and Marie Smith. (SS.)

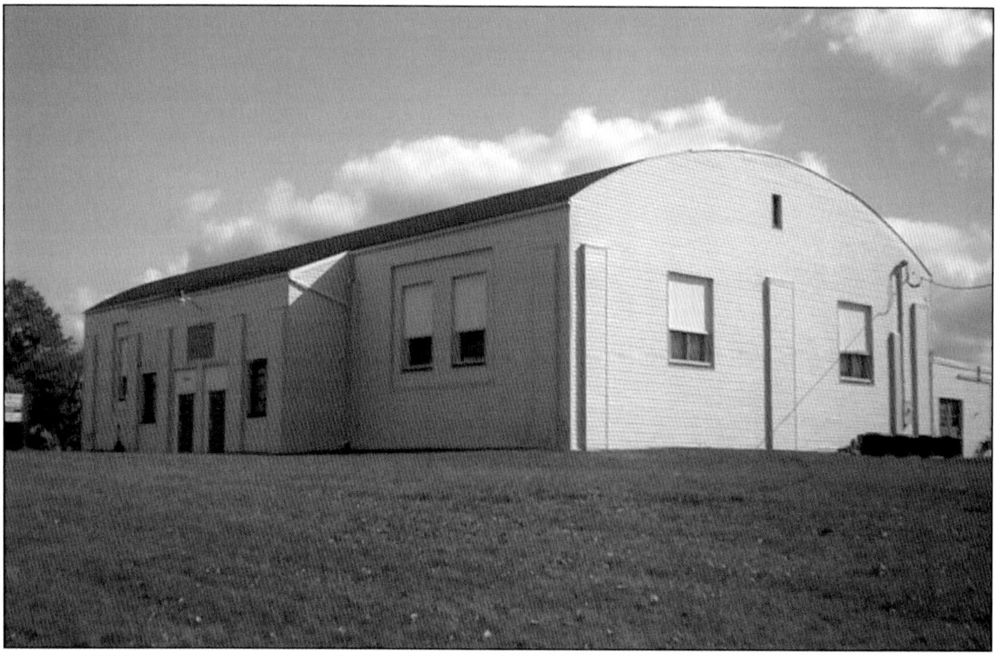

Benner Hall was constructed by the Richlandtown Playground Association, which was founded in 1931 to sponsor local baseball and basketball teams. After the Second World War, the association purchased 13 acres and put up the building, which served multiple purposes. The structure was dedicated in May 1953 in memory of Charles E. Benner. (KF.)

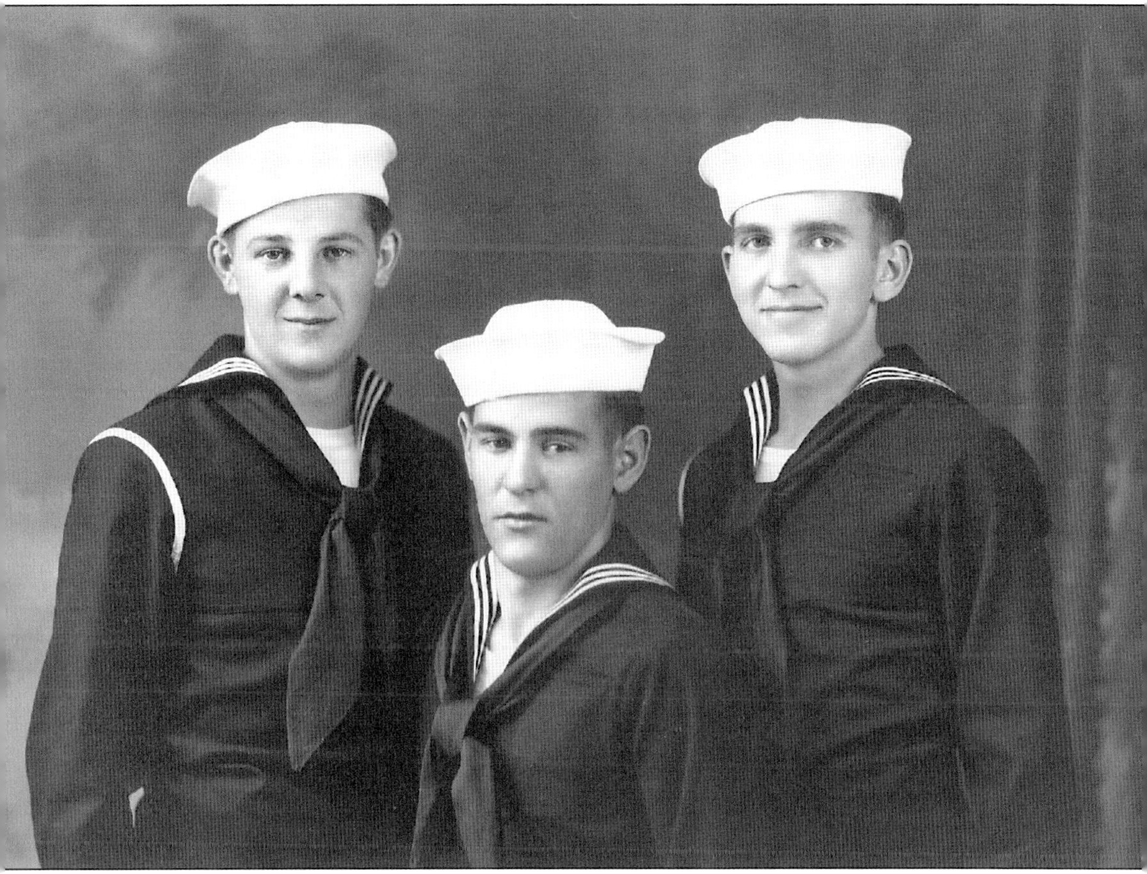

Marvin Refsnider (left), Charles Benner (center), and Forrest Wimmer (right) enlisted in the U.S. Navy during the Second World War. Charles Benner was killed during training exercise on an Launching Ship Tank (LST) shortly before D-day. A letter from his commanding officer to Benner's mother said, "Our ship was lost in the early morning hours of April 28, 1944, having been torpedoed by enemy E boats off the English coast. During the action, Charles was at his battle station, the radio control room, performing his duties with the highest degree of loyalty. He left the ship when it was abandoned and was not seen again until his body was taken from the water later that day. Charles . . . was a credit to his ship and to the Navy . . . he made the supreme sacrifice for his country." In 1950, the Richlandtown Athletic Association constructed a social hall, and it was named Benner Hall to honor the memory of Charles Benner. (MR.)

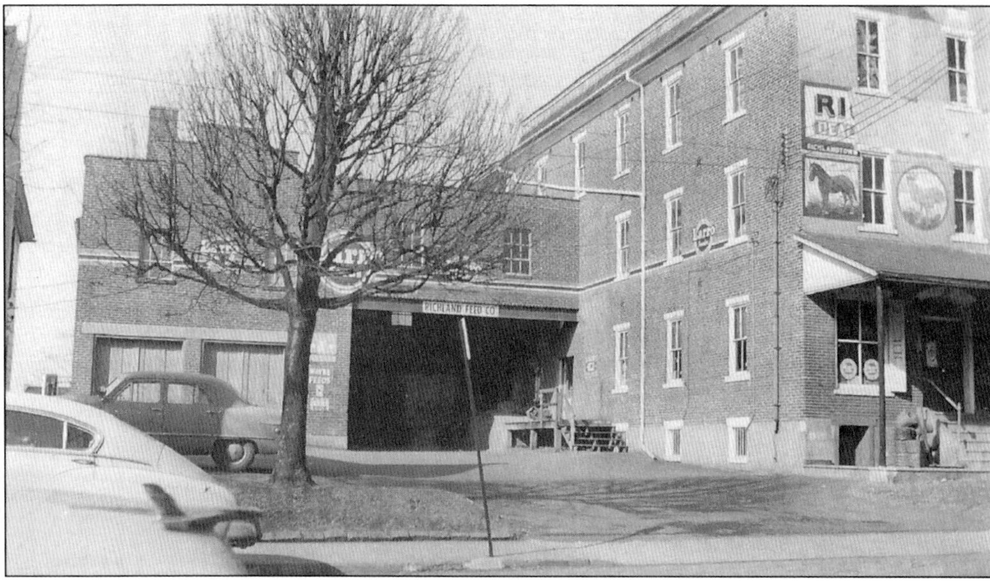

This photograph was taken in 1943, when the Freed factory was sold to Howard Erney and converted into a feed store. The business has been operated by the Sames family for several decades. After World War II, agricultural activity was vibrant and feed companies provided feed and other products for livestock. As the area has developed, Richland Feed has adjusted its products to serve its current clientele. (RFC.)

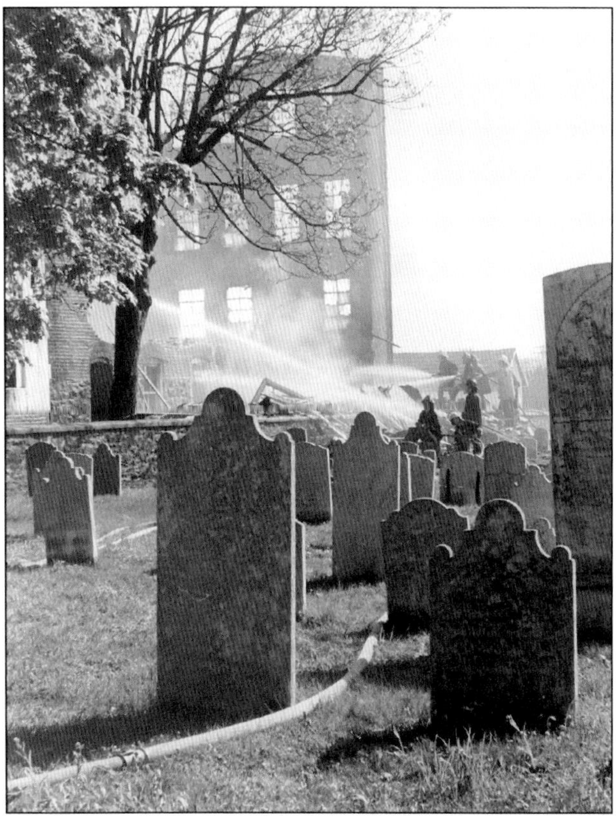

Fluck's Hall was purchased in the 1920s by Morris Trishon Manufacturing Company, which made Ship and Shore women's blouses. Fire destroyed the factory on April 29, 1976. The Richlandtown Fire Company snaked hoses among historic tombstones in the adjoining cemetery to fight the fire. It was rumored that because the material used in making blouses was not union-made, the fire was set deliberately. (CH.)

Three

VILLAGES

During the 18th and 19th centuries, the citizens of Richland Township created villages when they built homes, churches, stores, and factories close together, particularly at busy crossroads. The most important of these was Quakertown, which grew sufficiently large and sophisticated to achieve a separate identity from the township when it became incorporated as a borough. Richlandtown reached a similar point when it became a borough in 1890. There were five other settlements—Rich Hill, California, Paletown, Shelly, and Richland Centre. Photographs from these villages are included in the following pages.

Rich Hill is located on the Bethlehem Pike. First named Bunker Hill, it must have taken on the name shortly after the Revolutionary War from its location on a hill on the Bethlehem Pike at the border of Richland and Rockhill townships. Its name was changed to Rich Hill when it was awarded a post office. The main landmark is the Rich Hill Store, although there once was a tavern.

California takes its name from the hotel there. It was more diversified that Rich Hill, with a store, school, and mill. With its source not far from California, Tohickon Creek provided power for the mill. Paletown was primarily a cluster of farmhouses along what are now Paletown and Rocky Ridge Roads. Paletown at one time included a schoolhouse, blacksmith, and creamery.

The North Penn Railroad created two vibrant villages when it placed its stations in Shelly and Richland Centre. Shelly station was an enterprising, dynamic place. It had cigar factories, feed stores, a hotel, and a general store. During the early 1900s, the farms around Shelly became tourist destinations. Route 309 ran through the village in the 1930s. Richland Centre also was a product of the railroad, with several public houses (hotels), factories, and stores. Livestock was transported both to and from adjoining Richland Township through the station at Richland Centre. Richland Centre became the third ward of Quakertown when it became part of the borough.

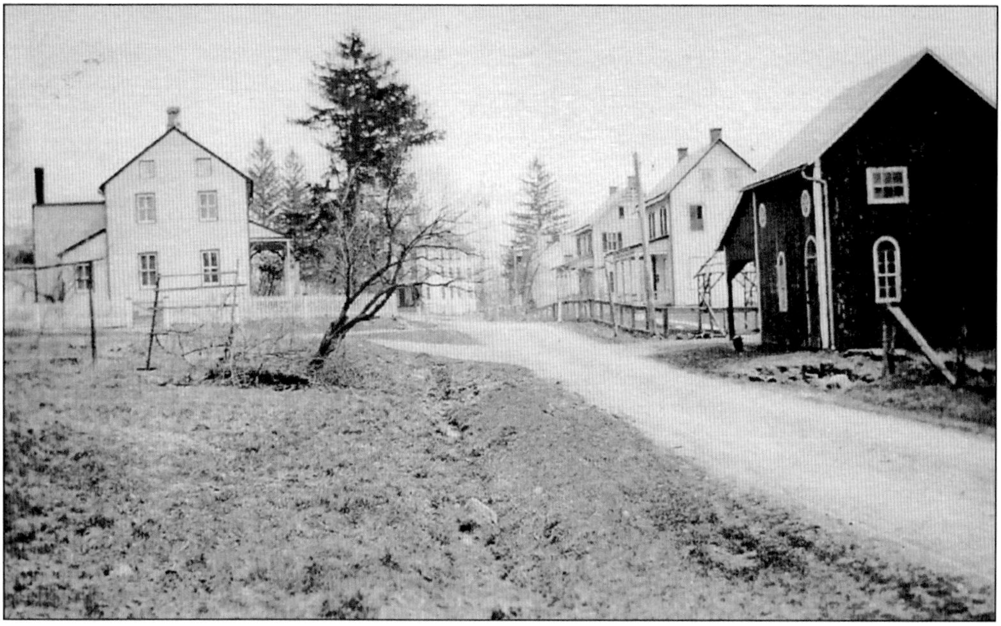

The village of California is a quiet community, where homes, farms, and businesses lie side by side. In 1963, a visitor to the village noted that "one side is a poultry farm, along another road is a butcher . . . the center of the intersecting roads is bordered by a large white frame hotel, on the roof of which something resembling a . . . widow's walk becomes the highest point in town." (LM.)

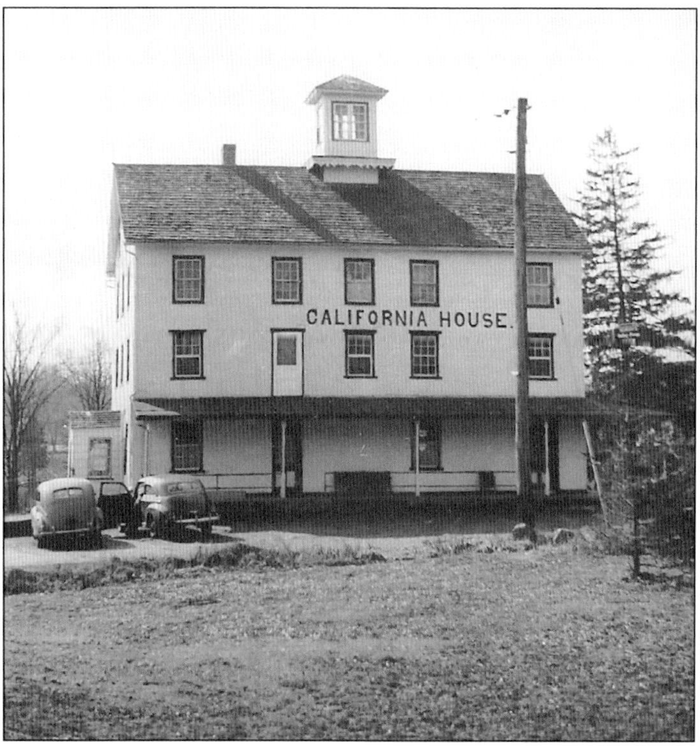

Frederick Wolf settled in Richland Township in 1847 and built a three-story hotel on his property. The structure was completed in 1849, the year of the gold rush in (the future state of) California. Wolf capitalized on this enthusiasm and called his place the California Hotel. The original sign boasted a man carrying a sack of gold over his shoulder. Locally, the village is known as Little California. (LM.)

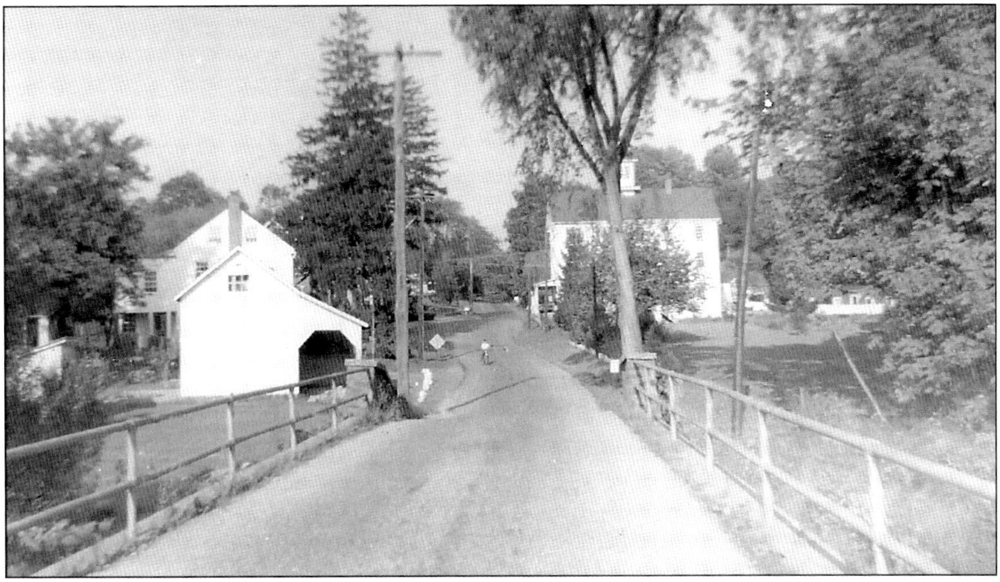

The road to California crosses a branch of the Tohickon Creek just south of the village. The creek powered a gristmill and a sawmill, but the area did not grow until the hotel was built. By the 1870s, the village boasted a store, a school, and over a dozen homes in addition to the hotel. (LM.)

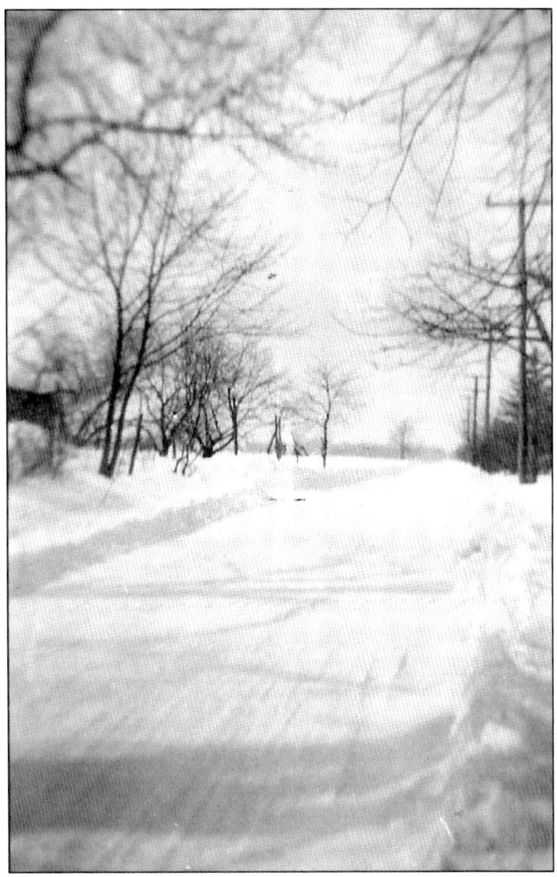

California Road is a very old thoroughfare; it was the colonial road that connected Richland to Durham Furnace. The photograph at right was taken after a snowstorm in 1958. Except for the electrical poles on the right side of the road, the scenery had not changed since the 1700s. (KF.)

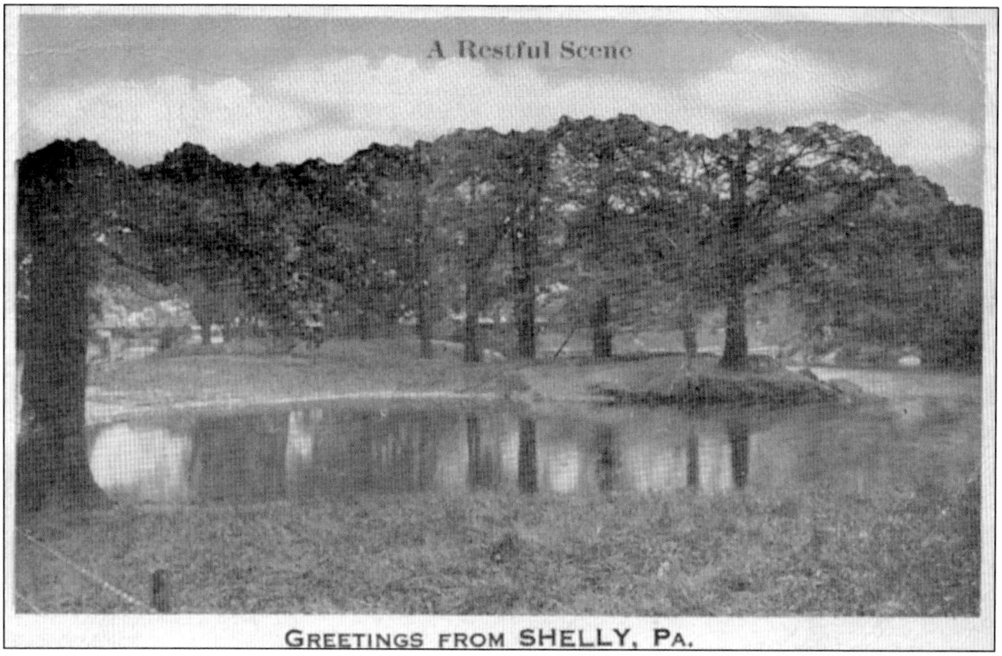

This postcard was sent to Anna Strawnsnyder who was in Sellersville (Grandview) Hospital in 1918. The area around Shelly Station was a favorite destination for vacationers who came from Philadelphia to Shelly or Quakertown by train, then were picked up by a farm family to spend a week as boarders in a farmhouse. (BH.)

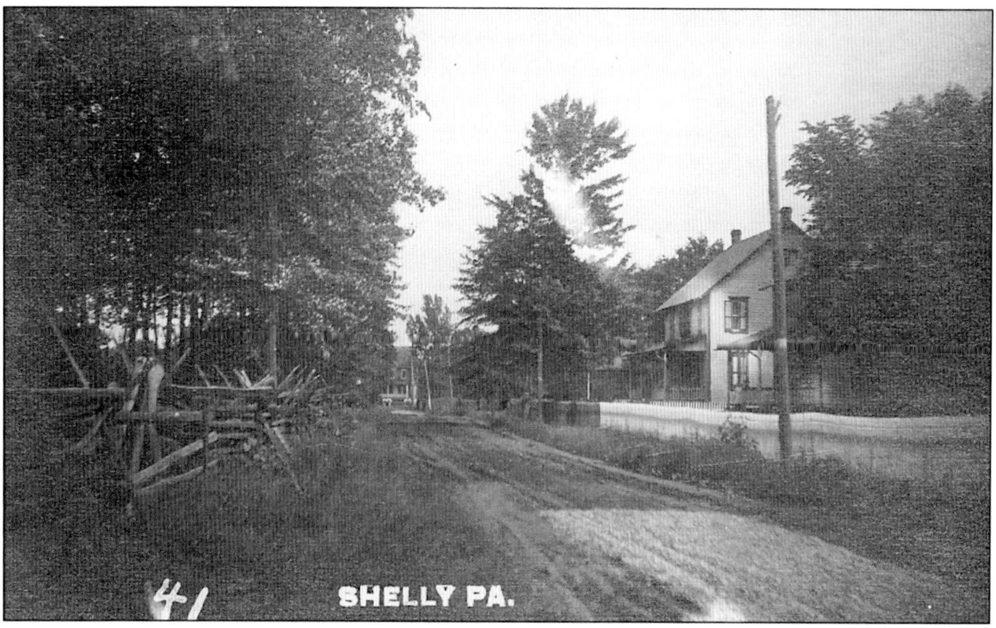

This idyllic view looking north into the village of Shelly was taken about 1907. The road is unpaved, and split rail fencing is to the left. Such fencing was easy to construct, as the rails were stacked upon one another in a zigzag fashion, with crossed supports. The fence required no hardware or nails, making it inexpensive and easy to maintain. (BH.)

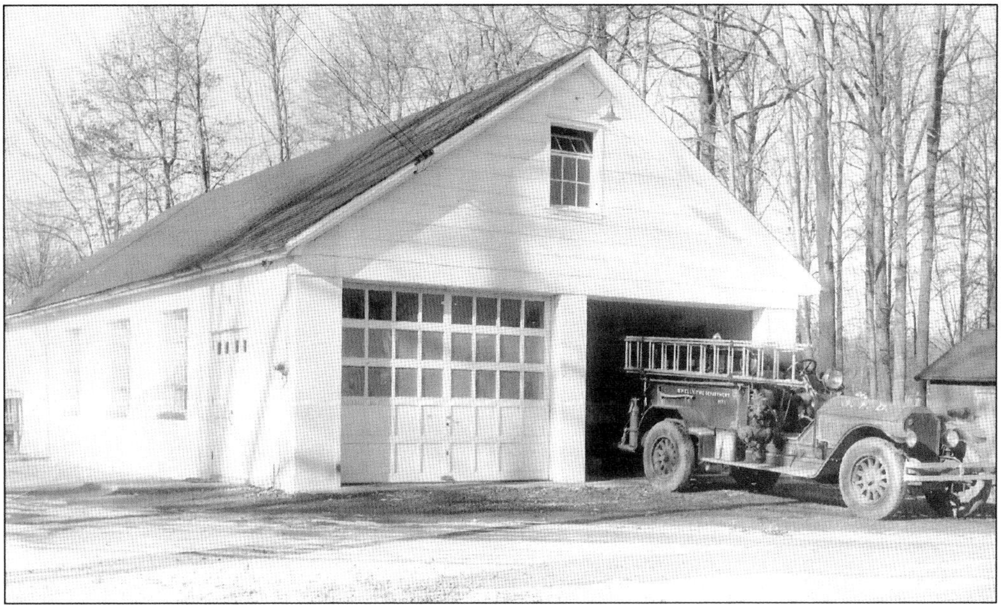

The impetus for a fire company in the village of Shelly began in 1933. Firemen worked out of a garage belonging to a local resident, and a siren was located on the third floor of the home. A fire call would be telephoned to the home, and a member of the family would climb to the third floor to crank the siren by hand. In 1948, the fire company purchased a lot along Shelly Road and utilized the above garage as a firehouse. By 1955, the name of the fire company was painted on the front of the building. In the photograph below, members of the company pose in front of their new 1954 International truck. (RTFR.)

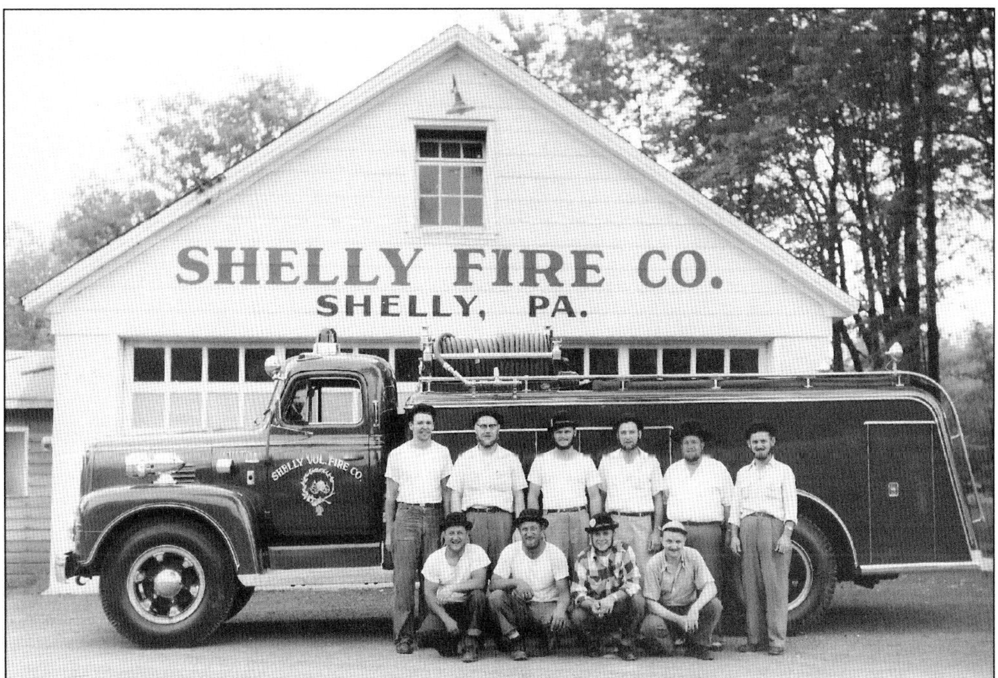

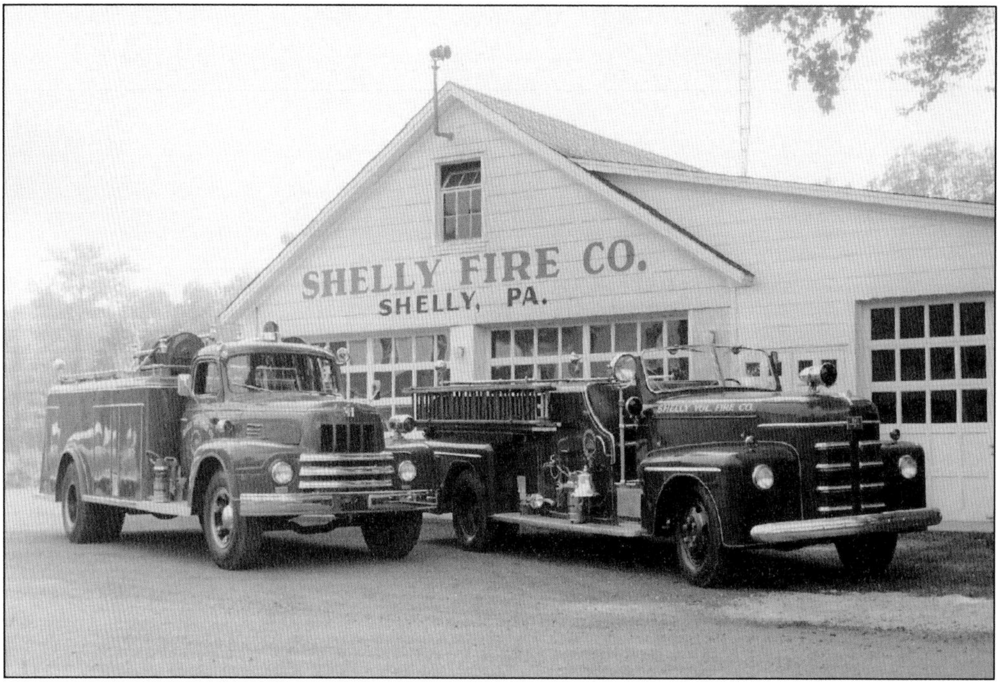

As the fire company grew, it became necessary to enlarge the firehouse. In the late 1950s, an additional bay was added to the north side. In 1977, the fire company built a new eight-bay fire station, and the above building was converted to a social hall. The Shelly Fire Company changed its name to Richland Fire and Rescue. (RTFR.)

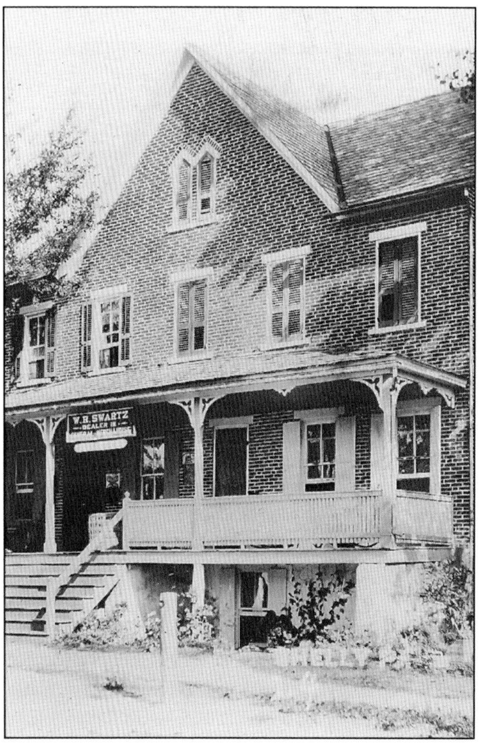

In the village of Shelly, a store was operated by the Dickert family during the second half of the 19th century. The store also served as Shelly's post office. The building was adjacent to the North Penn Railroad, and maps from the late 1800s refer to the village as Shelly's Station. (LM.)

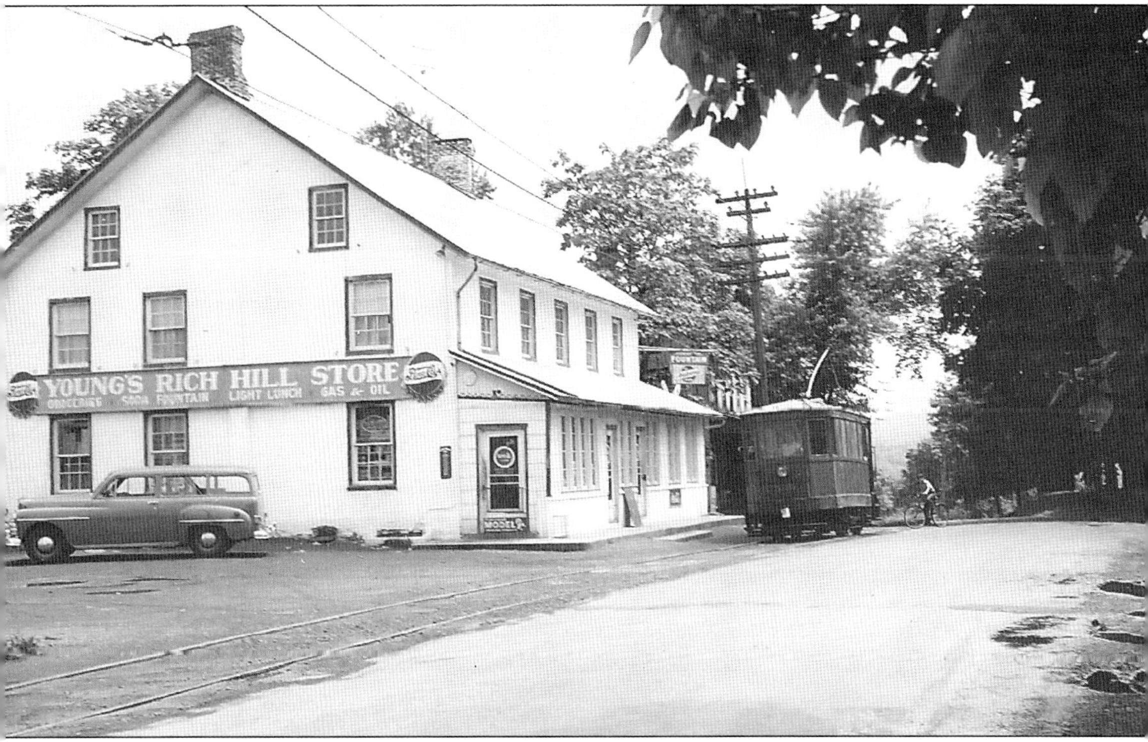

Rich Hill, a village along Bethlehem Pike on the Rockhill Township line, was once called Bunker Hill. The settlement grew in the early part of the 19th century around a popular public house operated by Anthony Amey. Eventually the inn lost its license and closed. The name Bunker Hill persisted until a post office was established in the village. Since a place named Bunker Hill, Pennsylvania, already had a post office, the name Rich Hill was assigned to the village. The Rich Hill store served as a post office for many years. During the 1940s, Rich Hill Store was famous for the largest and best double-dip ice-cream cone for a dime. The store also carried groceries, had a soda fountain, and served light lunches. Tickets for the trolley were sold, and there was even a passenger waiting room. The store closed in the 1960s. (LKW.)

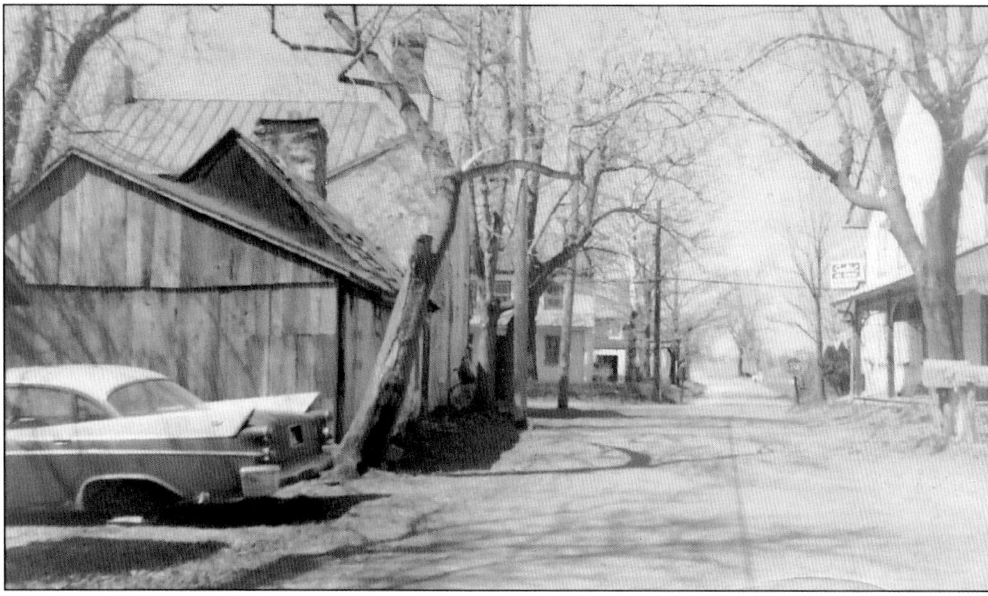

The Rich Hill store faces the Godon house, which was owned by Louise Godon. Godon was born in France in 1856 and came to the United States as a baby. She worked as both a schoolteacher and a postmistress in Queens County, New York. By 1920, Godon had retired and relocated to Richland Township, where her son Emile farmed. (CR.)

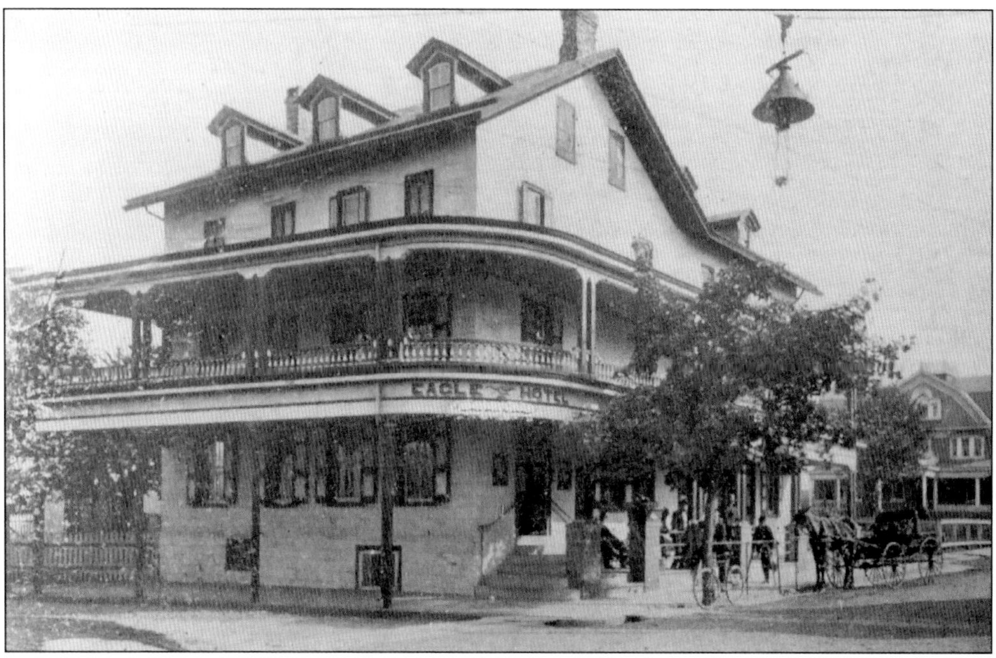

The Eagle Hotel is one of the oldest buildings in what was the village of Richland Centre. A store existed at this location as early as 1782, and a tavern at this spot called the Eagle was licensed in the 1830s. The village of Richland Centre was annexed by the Borough of Quakertown in 1874 but maintained its own post office as late as 1907. (RLC.)

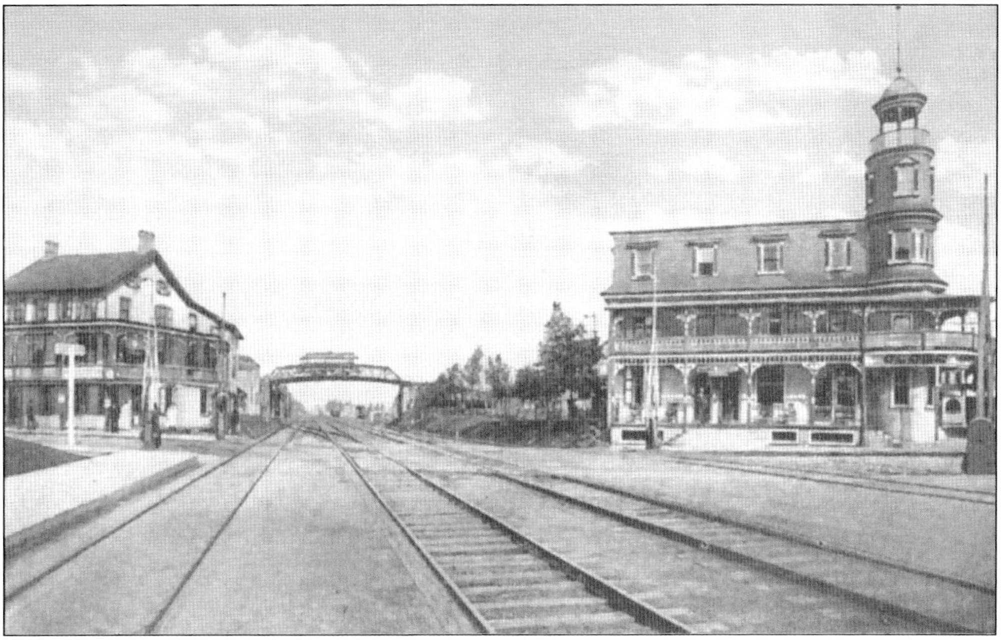

The North Penn Railroad was constructed through Richland Township in 1855, and the village of Richland Centre sprang up where the railroad crossed the Doylestown Road. In this view, looking north, the Globe Hotel appears on the right. It was the home of the Strawn family and was remodeled into a hotel the 1870s and the 1890s. (RLC.)

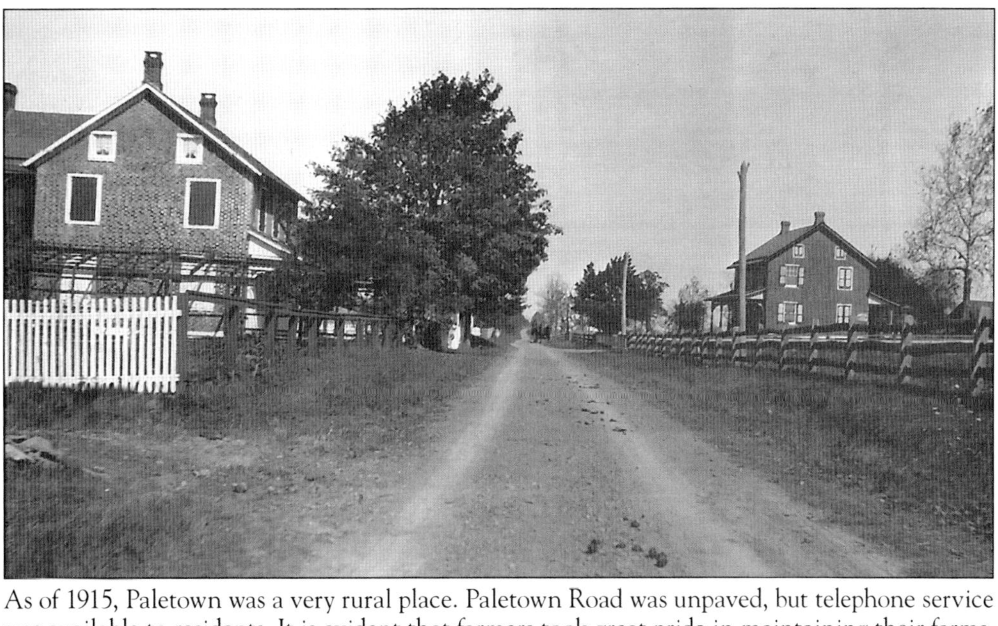

As of 1915, Paletown was a very rural place. Paletown Road was unpaved, but telephone service was available to residents. It is evident that farmers took great pride in maintaining their farms. Fences were kept in good repair, and houses and trim were painted frequently. (FFIM.)

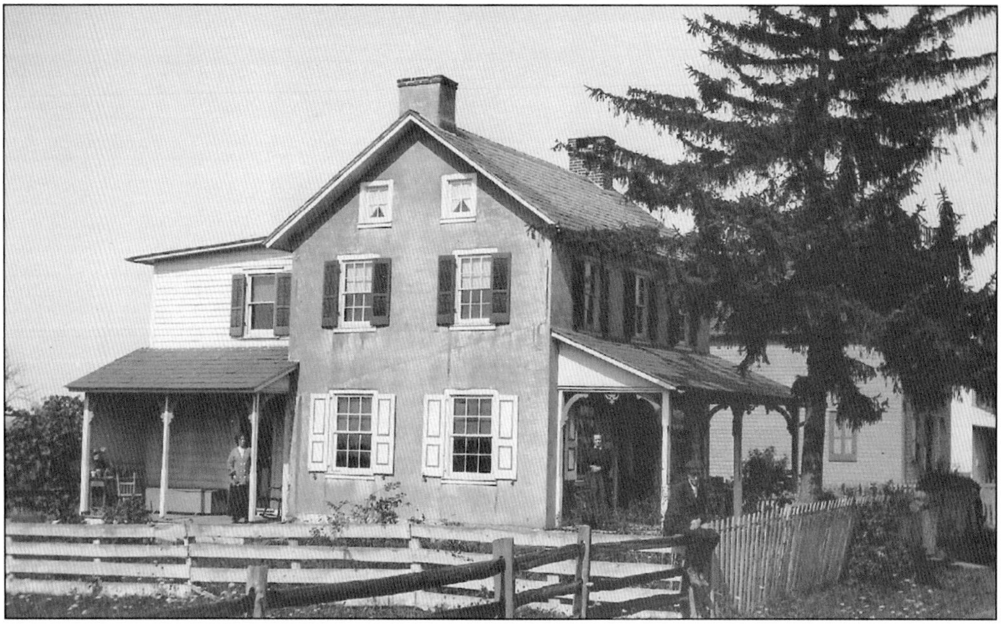

This is a prosperous farmer's home along Paletown Road about 1915. It had a fence made out of pales (slats), which gave Paletown its name. A whitewashed board fence is around the pasture. Shutters on the first floor are white with green trim; on the second floor they are green. Curtains can be seen in the attic windows. (FFIM.)

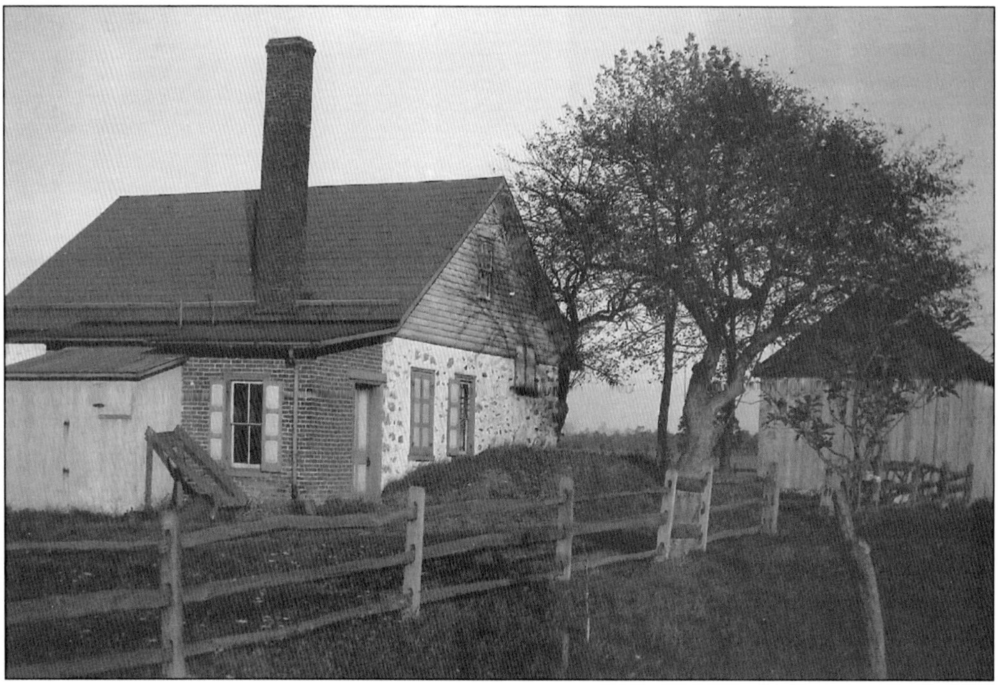

This creamery was located along Paletown Road in this 1915 photograph. Before modern refrigeration, raw milk had to be processed rapidly and bottled for sale to homes or stores, so creameries were located in almost every village. Many creameries such as this one were converted into homes when they were replaced by big dairy companies. (FFIM.)

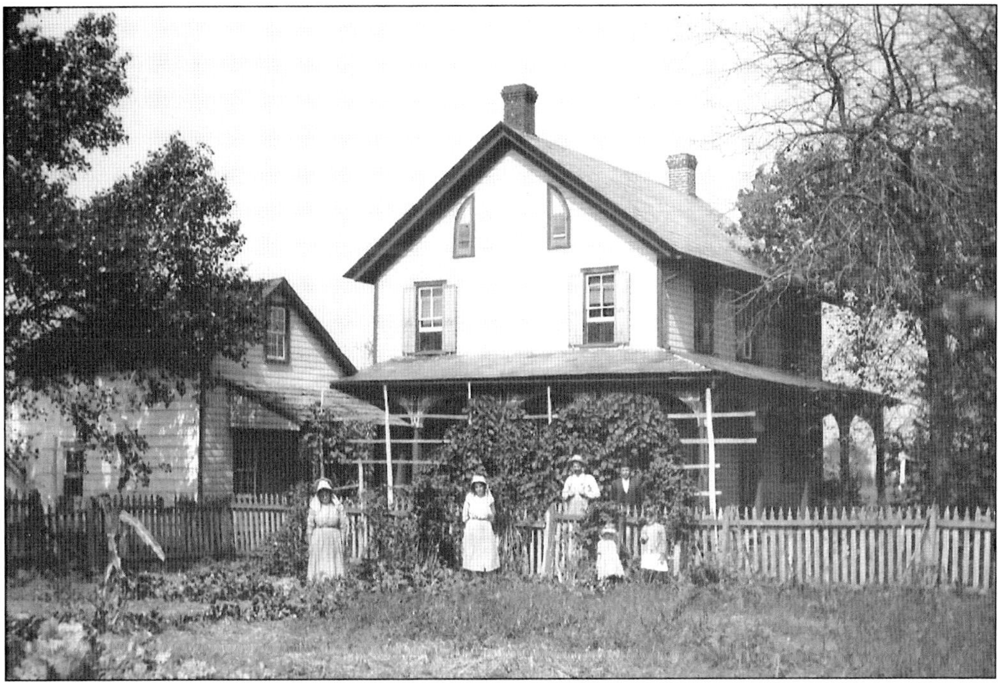

A family poses in front of the grape arbor at their farmhouse along Paletown Road about 1915. Purple Concord grapes were grown throughout the township and were a favorite for jelly and wine. A hand water pump is in the left foreground. This farm has the typical pale fence. (FFIM.)

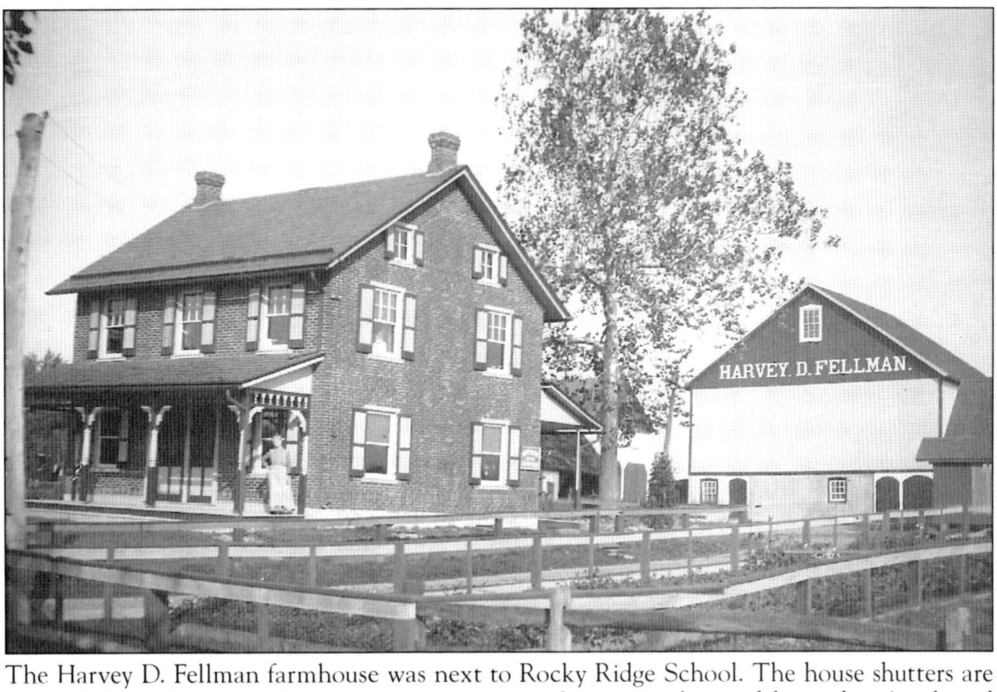

The Harvey D. Fellman farmhouse was next to Rocky Ridge School. The house shutters are painted white with green trim. Fences are necessary to keep animals out of the garden. A pole and wires on the left show that the Fellman family had a telephone even at that early date. Someone appears to be peering from the second floor window. (FFIM.)

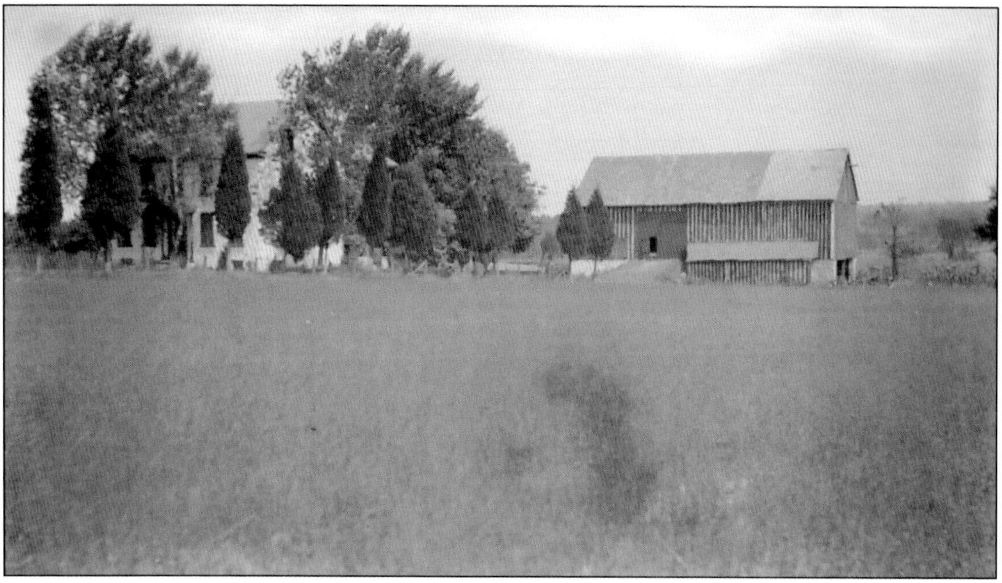

James and Rowena Lark were an African American couple who had been teachers in Washington, D.C. They moved to this farm (above) on Rocky Ridge Road in 1927 and became involved with the Mennonite mission that founded Rocky Ridge Church, which was on the edge of their farm. Because of their interest in the work of the Mennonite Church among African Americans in urban areas, they became superintendents of a mission in Chicago. In October 1946, Brother Lark was ordained in the Mennonite ministry. He was a leader of missionary work among African Americans. According to the Mennonite yearbook in 1981, James Lark was "fifty years ahead of his time in vision and concern for the growth of the Mennonite church in urban areas." (Above, FFIM; below, IM.)

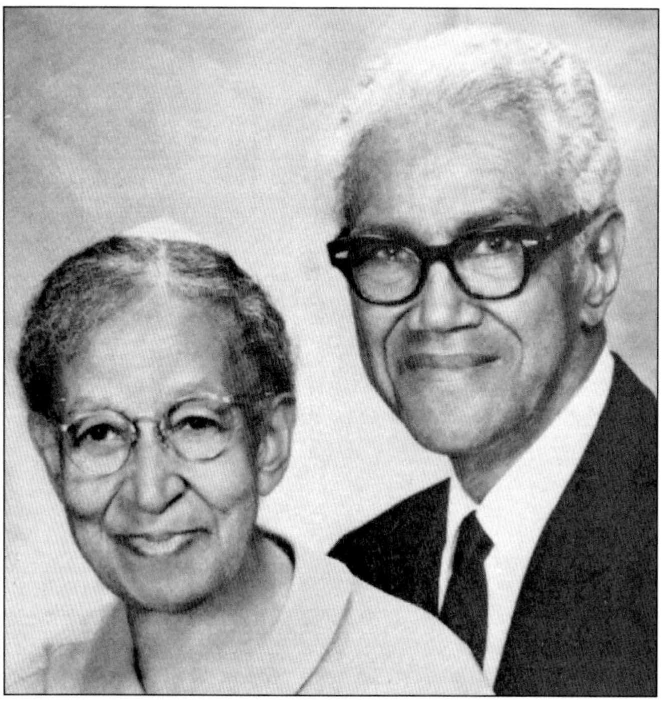

Four

SCHOOLS

The history of schooling in Richland Township goes back to the 18th century. At first, most children learned to read and calculate at home. Early in the 19th century, Richland Township had a number of teachers, such as Richard Moore, who conducted their own schools, probably in their homes.

The first formal schoolhouses were one-room structures. There were public schools in Richlandtown, California, and Paletown prior to 1850. A new brick schoolhouse was constructed in Richlandtown in 1855 at the corner of Main and Church Streets. In the next year, Shaw's School was built on California Road. The Society of Friends built a schoolhouse next to their meetinghouse in 1860.

It was necessary that the schools be within walking distance of the homes of the children. The following public schoolhouses were built in the years following the Civil War: Scholl's School (1867), Tohickon School (1868), Rocky Ridge School (1873), Shelly School on Richlandtown Pike (1885), California School (1890), Kaufman School (1890), Wimmer's School (1895), and Central School (1901). Richlandtown borough replaced its 1855 schoolhouse in 1909 with a four-room building. When Richlandtown discontinued its high school, its secondary students matriculated at Quakertown High School, as did Richland Township students.

With the pressure of the post–World War II baby boom, the era of the one-room schools ended in the 1950s. In cooperation with neighboring Milford Township, a modern elementary school, Tohickon Valley, was constructed to serve the students of both townships. But there were so many children of school age born in the 1950s that a second elementary school, Richland Elementary, was built. The former one-room schoolhouses were sold. The older Richlandtown School was used during the 20th century as a meeting place for community groups. It was razed after the Second World War in order to provide parking for St. John's United Church of Christ.

Quakertown Christian School is the only nonpublic school in Richland Township. It began as a one-room school in 1951 and is now a multiroom facility on Paletown Road.

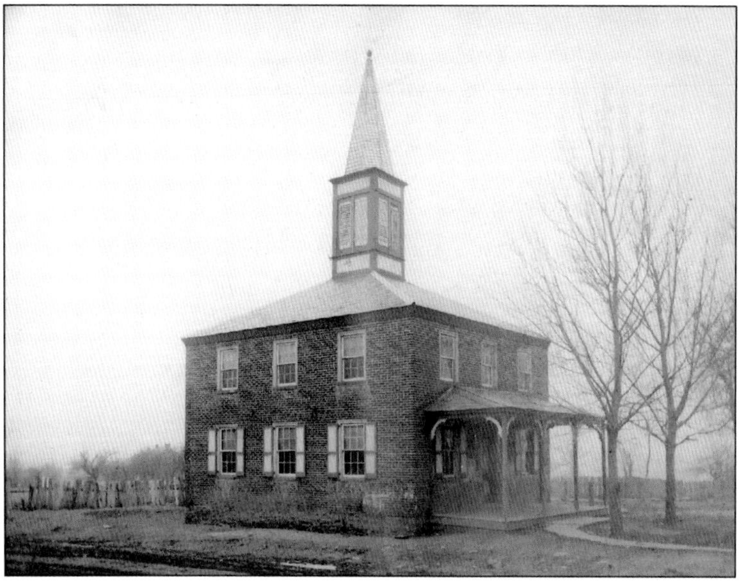

In 1854, the Richland Township School Board decided to build a schoolhouse and purchased a lot from the trustees of St. John's. A two-room brick building was completed in 1855. The students were organized into a primary school, consisting of grades one through four, and a grammar school of grades five to eight. (RHS.)

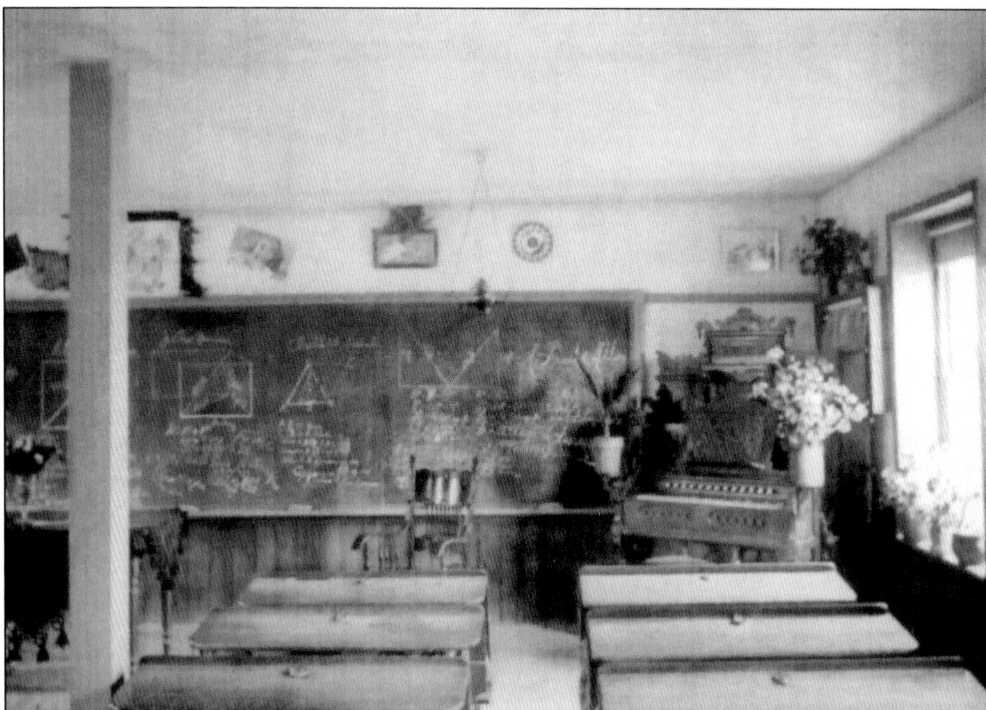

Several students in a geometry class in Richlandtown High School show their work on the blackboard in this photograph taken about 1900. The names of the students above their solutions to the problems are A. Frank Ahlum, J. Fred Neamand, Mabel A. Laubach, and James Rapp. The classroom had a pump organ, and it was lighted by a hanging oil lamp. (RHS.)

In 1856, the school board purchased a lot along California Road near the Red Lion Inn from Samuel Shaw. A brick schoolhouse was ready for students by the fall of 1856. For many years, students from all of the one-room schools in the township took their eighth-grade tests in Shaw's School. On the right is an ancient oak tree. (QCSD.)

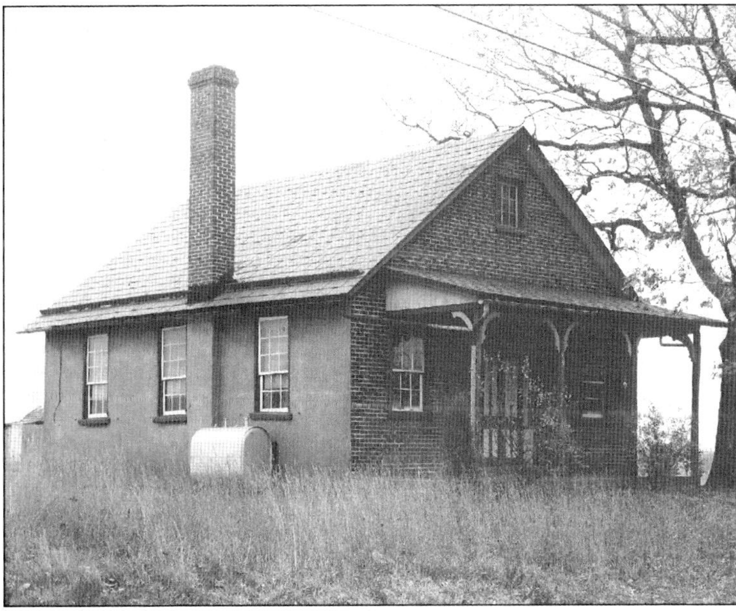

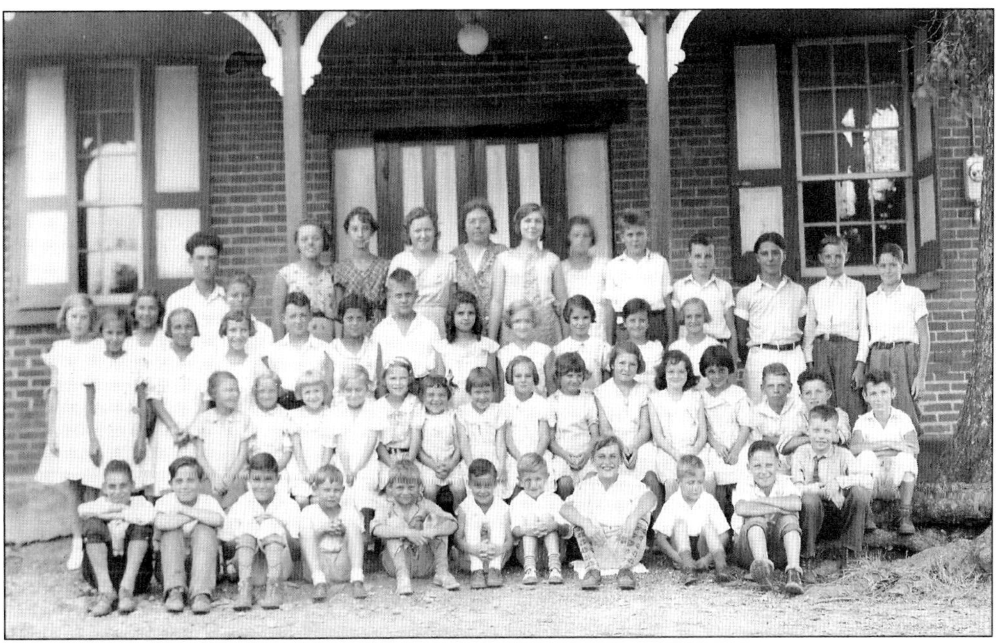

This photograph shows the students of Shaw's School on California Road with their teacher, Laura Stunk. Dressed in their best clothes, 48 students attended. Enrollment was so heavy in some of the township schools near Quakertown that Richland Township paid tuition to have the extra students attend elementary school in Quakertown. (RL.)

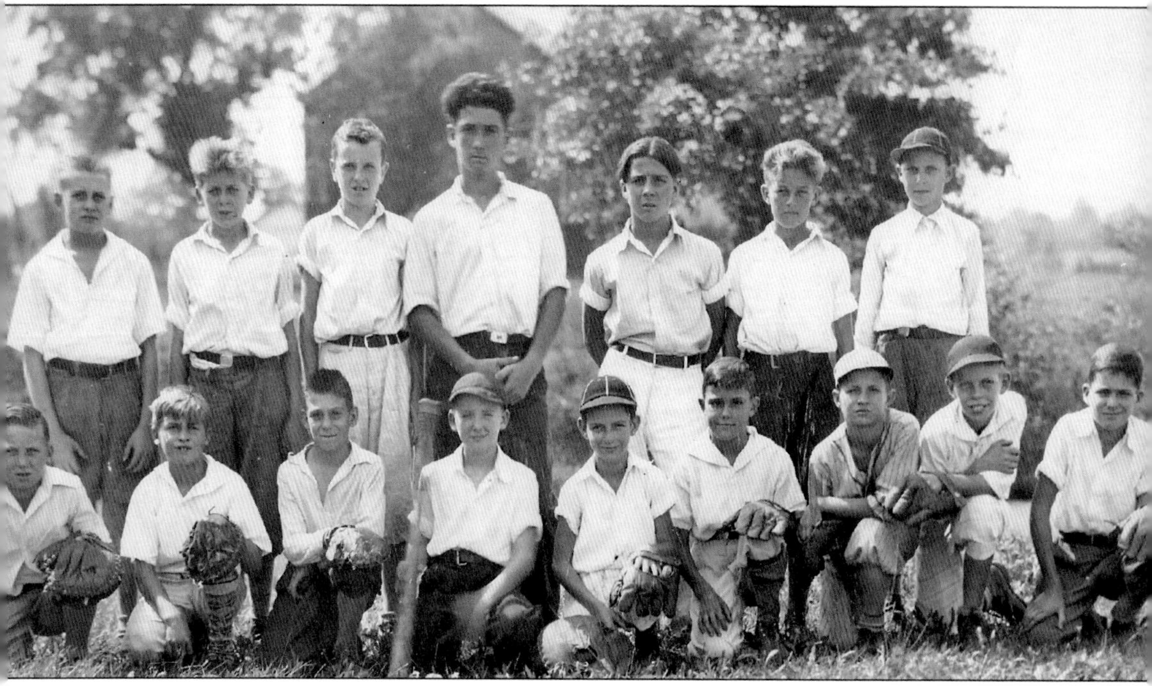

Shaw's School had enough boys to make up a baseball team, seen in this *c.* 1935 photograph. The ball field was on the farm of the Willauer family, across the California Road from the schoolhouse. The Willauers had a thriving business during the 1930s and 1940s manufacturing equipment for dairy barns and poultry houses. Their barn is in the background. The team includes, from left to right, (first row) Edward Novak, unidentified, William Harner, Jacob Fox, Raymond Lowman, William Leister, Vincent Cressman, Willard Landis, and Leonard Fox, (second row) unidentified, Raymond Foulke, Earl Fredrick, Howard Sholl, Raymond Sholl, Andrew Huyko, and Raymond Novak. Particularly after 1946, when three one-room schools had all of the seventh- and eighth-grade students, there were sufficient boys to form a team for informal competition with another of the one-room schools. One of the side benefits of having the eighth-grade examination at Shaw's School was that there were enough students to form teams during the break for lunch. (RHS.)

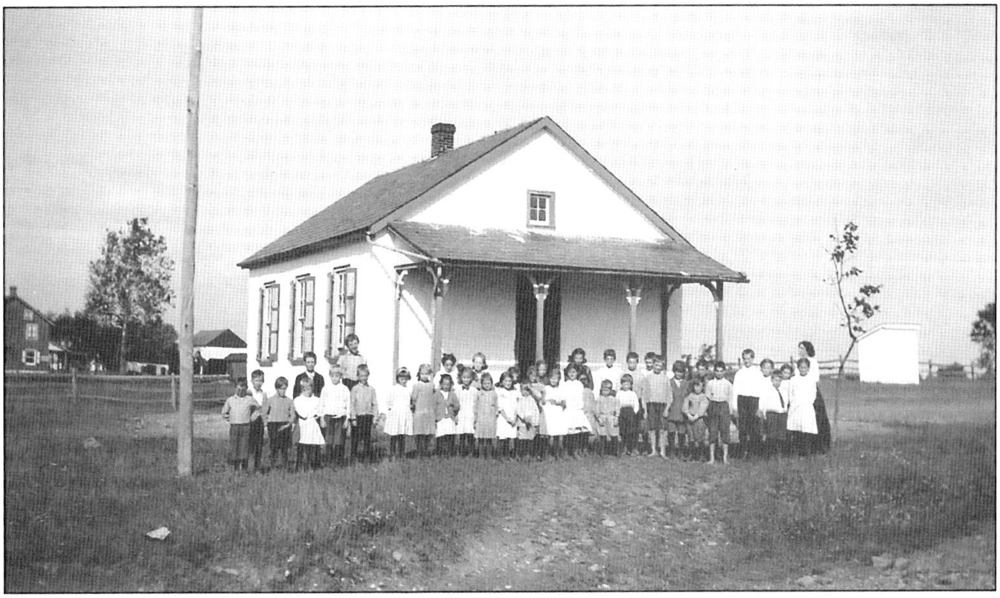

A public school was established on Paletown Road prior to 1853. This new building was erected in 1873. In the early days, it was called Fellman's School; it was later named Rocky Ridge School. Laura Fellman, who taught at Rocky Ridge, lived a few steps from the building. Her sister Flora captured many images of Paletown with her camera in 1914. (FFIM.)

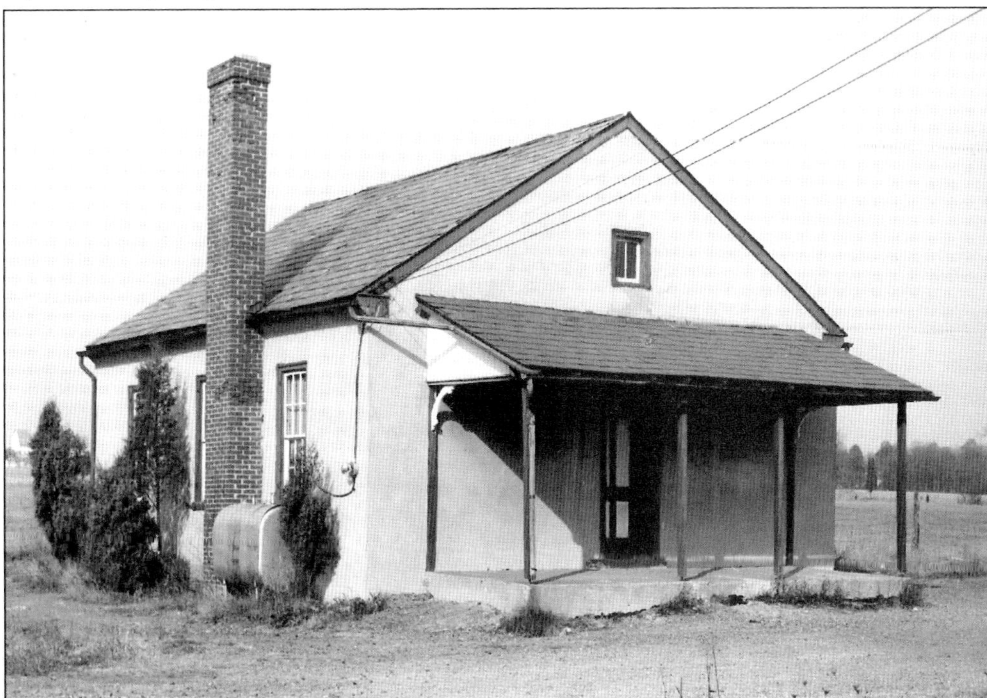

Scholl's School was located along a country road next to a stream that flooded the playground in rainy weather. A rusty barbed wire fence kept the students from playing in the adjoining cow pasture. Scholl's was reconstructed of stone on the site of a previous public school in 1867. The photograph was taken about 1950 by Quakertown High School teacher Warren Buck. (QCSD.)

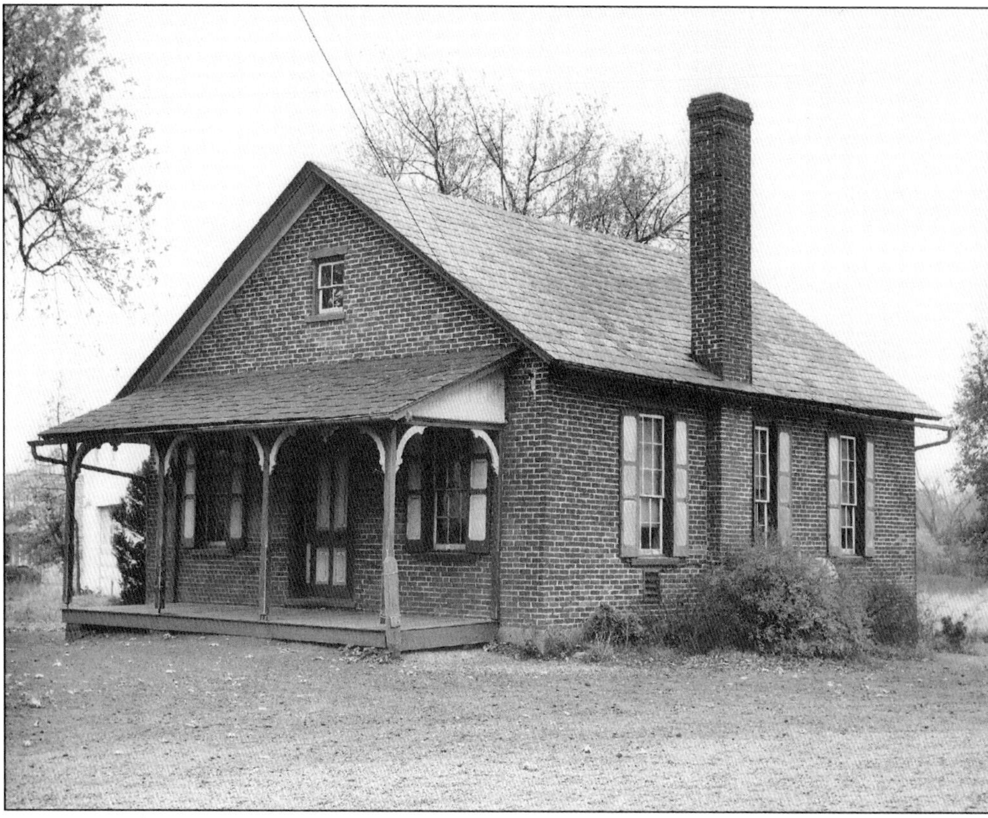

In 1885, students who lived between Richlandtown and Quakertown needed a convenient schoolhouse. A half-acre lot was purchased from Lewis Shelly along the Richlandtown turnpike. Contractor Sebastian Horne was the low bidder at $926. The Richland Historical Society purchased the Shelly schoolhouse in 1959 for $1,750 and has maintained it in its original condition. Cordelia Maier taught here in the 1940s and 1950s. (QCSD.)

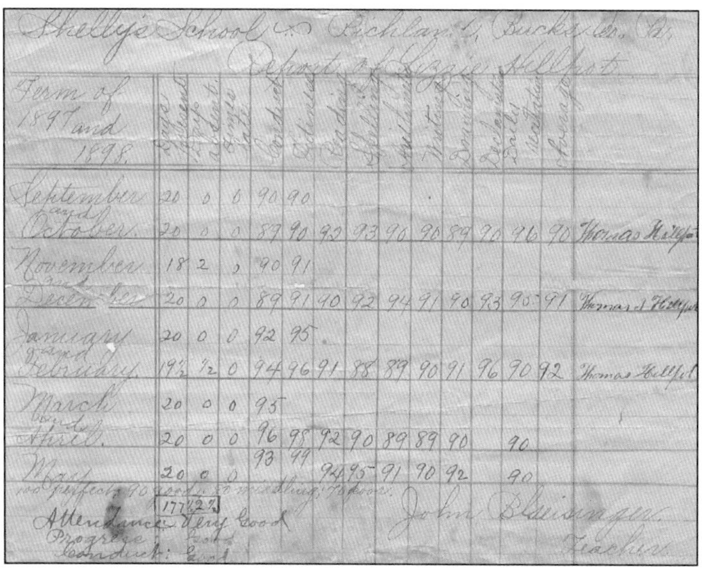

Shelly's School Richland, Bucks Co. Pa.

Report of Lizzie Hillpot

Term of 1897 and 1898														
September	20	0	0	90	90									
and October.	20	0	0	87	90	92	93	90	90	89	90	96	90	Thomas Hillpot
November	18	2	0	90	91									
and December	20	0	0	89	91	90	92	94	91	90	93	90	91	Thomas Hillpot
January	20	0	0	92	95									
and February.	19½	½	0	94	96	91	88	89	90	91	96	90	92	Thomas Hillpot
March	20	0	0	95										
and April.	20	0	0	96	98	92	90	89	89	90		90		
May	20	0	0	93	99	94	95	91	90	92		90		

100 perfect, 90 good, 80 middling, 70 poor.

177½ 2½

Attendance: Very Good

Progress: Good

Conduct: Good

John Blaisinger

Teacher

A report card from the 1897–1898 school term at Shelly's School shows that Lizzie Hillpot was graded on conduct, tidiness, reading, spelling, arithmetic, writing, drawing, declamation, and daily recitation. Hillpot was an excellent student; she attended 177.5 days of school and maintained averages above 90 percent. The report card was sent home for a parental signature every two months. (RLC.)

Keeping up the fire was one of the requirements of the one-room schoolteacher. Bringing wood or coal from the outside and tending the fire was often delegated to one of the older boys. Older students were paid to start the fire on Sunday evening so the room would be warm on Monday morning. (RLRF.)

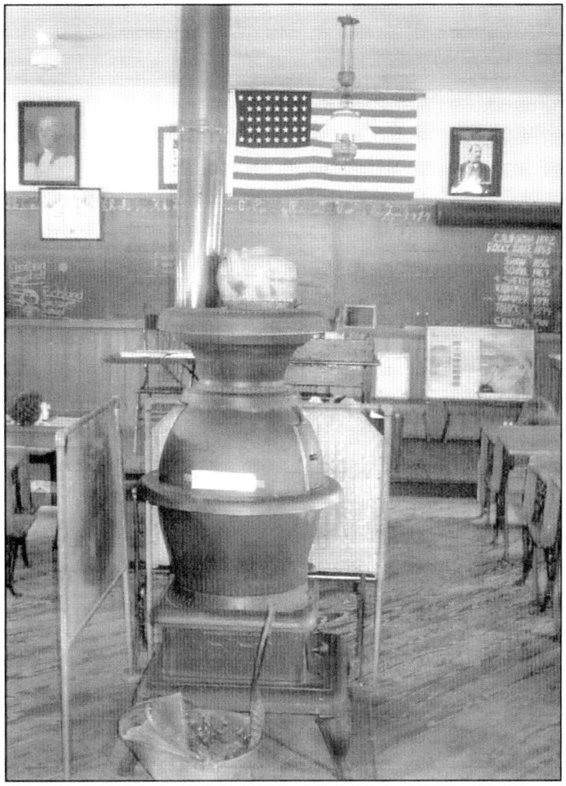

Students from the section of Richland Township east of Richlandtown needed a convenient school in 1890. A half-acre lot was purchased from Isaac Wimmer for $100. Contractor J. W. Stoneback won the contract to construct the Wimmer schoolhouse with a bid of $818. The school building was identical to Shelly School. The teacher during the 1950s when the school closed was Frank Novelli. (QCSD.)

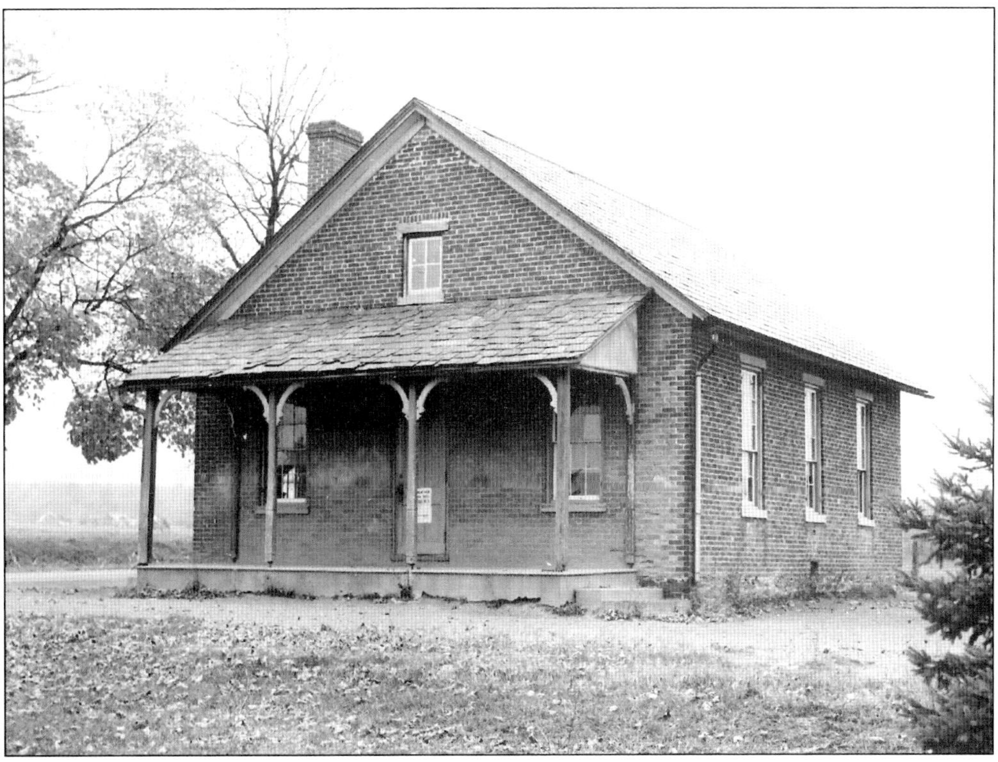

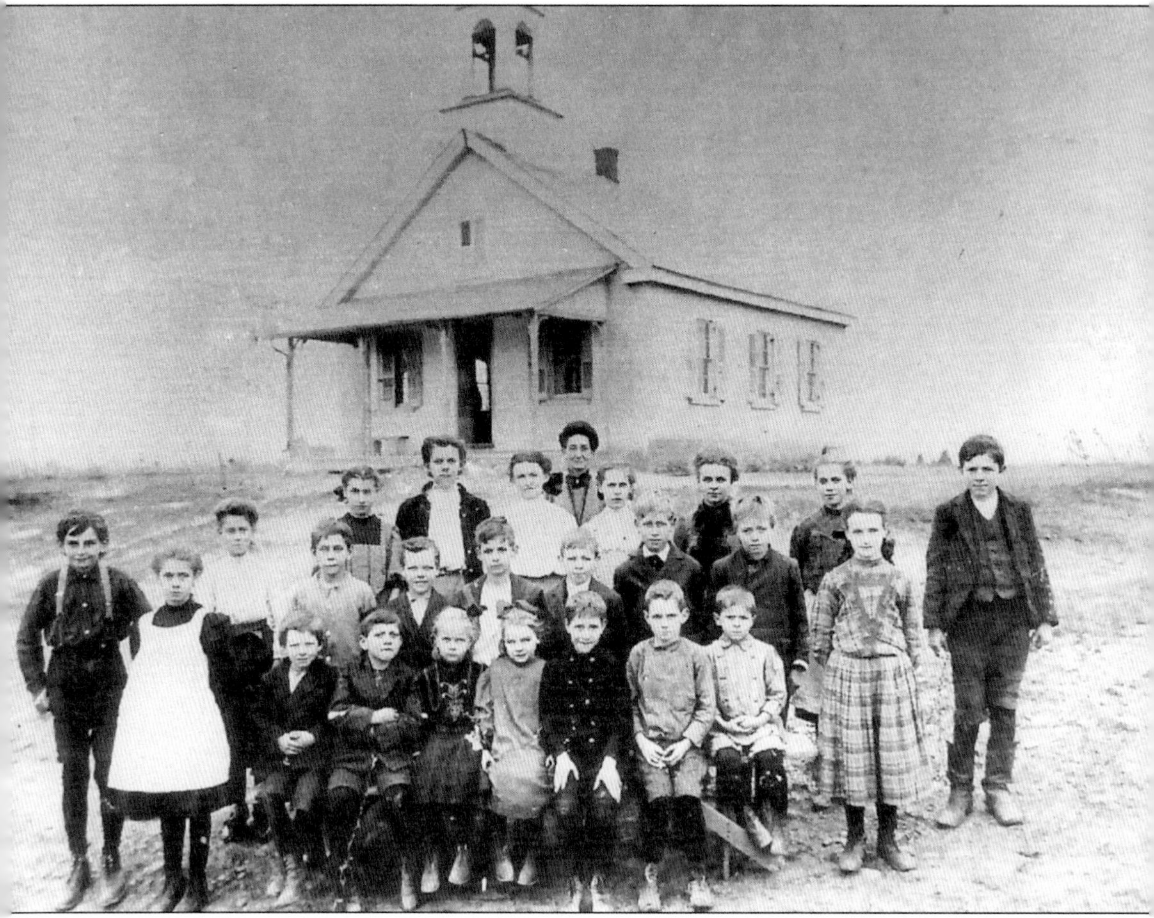

Rebecca Heller (back row center) posed with her students at Wimmer's School during the spring term in 1914. Students enrolled in the school at the time were: Gertrude Allem, Maggie Allem, Beatrice Behney, Alma Beidler, Arthur Clay, Alice Kelly, Susan Klimeck, Hiram Kulp, Granville Link, Maybelle Link, Catherine Neamand, Normand Neamand, Vincent Neamand, Fred Raub, Harvey Raub, Mabel Raub, Chester Sames, Stephen Schaffer, Myrtle Scheetz, Paul Scheetz, Arthur Slotter, Mildred Slotter, Charles Sloyer, Mamie Sloyer, Myrtle Sloyer, Laquitta Stahler, Emma Sterner, Marian Ulmer, Pauline Ulmer, Alice Walp, Norman Weiss, Bessie Youngkin, Edith Youngkin, and Norman Youngkin. Some schoolhouses were built with a bell tower, as shown in the photograph. However, the slate roof around the tower often leaked. During high winds, the tower could be damaged or even knocked down. When this happened, school boards often felt the practical decision was to repair the roof without a tower. (RLC.)

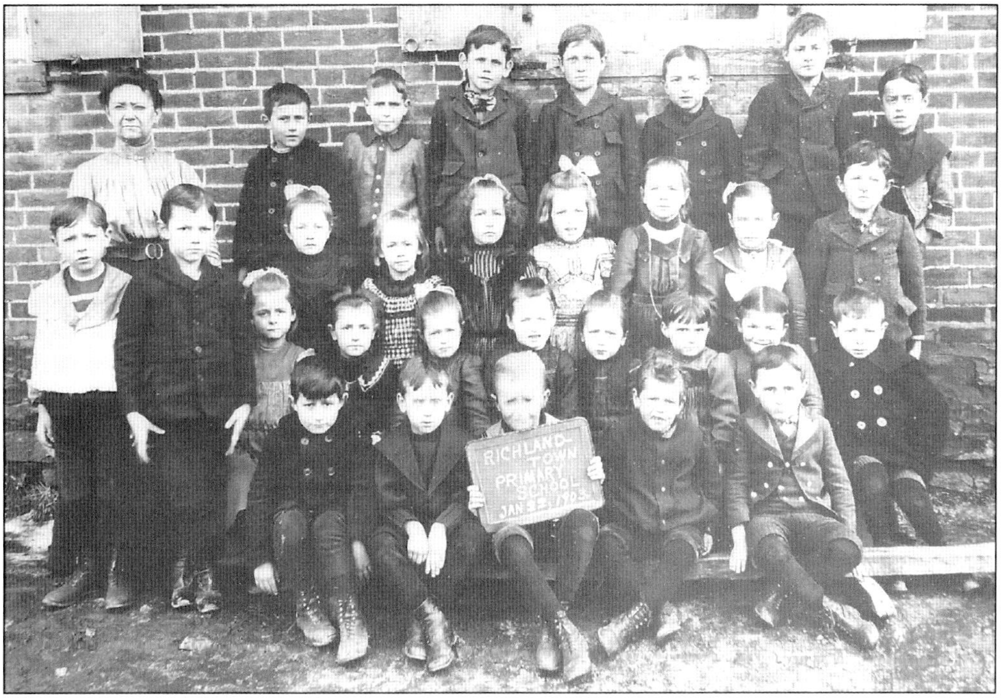

Emma Price, who taught for 40 years, stands with her students outside of the Richlandtown School in 1903. This photographs of Price with the primary class includes, from left to right, (first row) Harry Henry, Harold Hartman, Erwin Heller, Raymond Henry, and Harvey Weider; (second row) Verney Nace, Earl Ruth, Helen Jones, Amanda Frankenfield, Erwinna Price, Edith Gable, Esther Wilt, Mary Hartman, Maggie Shelly, and Ray Hartman; (third row) Mary Schroy, Myrtle Freed, Mabel Cressman, Mabel Freemoyer, Revena Hartman, Florence Wimmer, and Herbert Wimmer; (fourth row) Emma Price (teacher), Elmer Henry, Albert Cease, John Kemmerer, Milton Weaver, Holt Sterner, Charles Weaver, and Stuart Erdman. The grammar class, taught by Frank Hartman, posed for a picture the same day. Unfortunately, the names of his students were not recorded on the picture. (Both, RLC.)

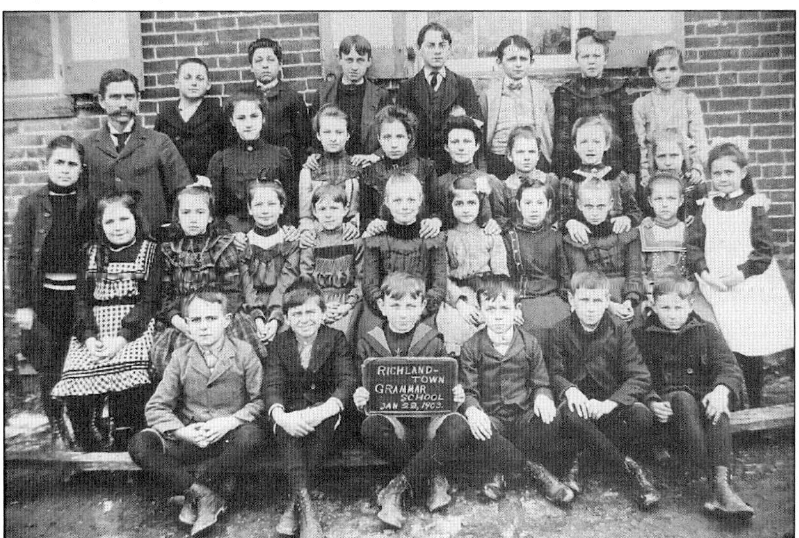

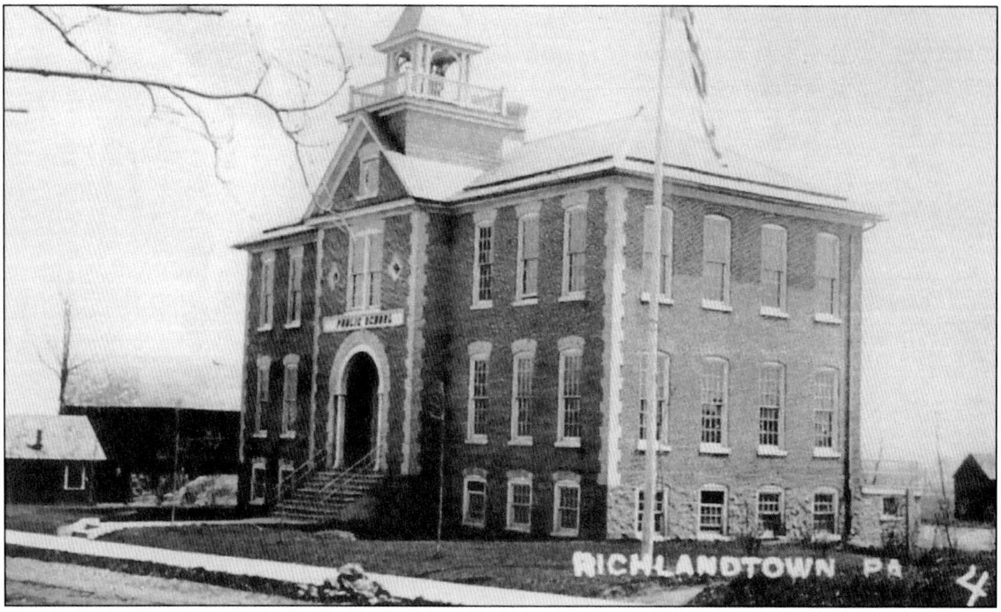

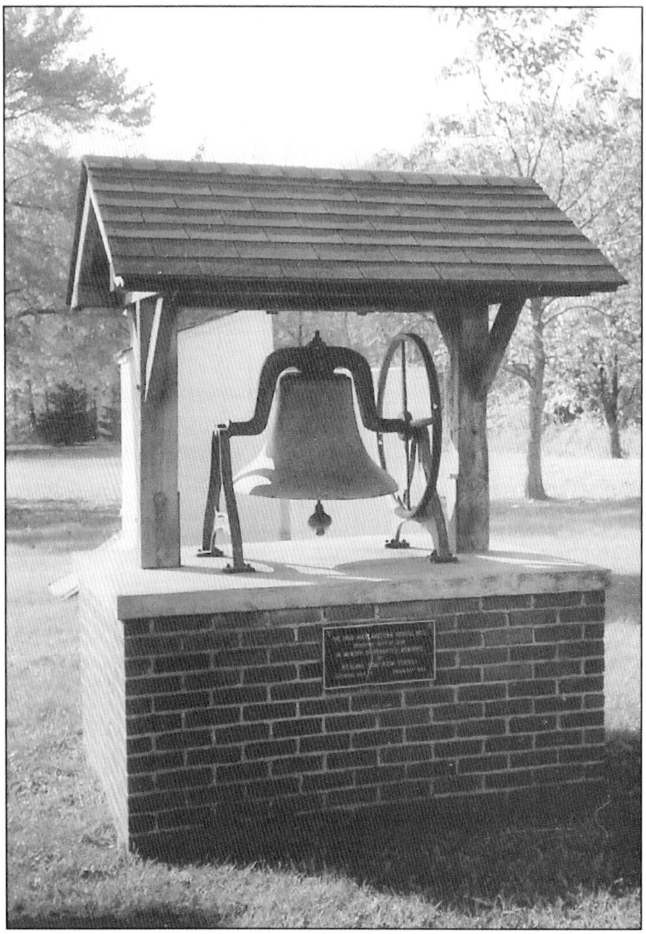

In April 1909, the Richlandtown School Board resolved to purchase a lot across from the cemetery to build a new school. A loan of $8,000 was secured to erect the new building, which was completed in less than a year. The school (above) opened in September 1910 and housed primary, grammar, and high school classes. High school classes ended in 1927, but elementary classes continued into the 1970s. Later the building was sold and converted into apartments. The bell from the tower was removed and in 1976 was placed outside the Shelly School (left). It serves as a memorial to deceased members of the Richland Historical Society. (Above, RB; left, RHS.)

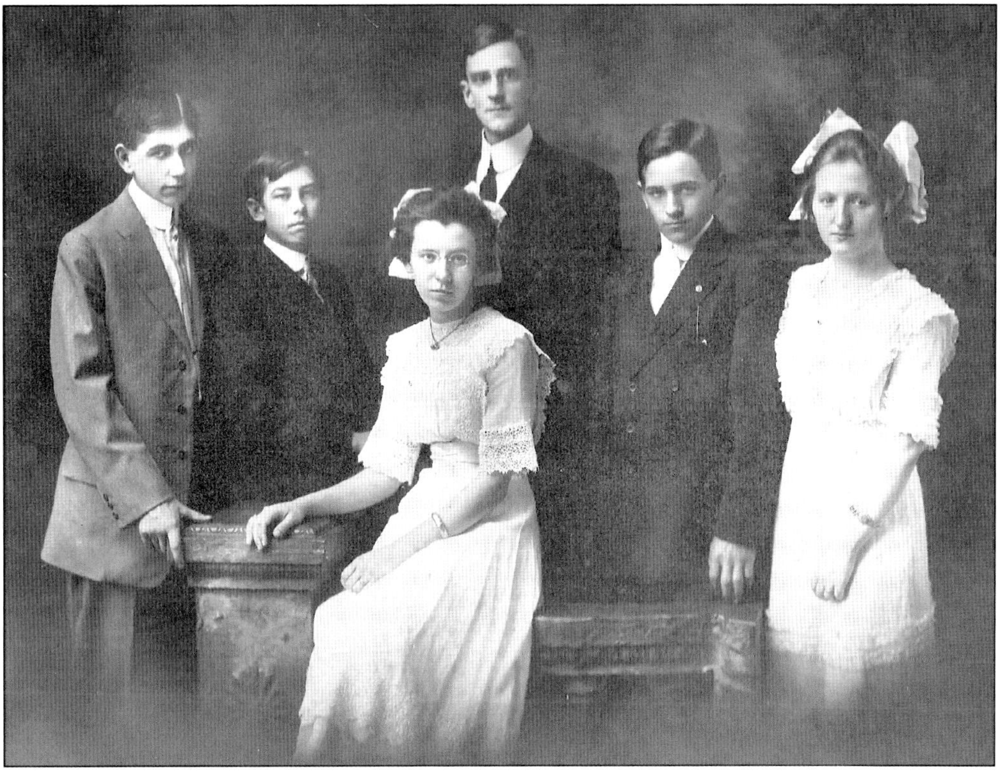

When the new Richlandtown School was opened in September 1910, high school classes were housed on the second floor. Five students graduated from Richlandtown High School in 1912. In this photograph are, from left to right, (sitting) Esther Saylor; (standing) Harry Landis, Raymond Kreuger, Prof. William Melchior, Robert Clark, and Naomi Clark. William Melchior also served as principal and drew a salary of $85 per month. The Richlandtown High School was able to field a basketball team (below). This photograph shows what was probably the last basketball team from the school. Richlandtown High School was closed in 1927, and students wishing to pursue secondary studies were sent to nearby Quakertown High School. (Above, RHS; below, RB.)

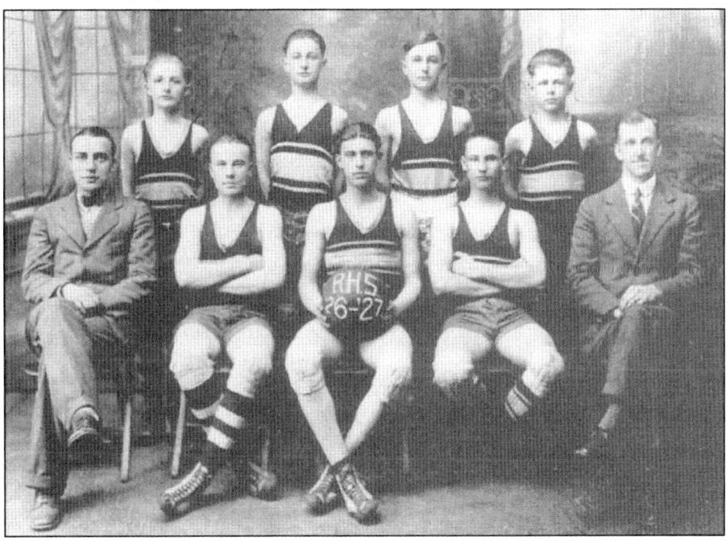

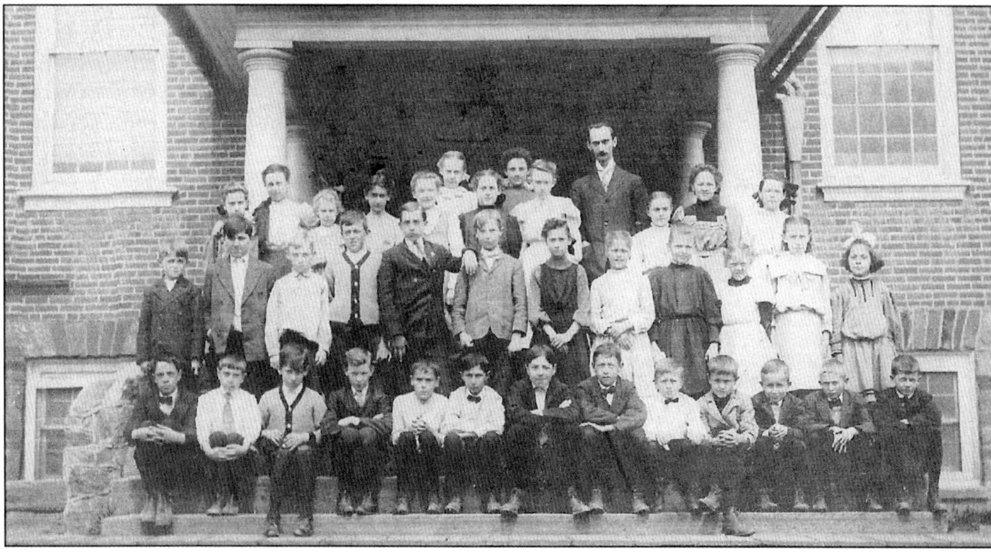

Frank Hartman served as the grammar school teacher in Richlandtown for many years. He taught grades five through eight in the old two-room schoolhouse and moved to the new school when it opened in 1910. In this picture, he poses with his students at the new facility. Frank Hartman earned $55 per month. His colleague, Cordelia Strouse, taught the primary grades for $50 per month. (RLC.)

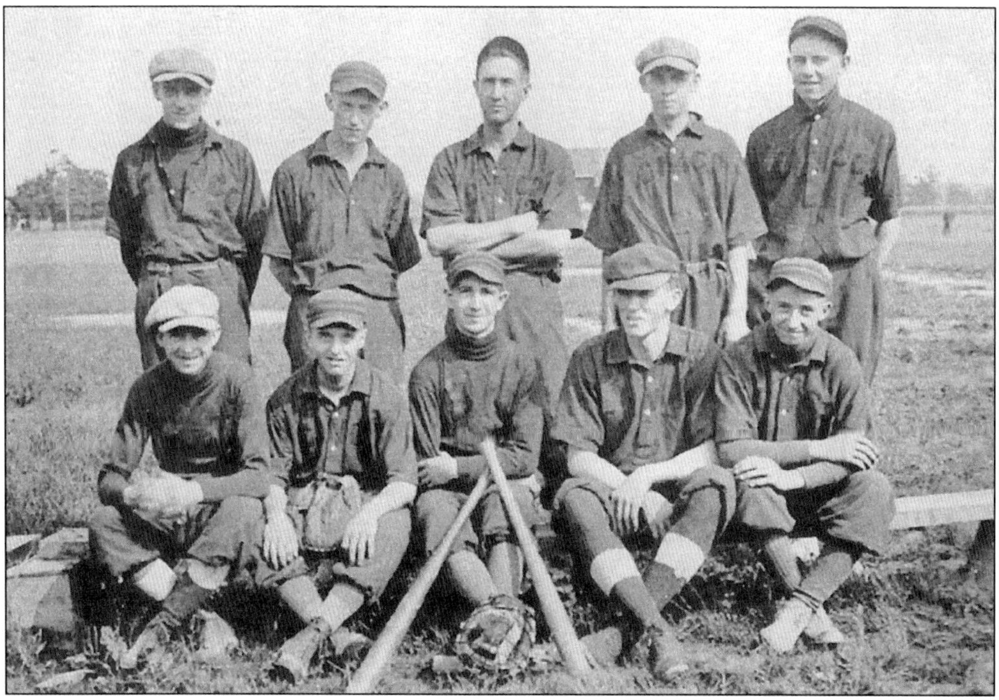

Athletics were not necessarily part of the curriculum in the early schools of Richlandtown. Local students had to look to community members to sponsor athletic activities. One such group was this baseball team, sponsored by the Richlandtown Athletic Association. The association was organized in the early 1930s to promote general recreation. The baseball team poses at the field built for them by the athletic association. (RB.)

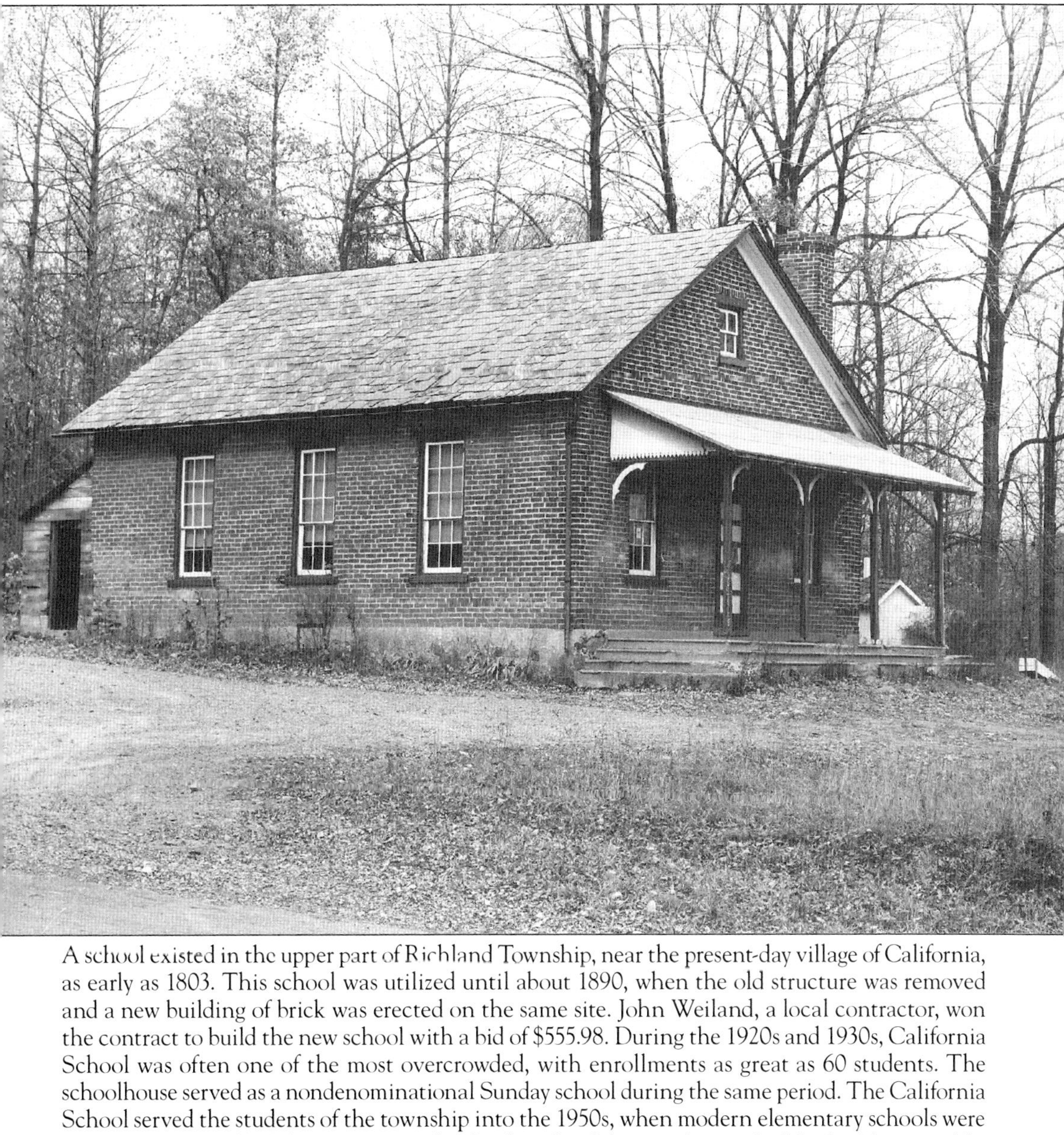

A school existed in the upper part of Richland Township, near the present-day village of California, as early as 1803. This school was utilized until about 1890, when the old structure was removed and a new building of brick was erected on the same site. John Weiland, a local contractor, won the contract to build the new school with a bid of $555.98. During the 1920s and 1930s, California School was often one of the most overcrowded, with enrollments as great as 60 students. The schoolhouse served as a nondenominational Sunday school during the same period. The California School served the students of the township into the 1950s, when modern elementary schools were opened. As with all of the one-room schools, the school district disposed of the building quickly. Unfortunately, the California School was razed by the new owners after it was sold. (QCSD.)

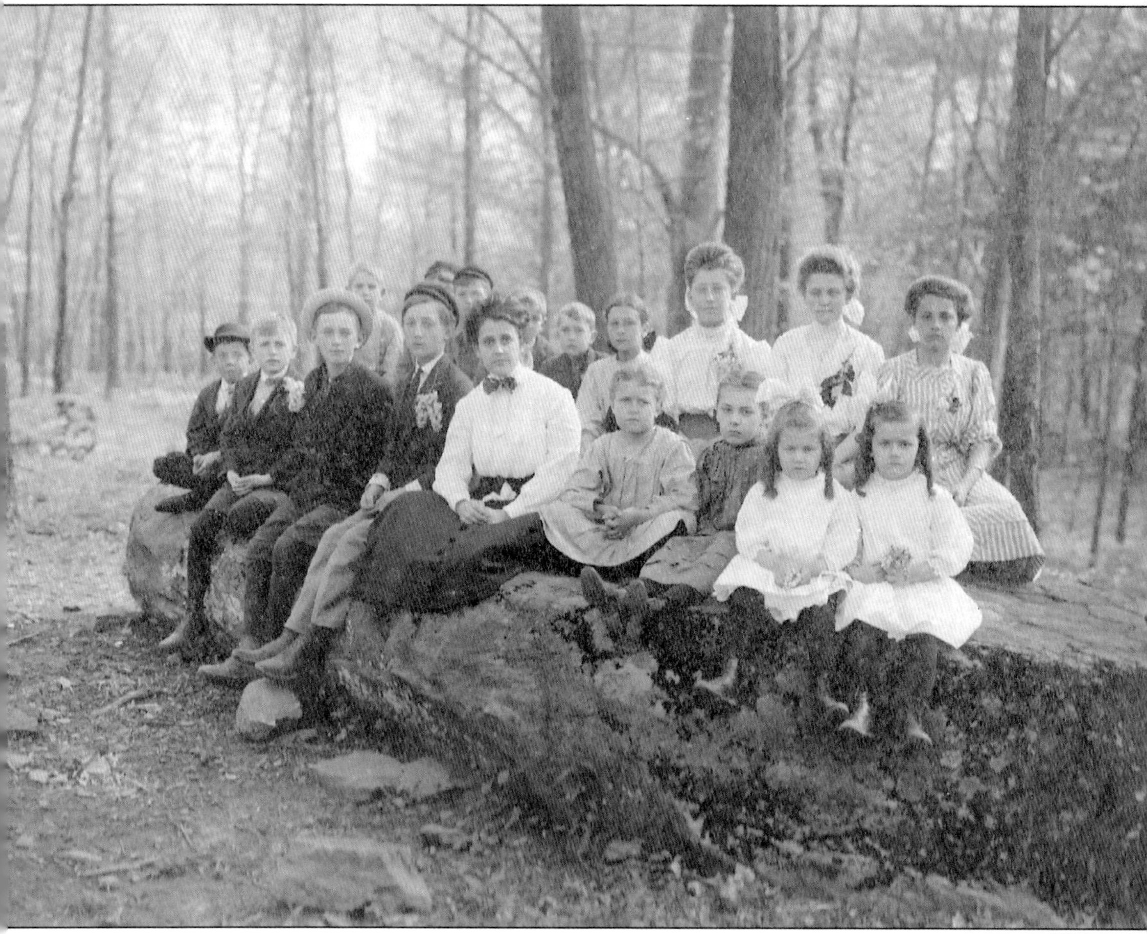

Students from Kaufman School enjoy a picnic in the woods with their teacher, Alda Moyer, during the 1908–1909 school year. Pictured are, from left to right, (first row) Wilson Charles, Earl Trumbauer, John Nice, William Nice, teacher Alda Moyer, Mabel Dewees, Edna Moose, Annie Miller, and Florence Miller; (second row) five unidentified, Pearl Collier, Estella Fluck, Ella Nice, and Jennie Cressman. The Kaufman School was built in 1890 to serve students living in the northwestern part of Richland Township. Land for the school was donated by Peter Kaufman, who owned an 86-acre farm. When U.S. Route 309 was constructed through Richland Township, the Kaufman School was cut off from the village of Shelly. During the construction, the school board took an unusual step and hired a private contractor, Harry Moose, to transport the students to school. It was the first time that transportation was provided for Richland students. (RHS.)

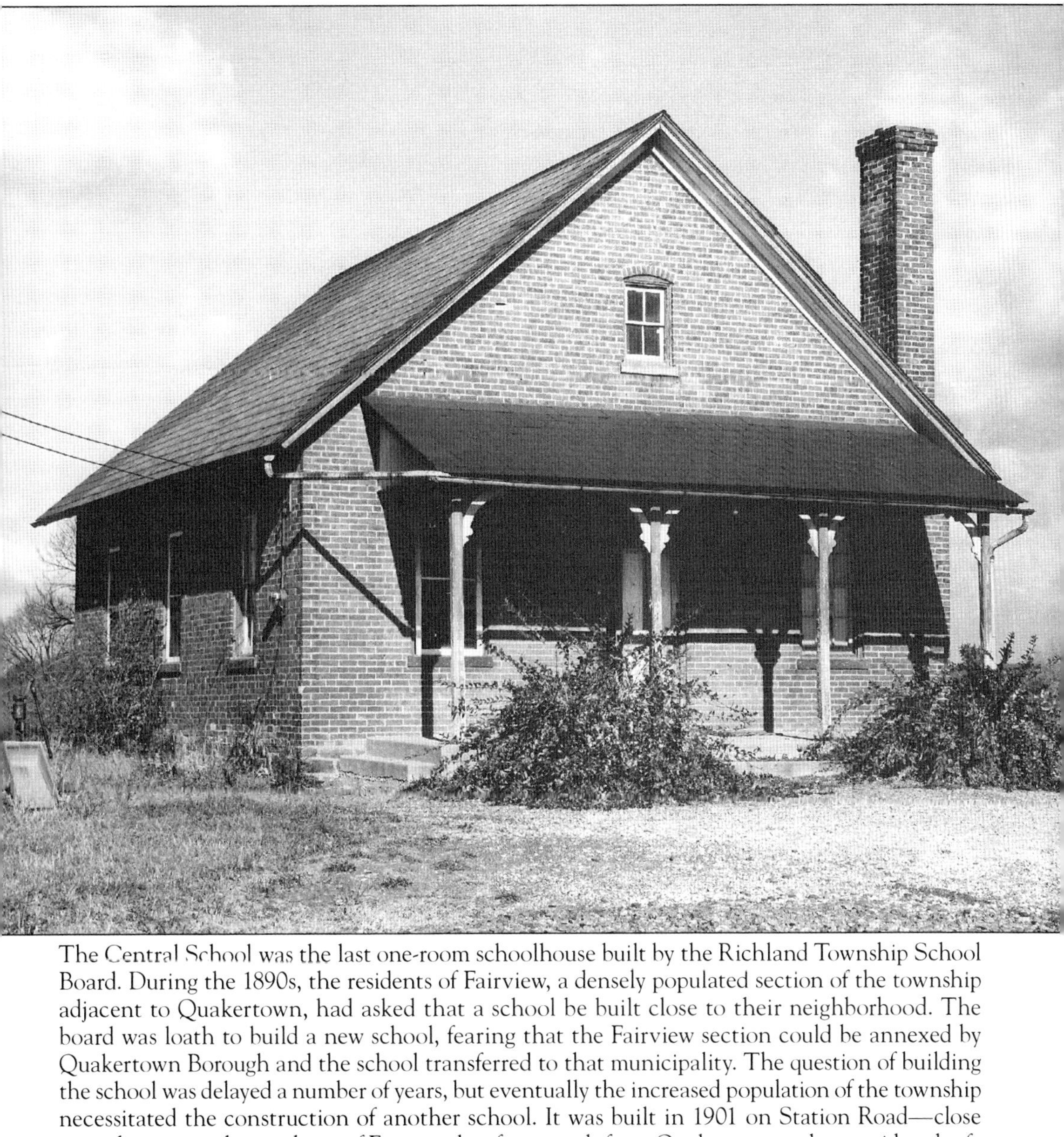

The Central School was the last one-room schoolhouse built by the Richland Township School Board. During the 1890s, the residents of Fairview, a densely populated section of the township adjacent to Quakertown, had asked that a school be built close to their neighborhood. The board was loath to build a new school, fearing that the Fairview section could be annexed by Quakertown Borough and the school transferred to that municipality. The question of building the school was delayed a number of years, but eventually the increased population of the township necessitated the construction of another school. It was built in 1901 on Station Road—close enough to serve the residents of Fairview but far enough from Quakertown to be considered safe from annexation. The Central School closed in 1957. It was disposed of at a private sale and still stands. (QCSD.)

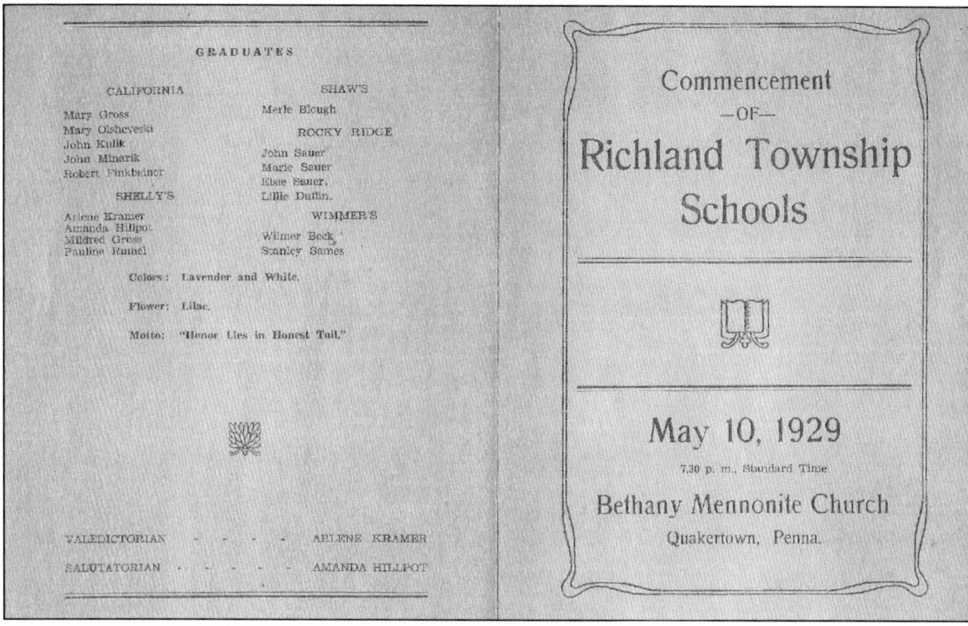

GRADUATES

CALIFORNIA

Mary Gross
Mary Olsheveski
John Kulik
John Minarik
Robert Finkbeiner

SHELLY'S

Arlene Kramer
Amanda Hillpot
Mildred Gross
Pauline Rumel

SHAW'S

Merle Blough

ROCKY RIDGE

John Sauer
Marie Sauer
Elsie Sauer.
Lillie Duffin.

WIMMER'S

Wilmer Beck
Stanley Sames

Colors: Lavender and White.

Flower: Lilac.

Motto: "Honor Lies in Honest Toil."

VALEDICTORIAN - - - - - ARLENE KRAMER

SALUTATORIAN - - - - - AMANDA HILLPOT

Commencement

—OF—

Richland Township Schools

May 10, 1929

7.30 p. m., Standard Time

Bethany Mennonite Church

Quakertown, Penna.

The formal program for grade eight graduation featured recitations and musical numbers by the graduates. As the matter of separation of church and state was not an issue in American public schools, a minister was often the major speaker. Pastor H. Jerome Leinbach offered the invocation, gave the major address, and offered the benediction. Diplomas were awarded by assistant county superintendent of schools Albert C. Rutter. The eighth-grade commencement was an important milestone, equivalent to high school graduation now, as many students concluded their formal schooling at this point. The ceremony typically was held in a church as none of the one-room schoolhouses could have held the crowd of families and friends. In 1929, the ceremony was on May 10 in Bethany Mennonite Church, on Juniper Street in Quakertown. (RL.)

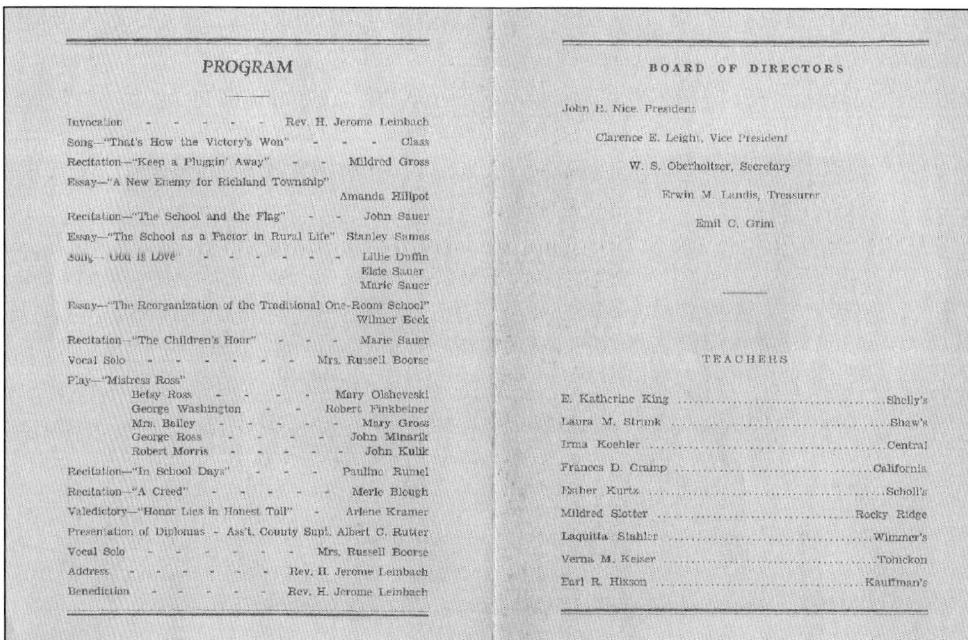

PROGRAM

Invocation - - - - - - Rev. H. Jerome Leinbach
Song—"That's How the Victory's Won" - - - Class
Recitation—"Keep a Pluggin' Away" - - Mildred Gross
Essay—"A New Enemy for Richland Township" Amanda Hillpot
Recitation—"The School and the Flag" - - John Sauer
Essay—"The School as a Factor in Rural Life" Stanley Sames
Song—"God Is Love" - - - - - - Lillie Duffin, Elsie Sauer, Marie Sauer
Essay—"The Reorganization of the Traditional One-Room School" Wilmer Beck
Recitation—"The Children's Hour" - - - Marie Sauer
Vocal Solo - - - - - - Mrs. Russell Boorse
Play—"Mistress Ross"
Betsy Ross - - - - Mary Olsheveski
George Washington - - Robert Finkbeiner
Mrs. Bailey - - - - - Mary Gross
George Ross - - - - John Minarik
Robert Morris - - - - - John Kulik
Recitation—"In School Days" - - - Pauline Rumel
Recitation—"A Creed" - - - - - Merle Blough
Valedictory—"Honor Lies in Honest Toil" - Arlene Kramer
Presentation of Diplomas - Ass't. County Supt. Albert C. Rutter
Vocal Solo - - - - - - Mrs. Russell Boorse
Address - - - - - - Rev. H. Jerome Leinbach
Benediction - - - - - Rev. H. Jerome Leinbach

BOARD OF DIRECTORS

John P. Nice, President
Clarence E. Leight, Vice President
W. S. Oberholtzer, Secretary
Erwin M. Landis, Treasurer
Emil C. Grim

TEACHERS

E. Katherine King .... Shelly's
Laura M. Strunk .... Shaw's
Irma Koehler .... Central
Frances D. Cramp .... California
Esther Kurtz .... Scholl's
Mildred Slotter .... Rocky Ridge
Laquitta Stahler .... Wimmer's
Verna M. Keiser .... Tohickon
Earl R. Hixson .... Kauffman's

Each spring, a test was given to all students who had completed eighth grade. All of the candidates gathered the same day at a central location in the township, usually Shaw's School (at right), to take the exam. Topics included history, English grammar, literature, mathematics, hygiene, geography, and spelling. Pastor Henry W. Fitting, of St. John's Lutheran Church, delivered the invocation, major address, and benediction at the 1931 commencement exercises (below). The valedictorian, Arthur Longacre, and salutatorian, Louise Barr, had scored highest in tests given by the county superintendent of schools (RL.)

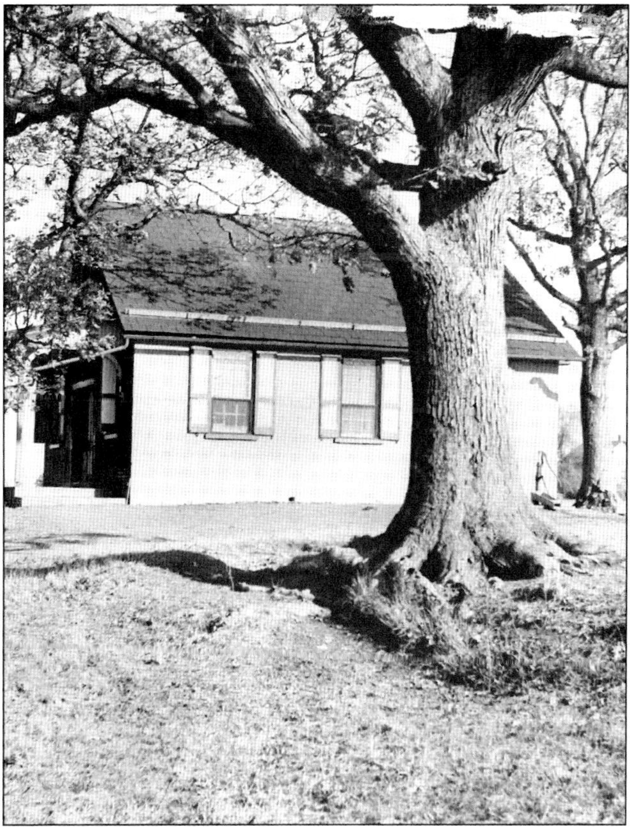

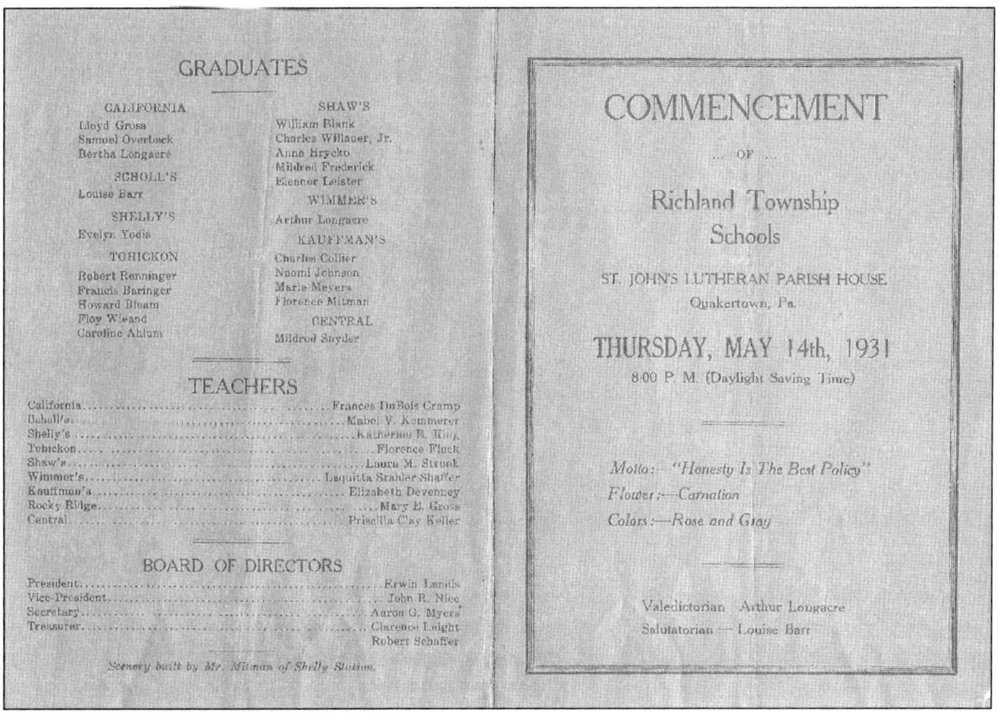

GRADUATES

CALIFORNIA
Lloyd Gross
Samuel Overback
Bertha Longacre

SCHOLL'S
Louise Barr

SHELLY'S
Evelyn Yodis

TOHICKON
Robert Renninger
Francis Baringer
Howard Bleam
Floy Wieand
Caroline Ahlum

SHAW'S
William Blank
Charles Willauer, Jr.
Anna Hrycko
Mildred Frederick
Eleanor Leister

WIMMER'S
Arthur Longacre

KAUFFMAN'S
Charles Collier
Naomi Johnson
Marie Meyers
Florence Mitman

CENTRAL
Mildred Snyder

TEACHERS

California....Frances DuBois Cramp
Scholl's....Mabel V. Kemmerer
Shelly's....Katherine B. [illegible]
Tohickon....Florence Fluck
Shaw's....Laura M. Strunk
Wimmer's....Laquitta Stahler Shaffer
Kauffman's....Elizabeth Devenney
Rocky Ridge....Mary E. Gross
Central....Priscilla Clay Keller

BOARD OF DIRECTORS

President....Erwin Landis
Vice-President....John R. Nice
Secretary....Aaron G. Myers
Treasurer....Clarence Leight
Robert Schaffer

Scenery built by Mr. Mitman of Shelly Station.

COMMENCEMENT

... OF ...

Richland Township Schools

ST. JOHN'S LUTHERAN PARISH HOUSE
Quakertown, Pa.

THURSDAY, MAY 14th, 1931
8:00 P. M. (Daylight Saving Time)

Motto:—"Honesty Is The Best Policy"
Flower:—Carnation
Colors:—Rose and Gray

Valedictorian Arthur Longacre
Salutatorian — Louise Barr

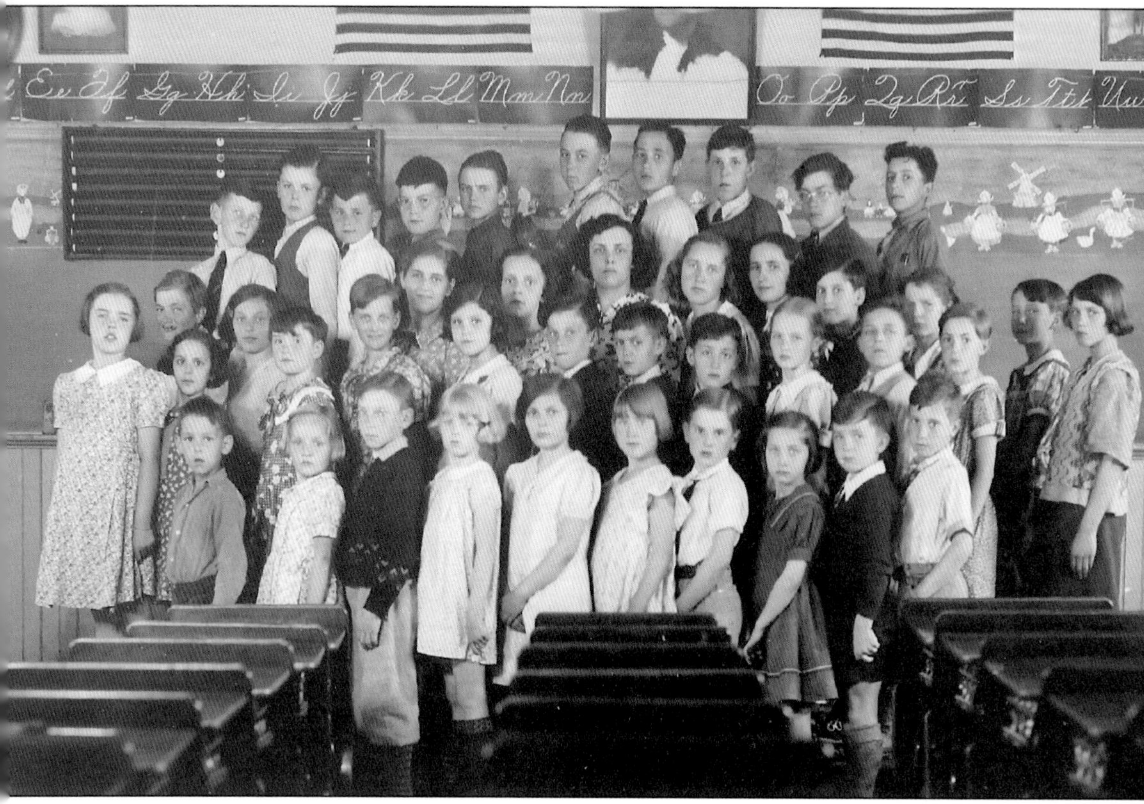

Students in Wimmer School pose with their teacher, Anna Neamand, during the 1937–1938 school term. From right to left are (first row) Richard Keller, Mary Ewaniuk, Allen Wimmer, Jean Parsons, Imogene Reichenbach, Betty Slifer, Gordon Hiestand, Dorothy Ritter, Lawrence Nice, and William Smith; (second row) Anna Sames, Bertha Kale, Alma Sherman, Annette Smith, Betty Raub, John Reichenbach, Russell Martin, Rowland Martin, Naomi Vokrot, Edwin Kale, Esther Crist, and Helen Slifer; (third row) Ralf Reichenbach, Dorothy Reichenbach, Margaret Landis, Arlene Sames, Anna Neamand, Nellie Vokrot, Ruth Bruckno, Estella Smith, Gloria Parsons, and Myrle Sherman; (fourth row) Ray Ritter, Richard Sames, Walter Bruckno, Chester Williams, Henry Slifer, Edward Lapinski, Herbert Bruckno, Andrew Crist, Stewart Afflerbach, and Francis Kale. In the 1930s, instructional materials were basic. A set of maps was mounted on the left side of the chalkboard, and examples of cursive letters were displayed across the top. The classroom was decorated with flags and a reproduction of Gilbert Stuart's unfinished portrait of George Washington. (RL.)

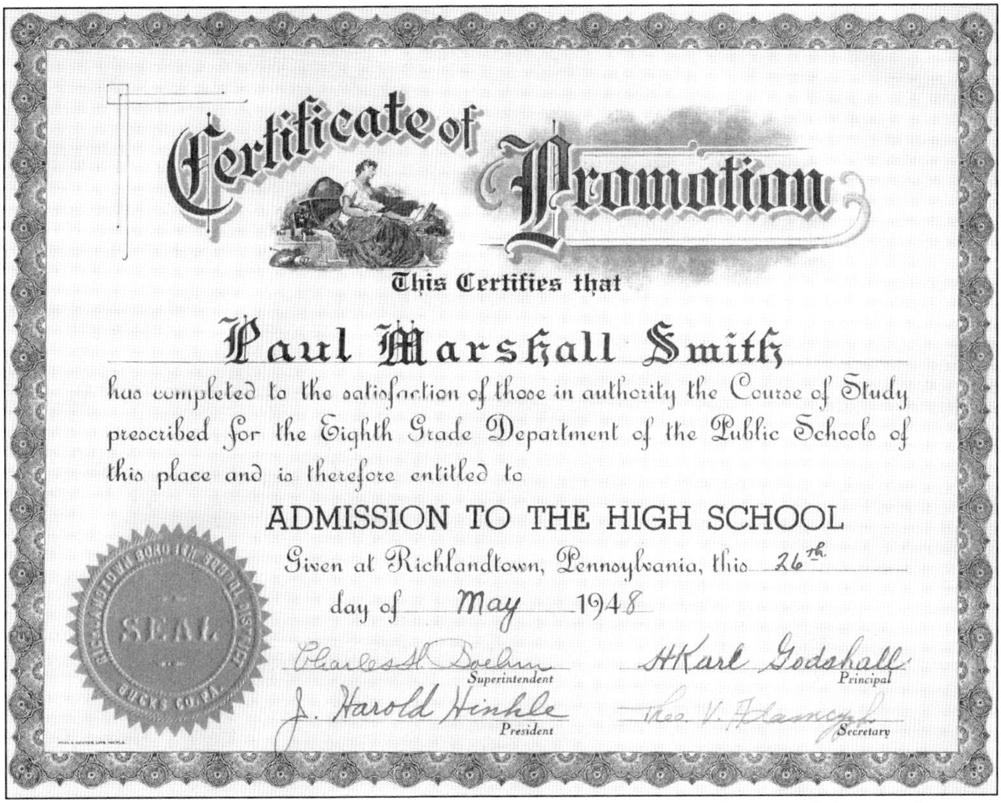

This diploma issued in Richlandtown in 1948 demonstrated the shared responsibility to education in small communities. The Bucks County Superintendent of Schools evaluated the eighth-grade exams, which determined if a student was ready for high school. Richlandtown Elementary was not large enough for a full-time principal, so the eighth-grade teacher assumed that capacity by signing the diploma. (RL.)

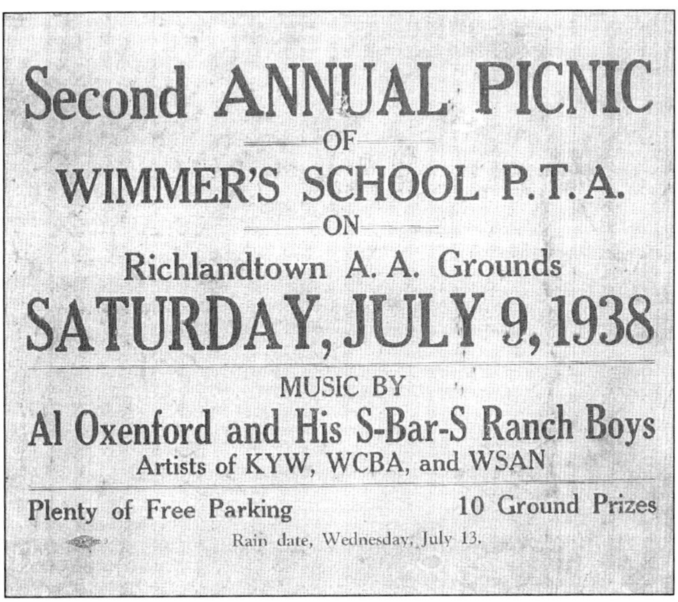

This poster announces the Wimmer School picnic. During the Depression, Parent-Teacher Associations (PTAs) gave a great deal of volunteer support to one-room schools. Wimmer's PTA held fund-raisers, such as picnics, to raise money. The PTA also installed electricity in Wimmer's School. Like most one-room schools, it did not have electric service until 1935. The school board did not have the funds to install electricity. (RHS.)

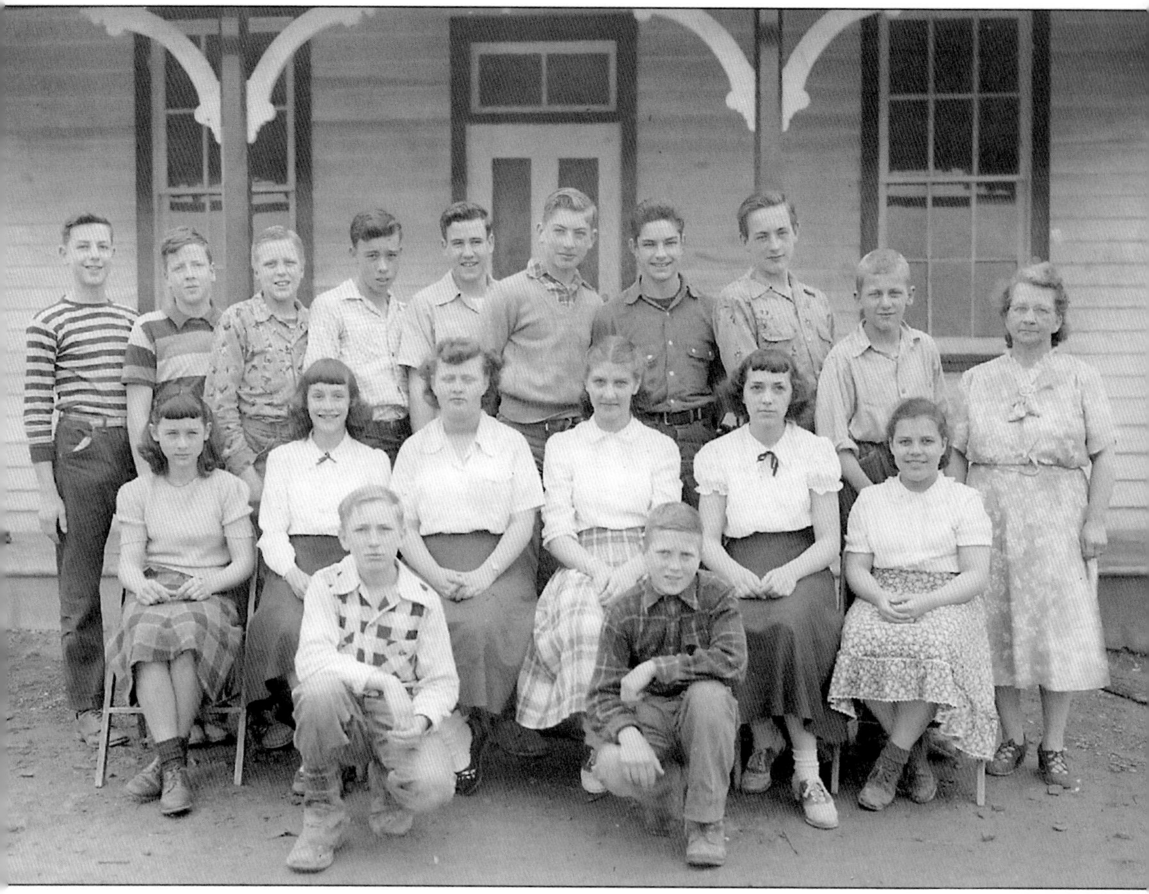

The Tohickon School was located on Thatcher Road. Of all the one-room schools to serve the township, Tohickon was the only one built of wood framing and clad with clapboard siding. Seventh- and eighth-grade students pose in front of Tohickon during the school term of 1949–1950. In 1946, Richland Township began to bus all of its school students. Bussing allowed the nine schools to be organized into three clusters. In each cluster, one school would have students from grades one to three; another had grades four through six, and the third had grades seven and eight. Students in this photograph are, from left to right, (first row) unidentified and Stanley Winkler; (second row) Dorothy Fields, Anna Herstine, Myrna Baringer, Gertrude Braunle, Shirley Schnable, and Joan Headman; (third row) Donald Webster, Marcus Hockman, Wilhelm Scheutz, Richard Leight, Raymond Kooker, Donald Shelly, Ronald Zackeosian, Bernard Breiner, David Faul, and teacher Irma Koehler. (RHS.)

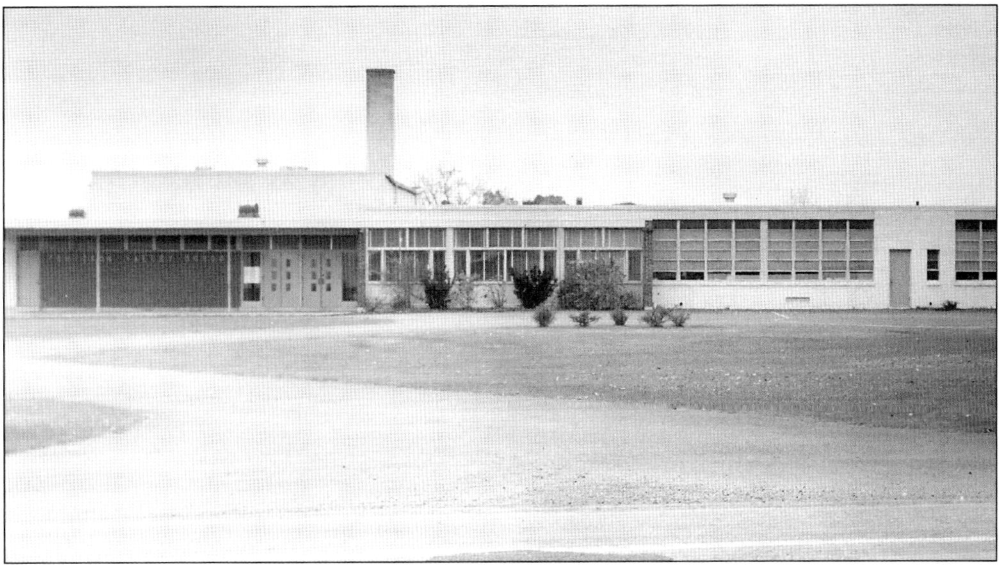

Tohickon Valley Elementary School was constructed by Milford and Richland Townships in order to educate the many children coming to school during the baby boom after the Second World War. Built in 1953, it is located on Old Bethlehem Pike near the boundary of the two townships. Several one-room schools were closed when the first students entered Tohickon Valley. (QCSD.)

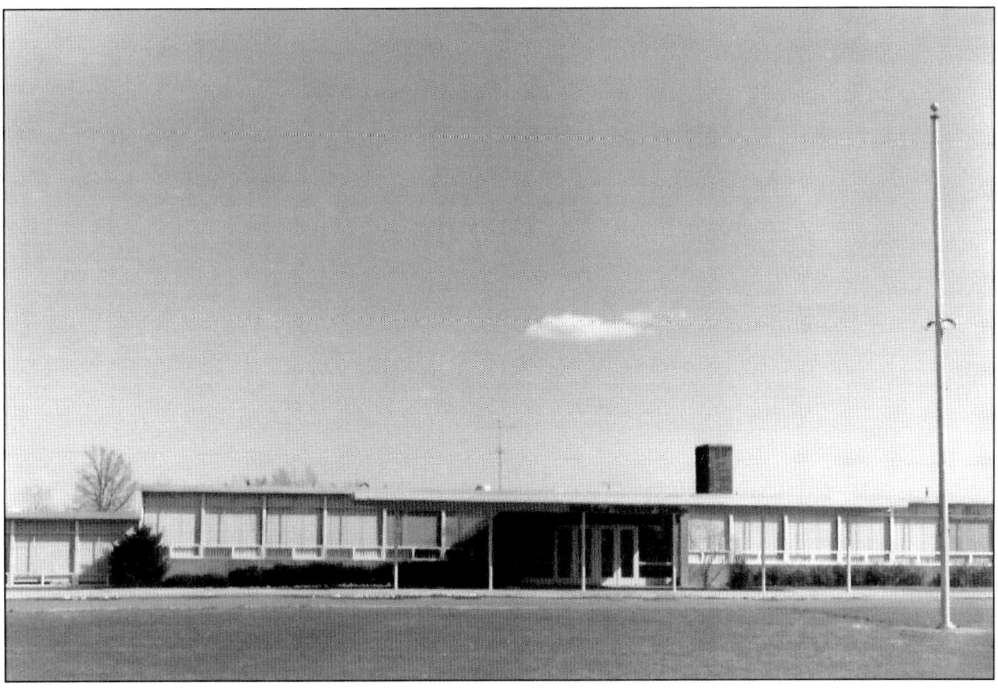

Tohickon Valley Elementary School was unable to accommodate the large number of baby boomers, so the Richland School Board decided to build a new 12-room elementary school for grades one through six on Fairview Street. It opened in September 1957. With the completion of Richland Elementary, the one-room schools were all sold, and the era of the one-room schoolhouse in Richland Township was over. (QCSD.)

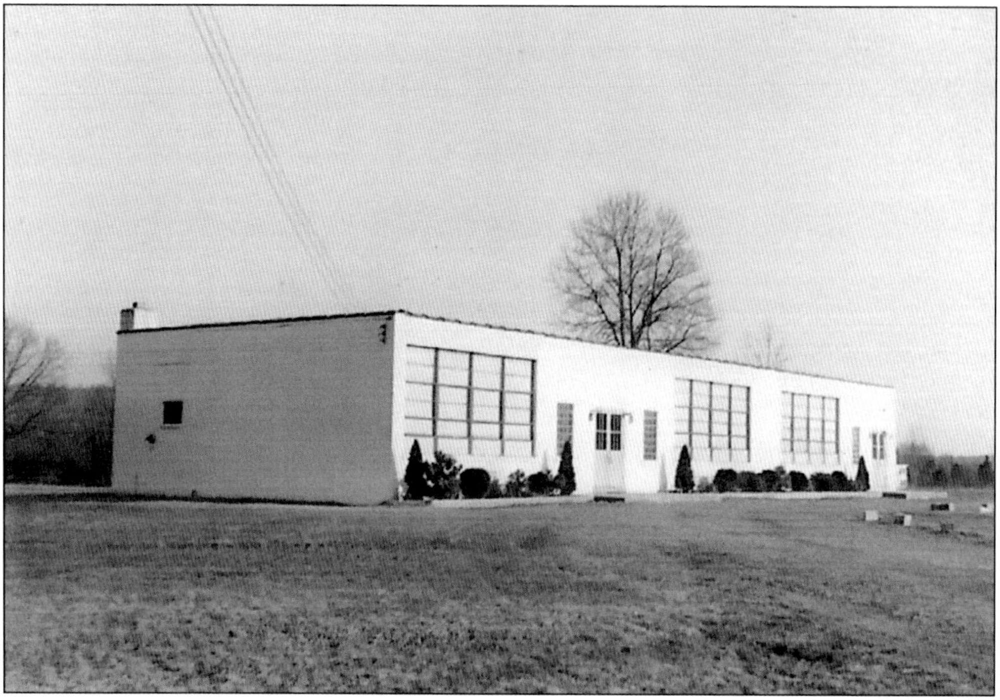

Quakertown Christian School grew out of its relationship with the Rocky Ridge Mennonite Church. It was founded in 1951 in the basement of the church, possessing a single classroom with one teacher for eight grades. Enrollment grew rapidly, necessitating the addition of a second classroom in 1952. The growth of the school was such that a new multiroom school on Paletown Road was constructed in 2000s. Quakertown Christian now offers educational programs for elementary, middle, and high school students. The original building is now utilized as an early childhood center. (Above, IM; below, QCS.)

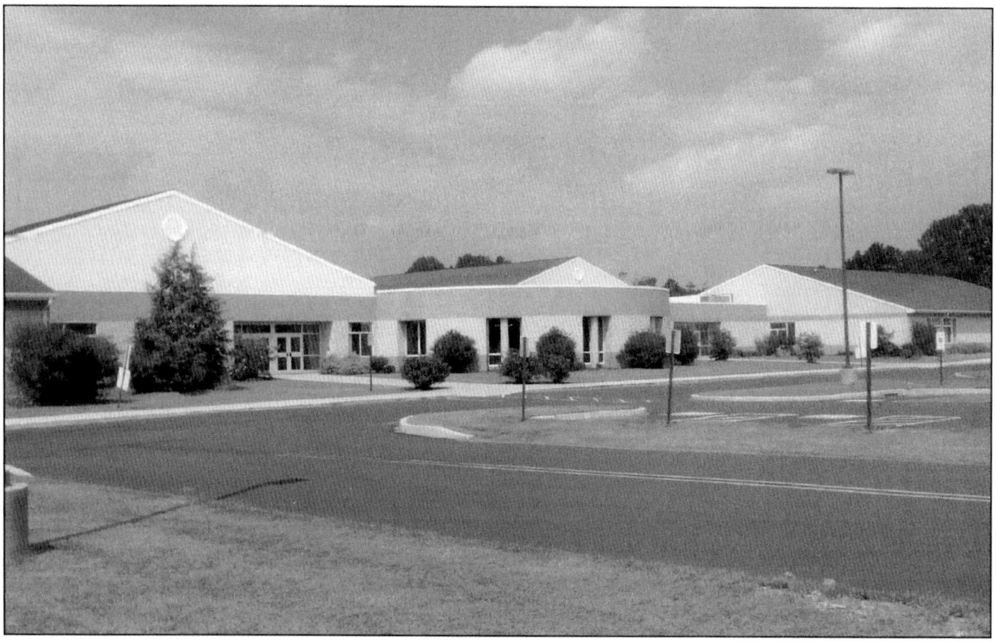

Five

CHURCHES

During the 18th century, members of the Society of Friends were the dominant group in Richland Township. Another ethnic group settled in Upper Bucks that, during the 19th century, outnumbered the Quakers. German immigrants had migrated to Pennsylvania to find religious freedom. About 1809, Lutheran and German Reformed congregations built a stone church building in present-day Richlandtown. A more substantial brick building replaced the original St. John's Union Church in 1859. Each congregation shared a pastor with other groups of their denomination. They held services on alternate Sundays but shared a union Sunday school. In 1932, the Lutheran congregation withdrew from the union and constructed a stone church building on Main Street. In 1937–1938, the Reformed congregation undertook major renovations to the older church. The historic church building in Richlandtown is now St. John's United Church of Christ.

The Mennonites were another German ethnic group. A congregation of Mennonites constructed Flatland meetinghouse at Erie and Thatcher Roads in 1837. Another Mennonite group, Bethany, worshipped in Quakertown. Bethany joined with Flatland in 1987, and they built United Mennonite Church next to the Flatland meetinghouse. Rocky Ridge Mennonite Church emerged from a mission charge in neighboring East Rockhill Township and constructed a church on Rocky Ridge Road. Salem Mennonite began worship in a former factory prior to constructing its church building in Shelly.

After World War II, several congregations moved from original locations in Quakertown to Richland Township. First Church of the Brethren moved from its building on Juniper Street in Quakertown to larger facilities on Trumbauersville Road in 1960. Grace Bible Fellowship also relocated from Juniper Street to a new spot on Bethlehem Pike in 1975. Most recently, St. Isidore's Roman Catholic Church transferred to a new property on West Pumping Station Road.

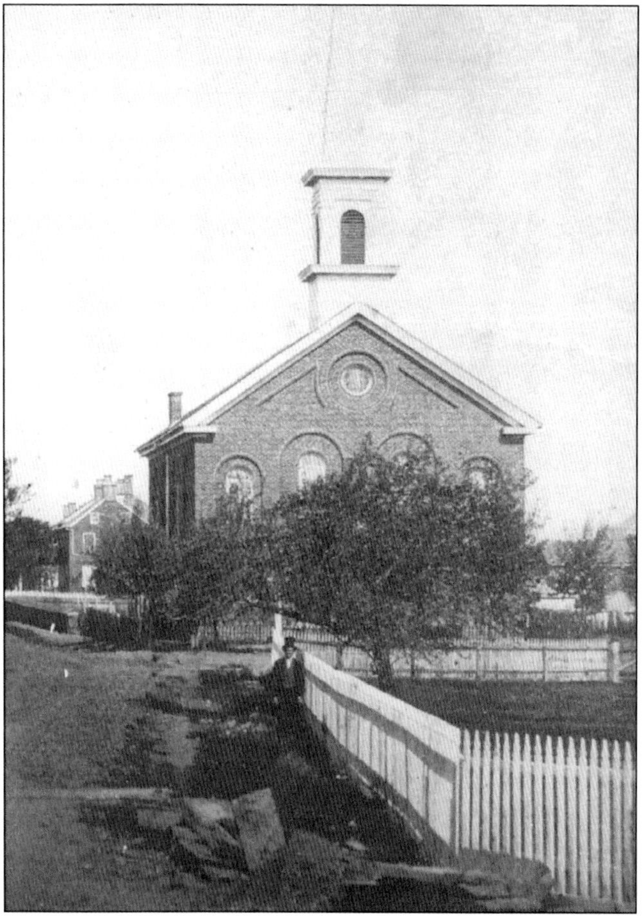

Lutheran and Reformed congregations were organized in Richlandtown around 1808, when the first union church was built. A larger brick edifice, pictured at left, was erected in 1859. Over the years, the building has been remodeled and the exterior clad in stucco, but the church continues to be an unmistakable landmark in the town. (RB.)

The cemetery shown here is on land donated by John Schmidt, who had been a soldier in the Revolutionary War. It is adjacent to St. John's United Church of Christ in Richlandtown. There are records of an earlier burying ground on the farm of Michael Croman, which would be in the 200 block of Main Street. The first inhabitants of Richlandtown were buried in unmarked graves. (UCC.)

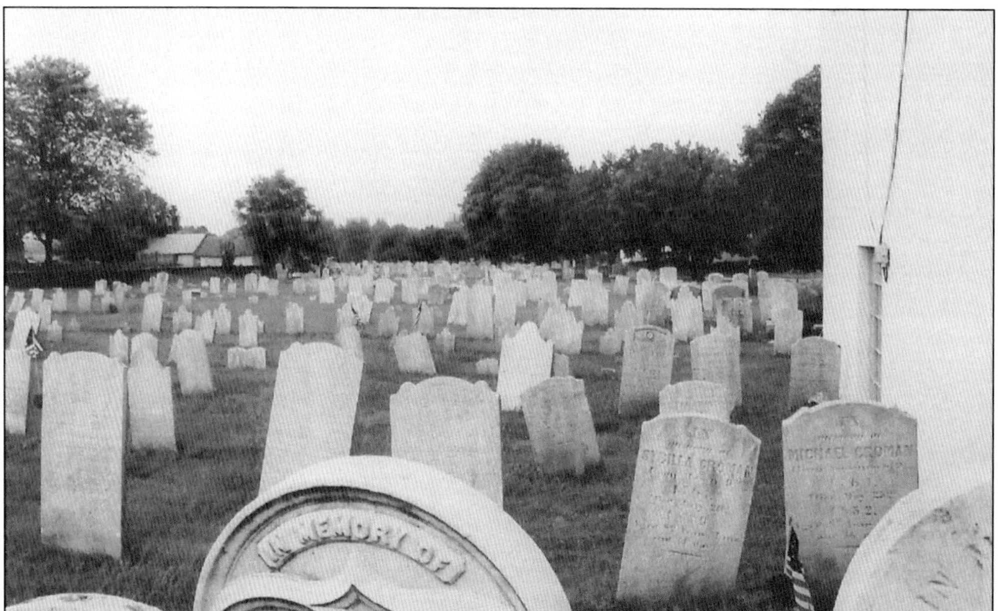

Rev. William B. Kemmerer served the Lutheran congregation in Richlandtown for 40 years. He, along with the Reverend Samuel Hess of the Reformed congregation, officiated at the laying of the cornerstone of a new sanctuary in 1859. This building still serves St. John's United Church of Christ. Reverend Kemmerer died August 5, 1860, and is buried behind the church. (RLC.)

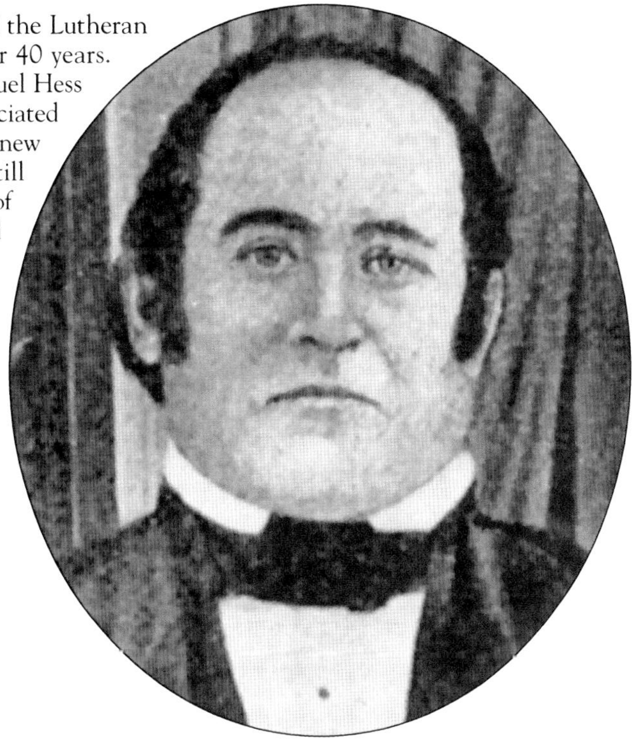

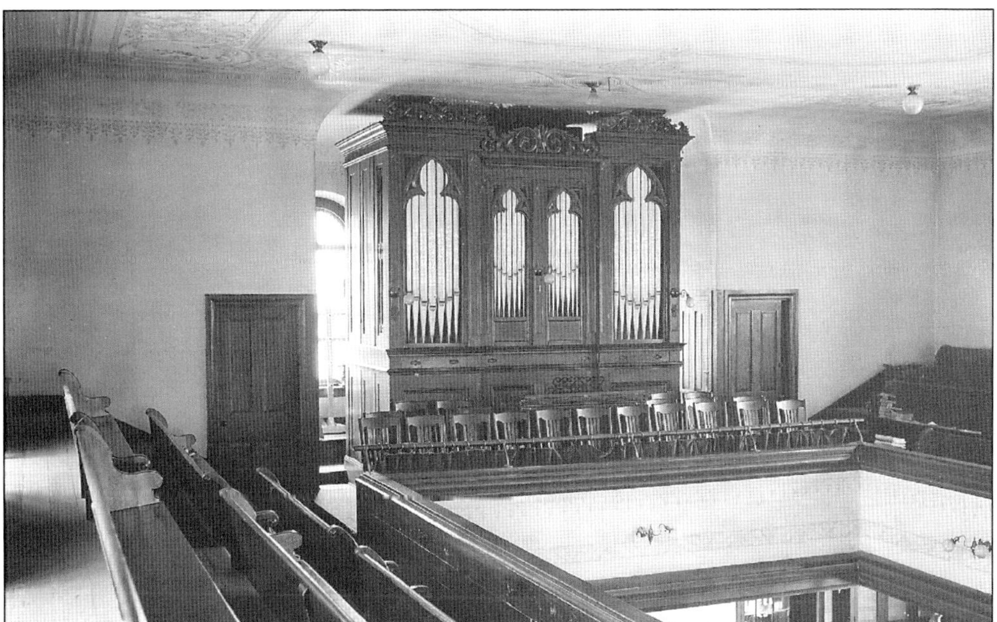

A large pipe organ was installed in the balcony of St. John's Union Church, Richlandtown, in 1870. The organ was crafted by the Charles Durner Organ Company of Quakertown and was purchased for the princely sum of $2,000. This organ was rebuilt and relocated in 1937 and continues to serve the congregation of St. John's United Church of Christ. (UCC.)

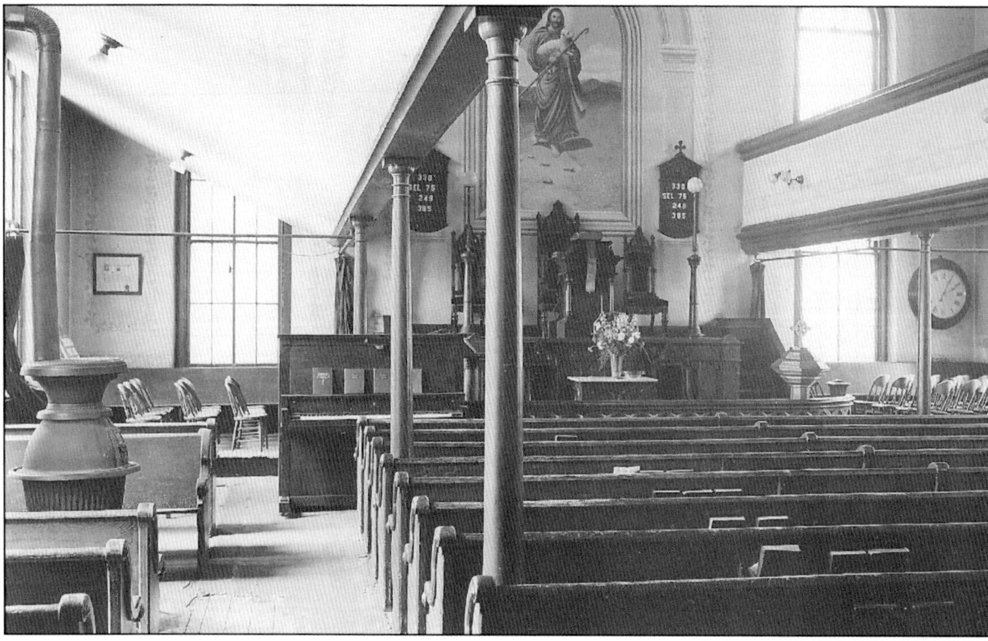

The interior of St. John's Union Church was typical for churches built in the mid-19th century: stoves provided heat and large windows allowed light into the building. Oil lamps supplied additional light. The pastor had to rely on the natural acoustics of the chancel to amplify his message. (UCC.)

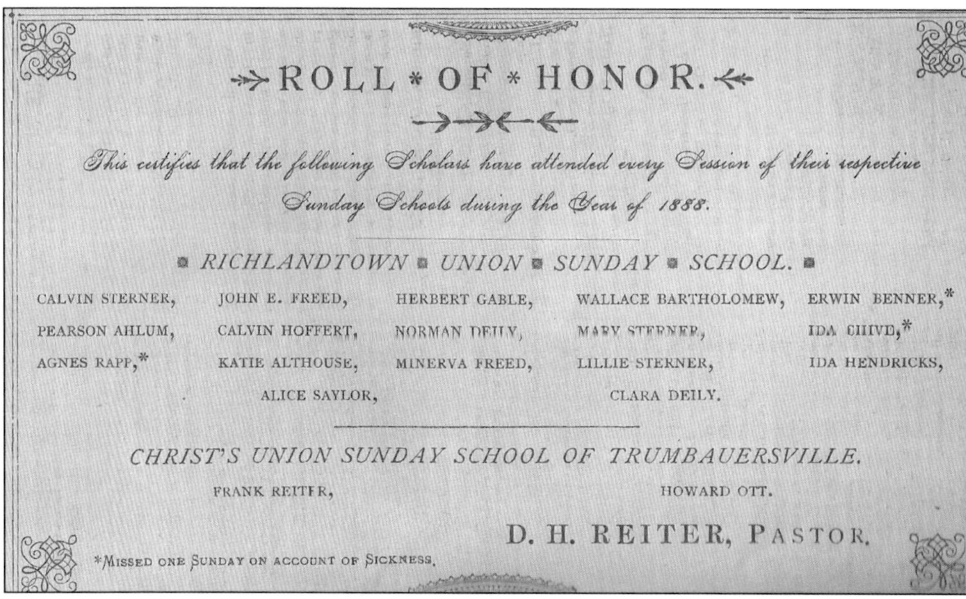

ROLL * OF * HONOR.

This certifies that the following Scholars have attended every Session of their respective Sunday Schools during the Year of 1888.

RICHLANDTOWN ▪ UNION ▪ SUNDAY ▪ SCHOOL.

CALVIN STERNER, JOHN E. FREED, HERBERT GABLE, WALLACE BARTHOLOMEW, ERWIN BENNER,*
PEARSON AHLUM, CALVIN HOFFERT, NORMAN DEILY, MARY STERNER, IDA SHIVE,*
AGNES RAPP,* KATIE ALTHOUSE, MINERVA FREED, LILLIE STERNER, IDA HENDRICKS,
ALICE SAYLOR, CLARA DEILY.

CHRIST'S UNION SUNDAY SCHOOL OF TRUMBAUERSVILLE.

FRANK REITER, HOWARD OTT.

D. H. REITER, PASTOR.

*MISSED ONE SUNDAY ON ACCOUNT OF SICKNESS.

In addition to sharing premises, it was common for union churches to combine forces and hold union Sunday school classes. To encourage attendance, rolls of honor were published to recognize those who had come to the school faithfully. The above certificate was published in 1888 and honors 17 youngsters with perfect, or near perfect, attendance. This certificate carried the printed signature of Rev. D. H. Reiter. (RLC.)

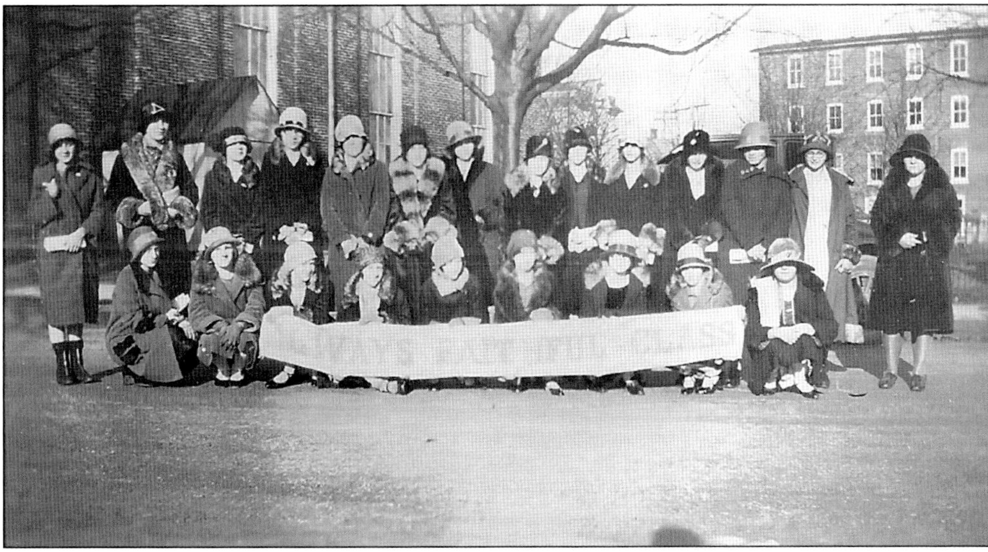

During the 1920s, St. John's had a union Sunday school composed of adult members of both the Lutheran and Reformed congregations. These women from the Always Faithful class pose outside the church building on a winter day in 1920. In the background on the right is the Eisenlohr Cigar factory, which was later converted into the Swan-Lee clothing factory. (UCC.)

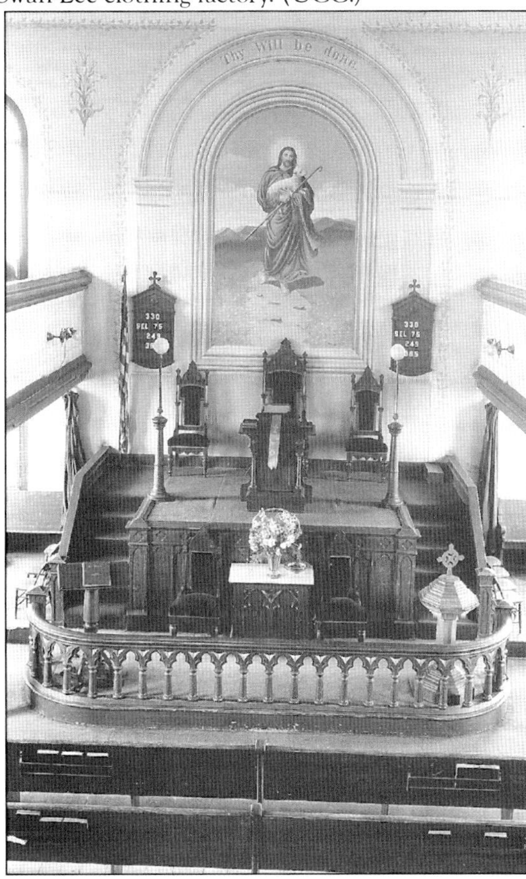

When St. John's Union Church was built in 1859, the balcony girded the church on three sides and the pulpit was placed on a raised platform in the chancel. The front of the church boasted a fresco, and the windows were of clear glass. This picture was taken prior to the renovations in 1937. (UCC.)

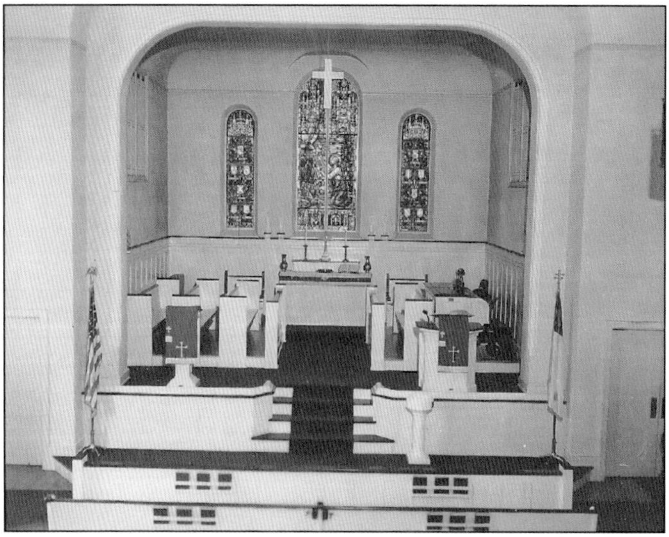

When St. John's Lutheran congregation left the union church arrangement in the 1930s, the Reformed congregation remained in the old sanctuary built in 1859. The interior was extensively remodeled and altered in 1937. The organ console was relocated to the front of the church, and the side balconies were removed. The photograph at left shows new stained-glass windows in the chancel. (UCC.)

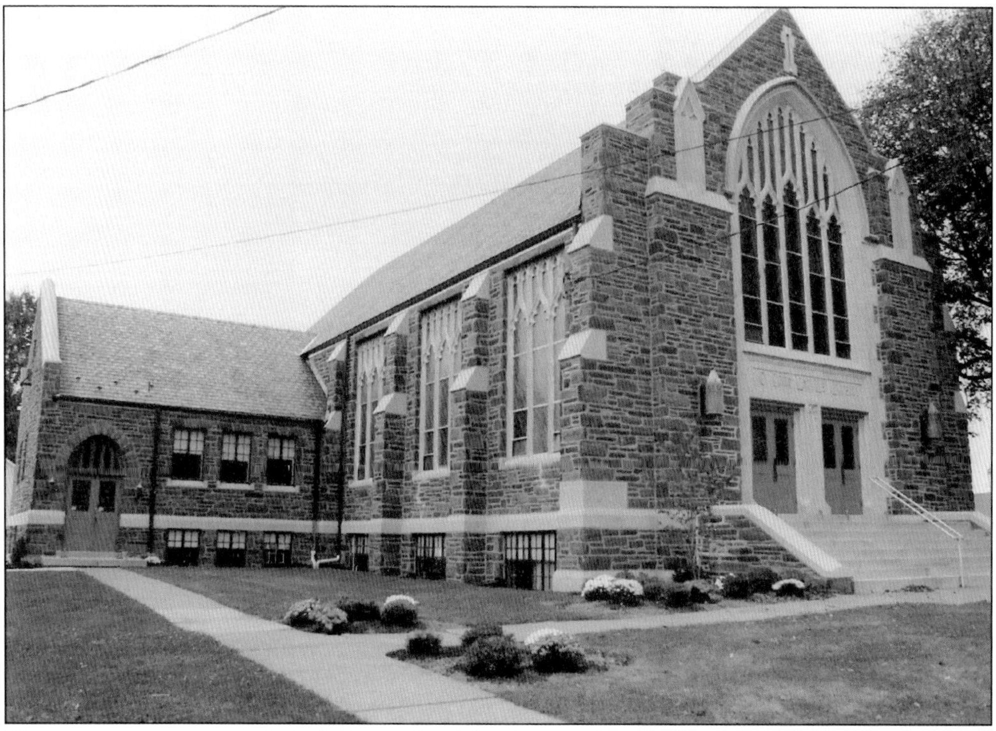

The congregation of St. John's Evangelical Lutheran Church decided in September 1929 to terminate the union relationship with the Reformed congregation and to build a new sanctuary. This edifice was dedicated during the week of April 3–7, 1932. Leadership for this ambitious project was provided by pastor Elbert Landis. The Reverend Charles C. Schlitzer was installed as the pastor of the parish on December 9, 1934. (SJL.)

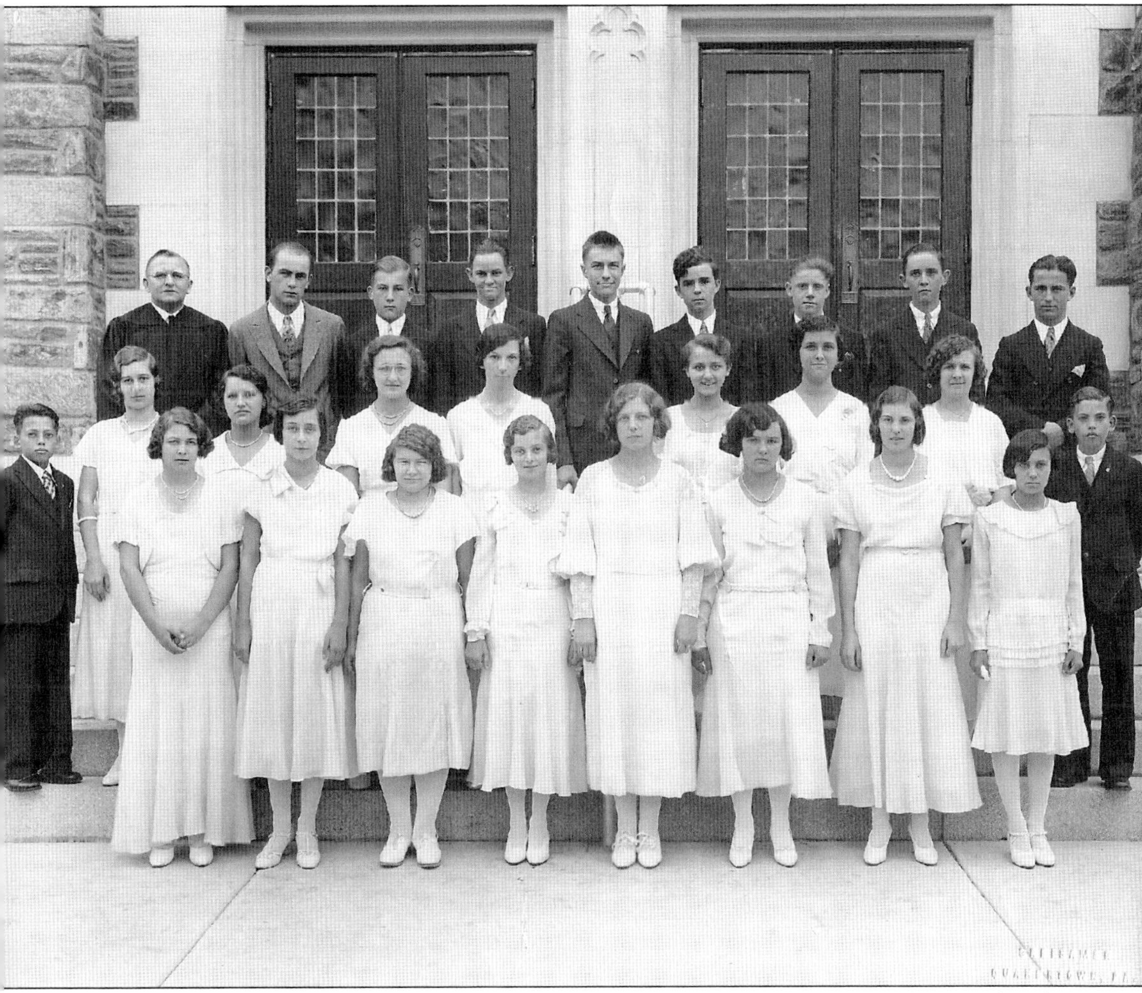

This was the first class to the confirmed in the newly constructed St. John's Lutheran Church in 1932. The group of young people poses on the steps in front of the red doors with their pastor. They had been instructed by pastor Elbert Landis. In this image are, from left to right, (first row) unidentified, Irene Banes, Anne Riechenbach, Melba Slotter, Beatrice Weaver Conway, Rose Baringer, Gertrude Taylor, and Lizzie Baringer; (second row) John Bartholomew, Ruth Schultz, Hazel Sommers, Dorothy McNair, Marion Bleam, Henrietta Landis, Dorothy Crouthamel, Helen Hager, and Arthur Bartholomew; (third row) pastor Elbert Landis, Kenneth Hinkle, Paul Ackerman, Ernest Hendrick, Henry Ahlum, unidentified, Samuel Wierbach, Harold Bleam, and Francis Baringer. Henrietta Landis was the daughter of pastor Elbert and Henrietta Landis. Later she married James Jahnsen and became a highly respected music teacher in the Quakertown Community School District. (SJL.)

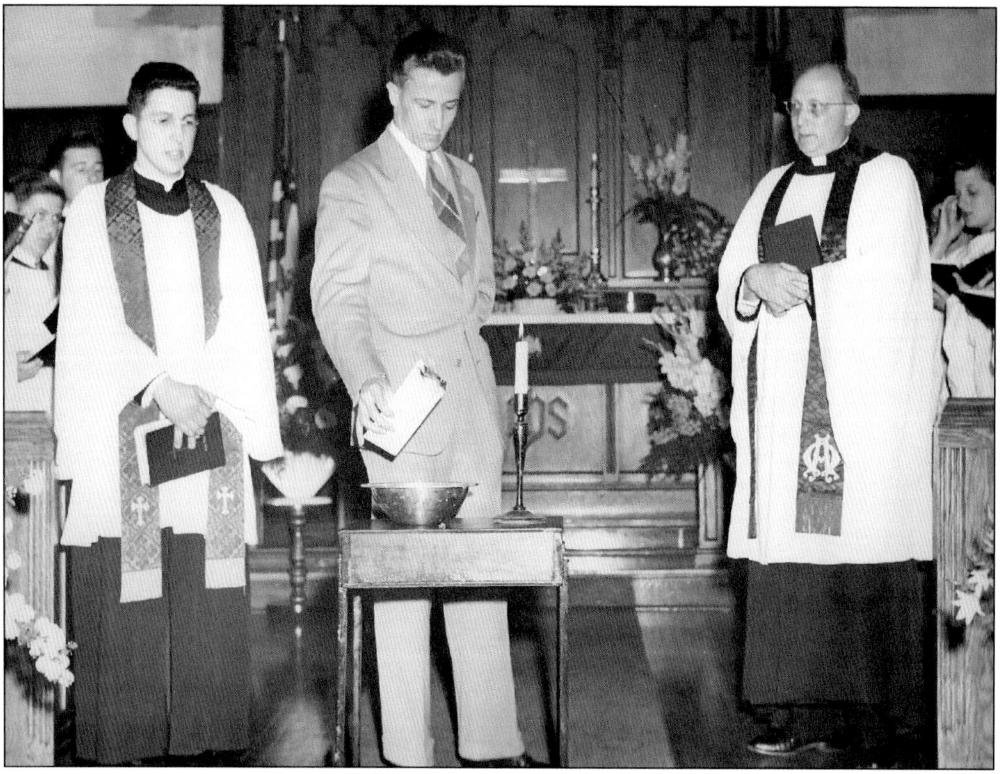

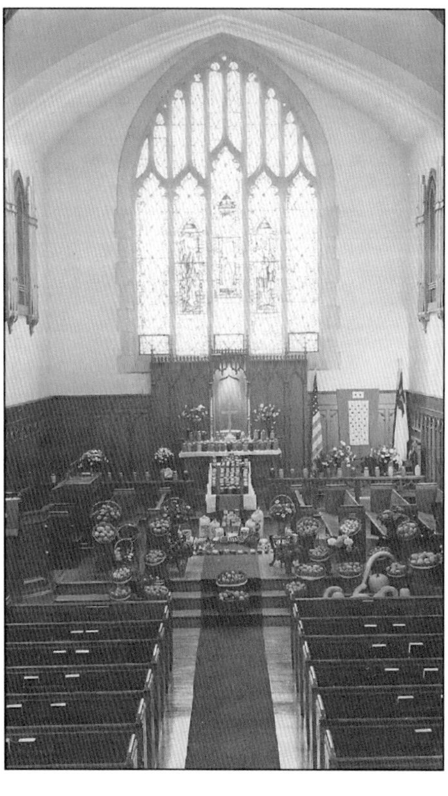

The Lutheran congregation took on a heavy financial obligation when it constructed the new church building. The cost of the church, property, furniture, pipe organ, and parsonage was approximately $61,000. Generous donations and fund-raising activities repaid the debt. On May 25, 1948, a special mortgage-burning service was held. Officiating were pastor Luther Vogel; Oliver Landis, son of pastor Elbert Landis; and former pastor Charles C. Schlitzer. (SJL.)

In the late fall, country churches such as St. John's Lutheran decorated the chancel with the fruits and produce that had been grown in gardens and orchards of members of the congregation. The foodstuff was then donated to institutions such as children's homes. This photograph shows food displayed under the stained-glass window in the front of the church. (SJL.)

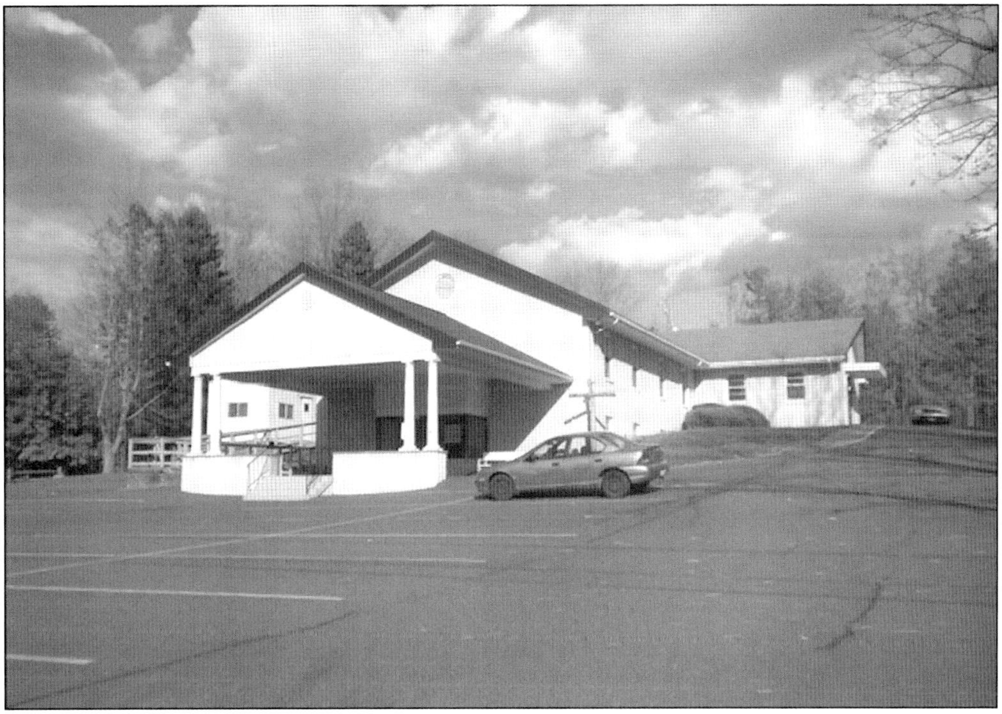

Salem Mennonite congregation began as a mission church in the Salem one-room schoolhouse in Springfield Township in 1946. They soon outgrew the schoolhouse, and in 1948, a former cigar factory in Shelly was purchased for use. As the cigar factory was not an efficient place of worship, planning began for a new church building in 1969; it was ready in 1971. (KF.)

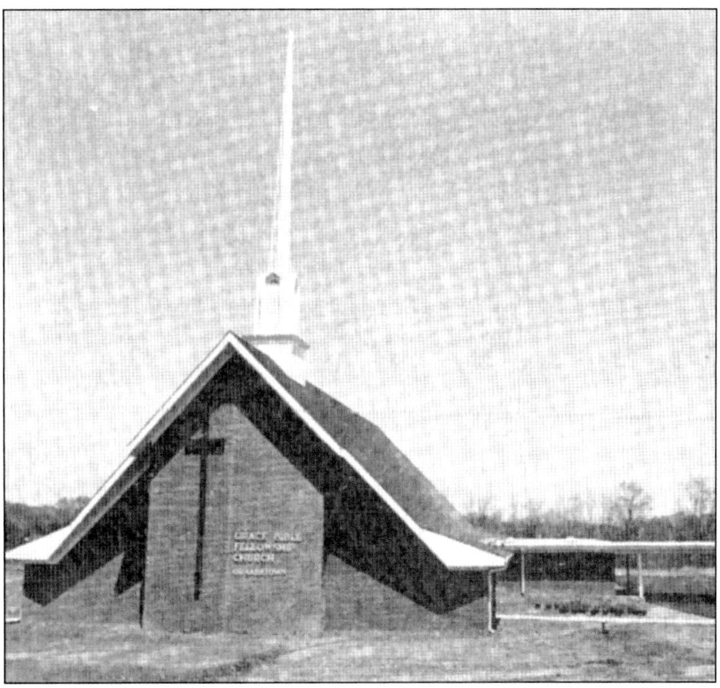

Grace Bible Fellowship Church began in an old church building in Haycock Township. In 1872, materials from the Haycock church building were used to construct a brick house of worship at 27 Third Street in Quakertown. In order to expand its facilities, the congregation constructed the present building on its campus on Bethlehem Pike in Richland Township. This church building was dedicated on May 16, 1975. (SS.)

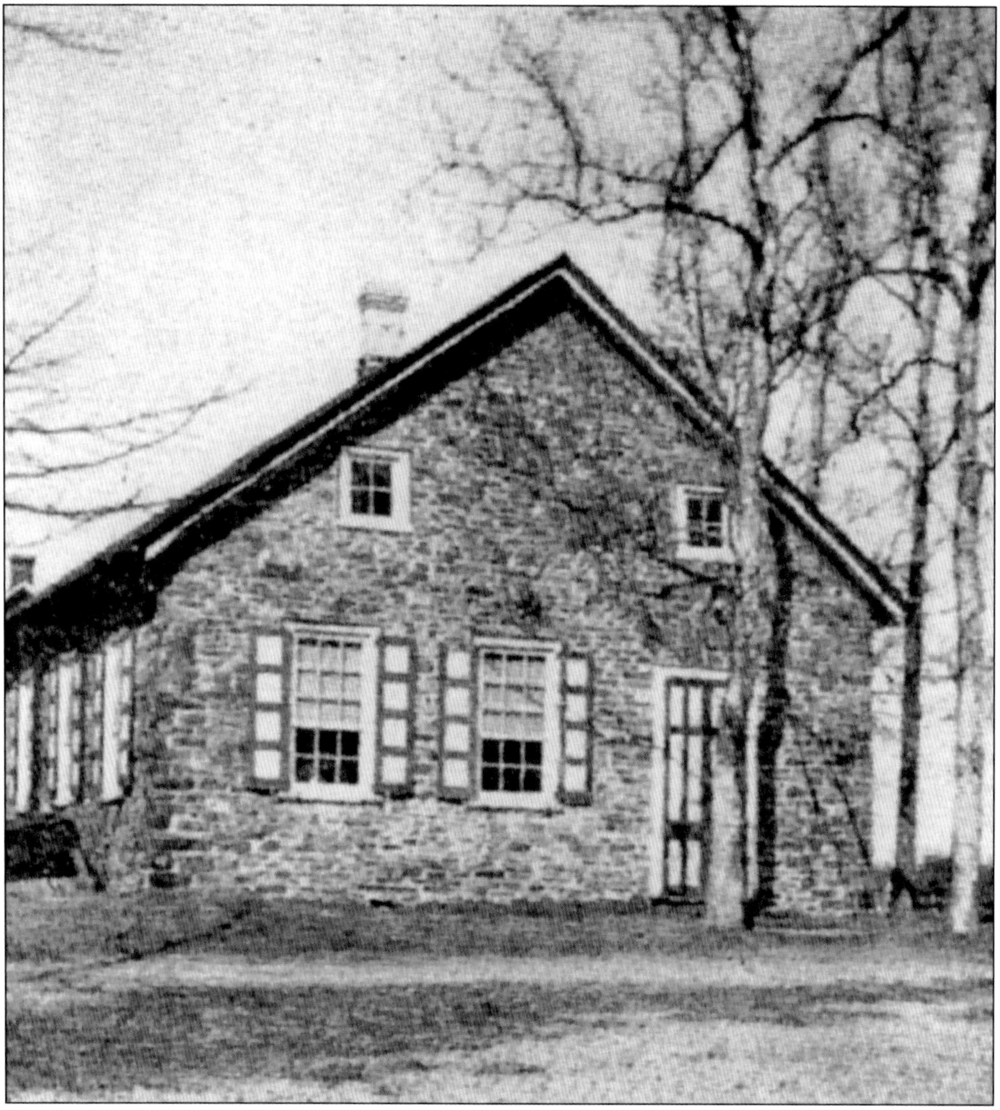

The meetinghouse of Flatland Mennonite Church was erected in 1837. Prior to construction of the meetinghouse, Mennonites in the Richland area had to travel to meetinghouses in Springfield, Saucon, Swamp, or Deep Run. At first, services were held on Sunday afternoons every four weeks so they did not interfere with attendance at Swamp or Springfield churches. A Sunday school was organized as early as 1853. The congregation remained small but had grown sufficiently so that an addition was constructed in 1961. For a number of years, Bethany Mennonite Church on Juniper Street in Quakertown and Flatland shared a pastor. The two groups merged to form United Mennonite Church when both outgrew their buildings. They worked together to build the present structure next to the former Flatland Church on Thatcher Road in 1987. (UMC.)

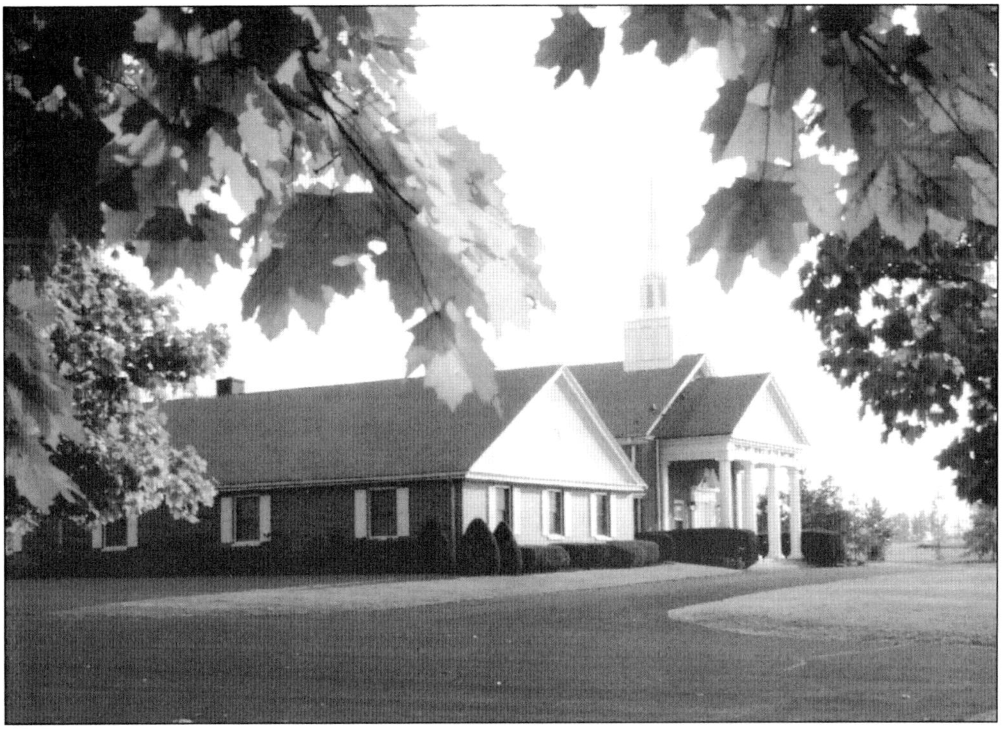

The Brethren congregation first met in 1908 in its original church building at 424 Juniper Street. When the congregation outgrew this structure after the Second World War, a new site was purchased at 455 Trumbauersville Road. The present church building was dedicated on September 25, 1960. (DS.)

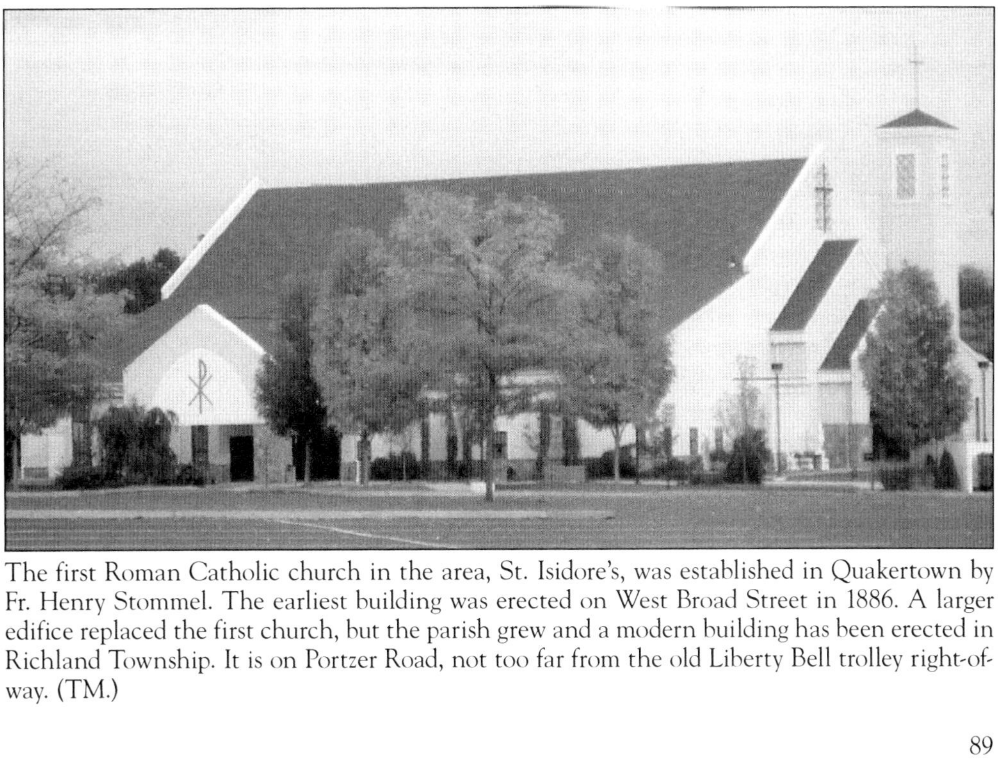

The first Roman Catholic church in the area, St. Isidore's, was established in Quakertown by Fr. Henry Stommel. The earliest building was erected on West Broad Street in 1886. A larger edifice replaced the first church, but the parish grew and a modern building has been erected in Richland Township. It is on Portzer Road, not too far from the old Liberty Bell trolley right-of-way. (TM.)

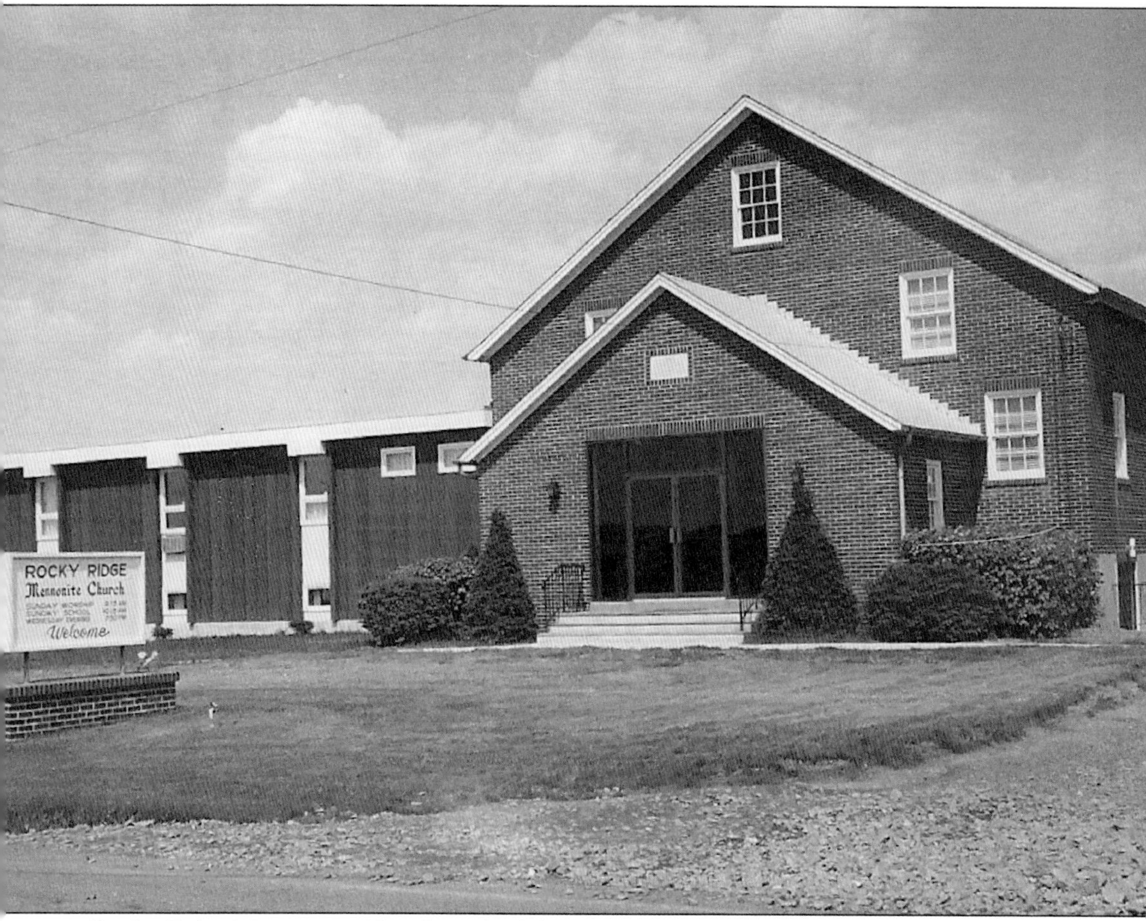

Rocky Ridge Mennonite Church evolved from a mission congregation that began meeting in private homes in East Rockhill. As interest grew, a Sunday school was organized in 1931 and began to meet in a log house. In the early 1940s, a lot was purchased on Rocky Ridge Road and dedicated for the erection of a new church building. Work was delayed during the Second World War due to shortages of manpower and construction materials. Efforts began on the present building in June 1948. It was completed by January 2, 1949, when dedication services were held. An article in *Mission News* of the Franconia Mennonite Conference notes, "The congregation has spent almost eighteen years in a temporary building. Coming into a new building almost seems like a dream." The congregation continued to grow, and two additions have been made to the original edifice. (IM.)

Six

Transportation

Richland Township, located between Philadelphia and the Lehigh Valley, was linked to them by three major transportation routes. During the 18th century, the Bethlehem Pike was the main path for travel between Philadelphia and Bethlehem. The pike entered Richland Township at Rich Hill and exited in Springfield Township on the north. In mid-19th century, railroad tracks were laid to the east of the Bethlehem Pike. During the 20th century, a major highway, Route 309, ran just to the west of the winding and narrow Bethlehem Pike. Each route had major implications for Richland Township.

The core of original Quakertown was on the Bethlehem Pike, and the railroad was about a mile away. In the 1890s, another railroad line ran through Richlandtown almost to the Delaware River. At the same time, a trolley ran from Quakertown to Richlandtown. Another trolley line ran along side of the Bethlehem Pike, providing an alternative to the railroad.

During the 1800s, an infrastructure of country roads linked the farms and villages of the township. An 1890s map of the township shows the same secondary roads as those in 1950. They had been improved with macadam paving during the 1920s and 1930s so that they were convenient for automobiles and trucks.

The most dramatic development in travel through Richland in the 20th century was the construction of Route 309 during the 1930s. The highway was built to support truck and automobile transportation between Philadelphia, the Lehigh Valley, and the coal regions. Its construction changed the future of Richland Township.

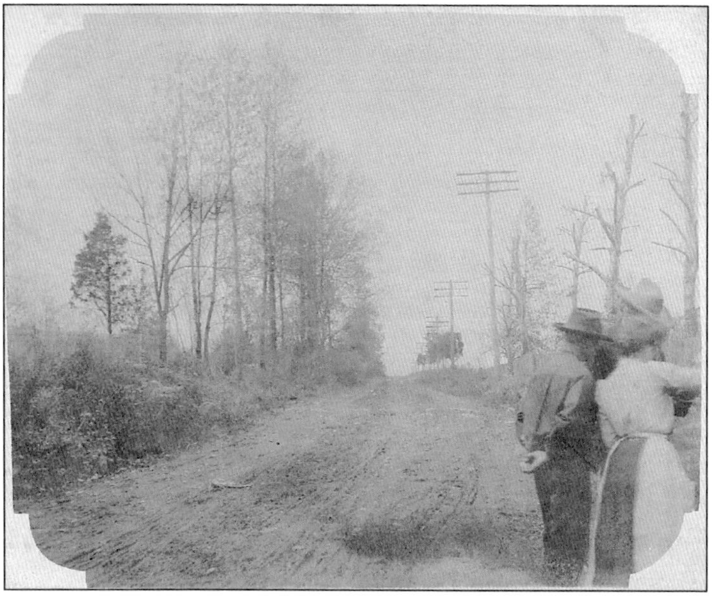

The Richland Turnpike or Plank Road Company, organized by local citizens in 1854, sought to improve and maintain a turnpike from the Doylestown Road (Route 313) to the Hellertown Road (Route 412). This early photograph, taken about 1905, depicts that portion of the road north of the borough. It appears that the highway was unpaved and somewhat rough well into the 20th century. (EF.)

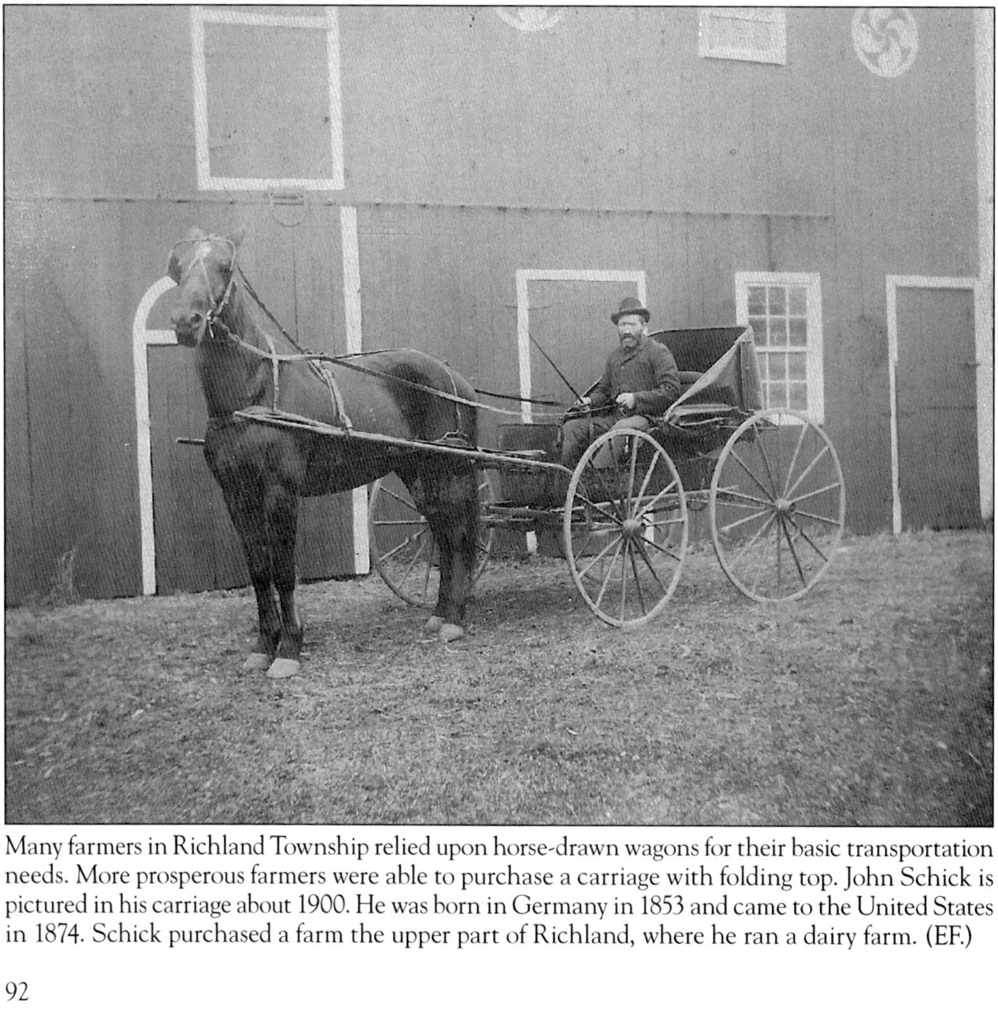

Many farmers in Richland Township relied upon horse-drawn wagons for their basic transportation needs. More prosperous farmers were able to purchase a carriage with folding top. John Schick is pictured in his carriage about 1900. He was born in Germany in 1853 and came to the United States in 1874. Schick purchased a farm the upper part of Richland, where he ran a dairy farm. (EF.)

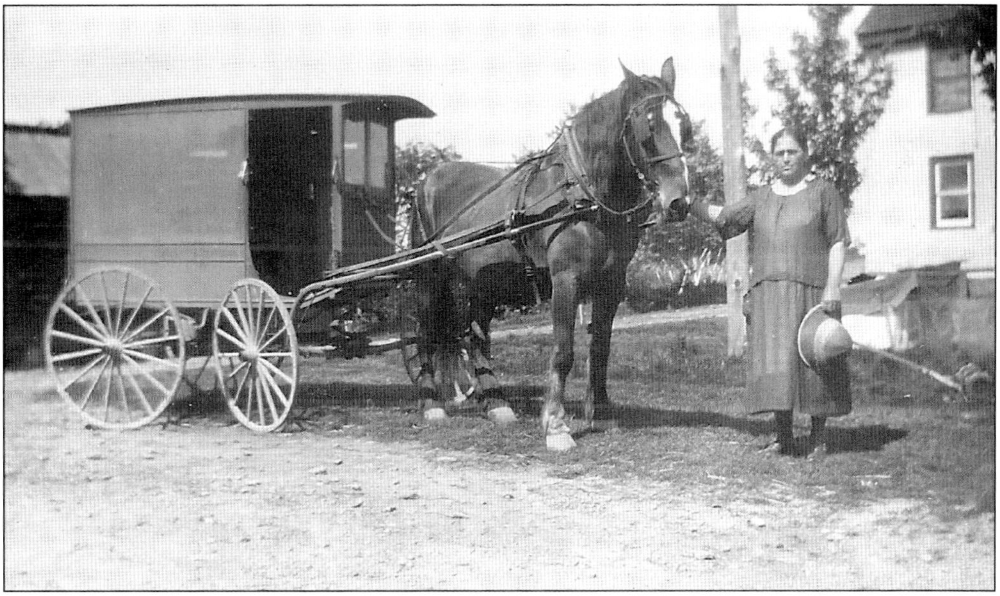

Hannah Cora Ritter holds the reins of a delivery wagon in this photograph from the 1920s. In rural areas, it was expeditious and profitable for merchants to bring their goods, wares, and foodstuffs to the consumers. Horse-drawn wagons were used by local farmers and traveling merchants well into the 1920s. (CH.)

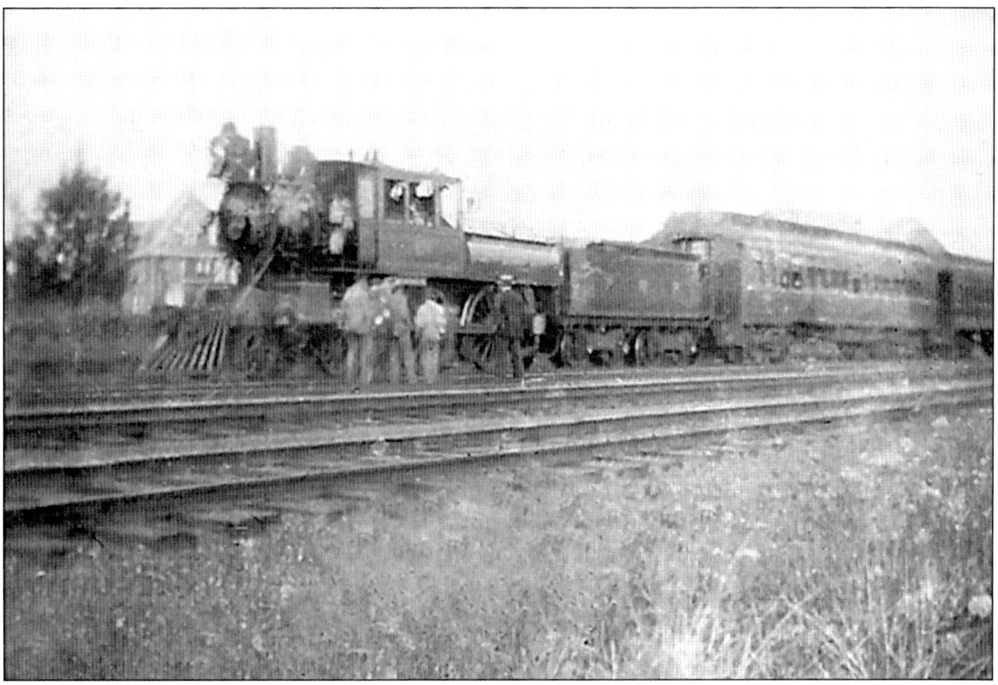

Local citizens formed the Quakertown and Eastern Railroad, which was chartered on July 6, 1897. The first passenger train was memorialized in this photograph dated August 12, 1897. The engine pulled two coaches. The train left Quakertown at 7:15 p.m. and arrived in Richlandtown some seven minutes later. Later the railroad was extended to Durham Furnace, 13 miles distant. The railroad ceased operations in 1936. (RLC.)

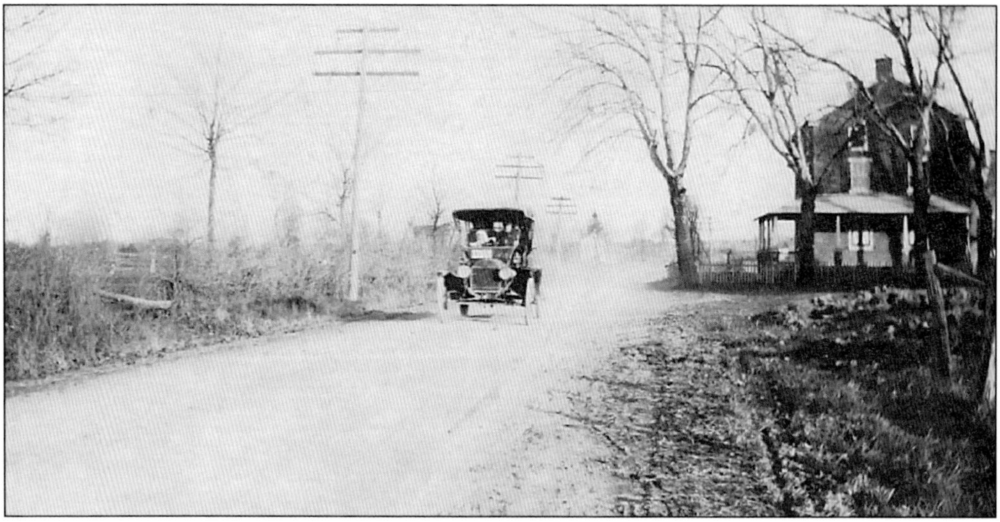

Jonas Harley is shown on the Doylestown Road in his automobile. Harley manufactured harnesses and was president of Quakertown Trust Company. His large factory, which employed 175 men, still stands at the corner of Main and Juniper Streets in Quakertown. Little did he know that the autos such as he was driving would eventually end the need for equipment for horses and bring an end to his industry! (CR.)

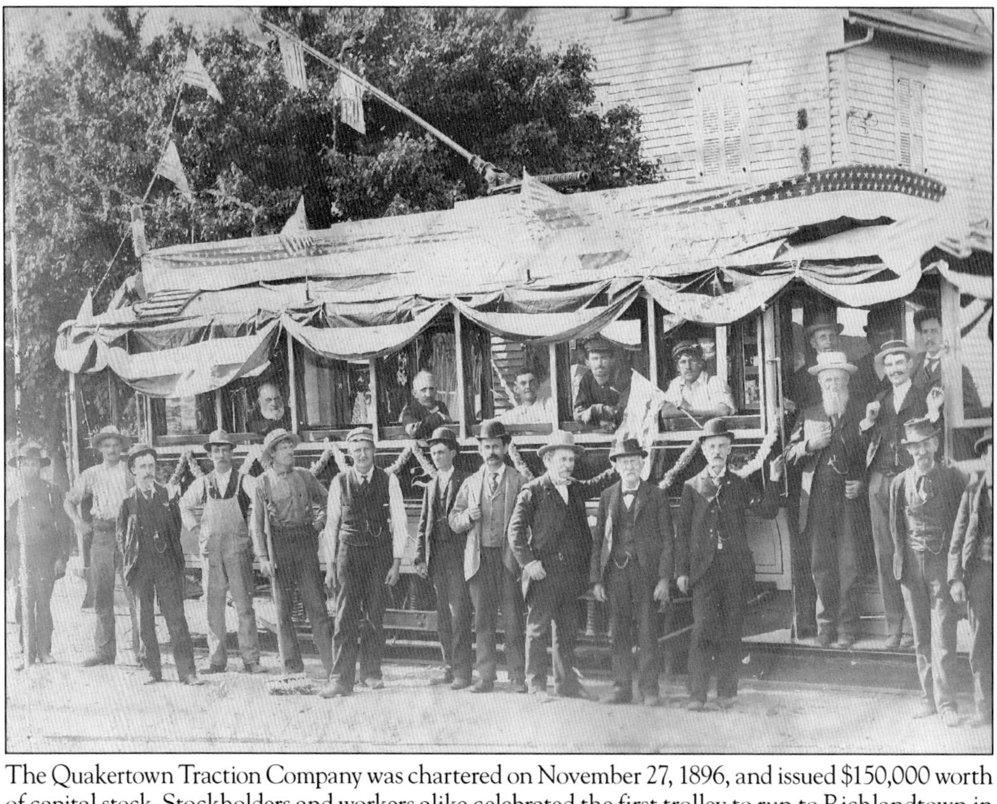

The Quakertown Traction Company was chartered on November 27, 1896, and issued $150,000 worth of capital stock. Stockholders and workers alike celebrated the first trolley to run to Richlandtown in 1898. The line ran from Main and West Broad Streets in Quakertown to just south of Richlandtown. The trolley to Richlandtown was known colloquially as the "Tripper." (RHS.)

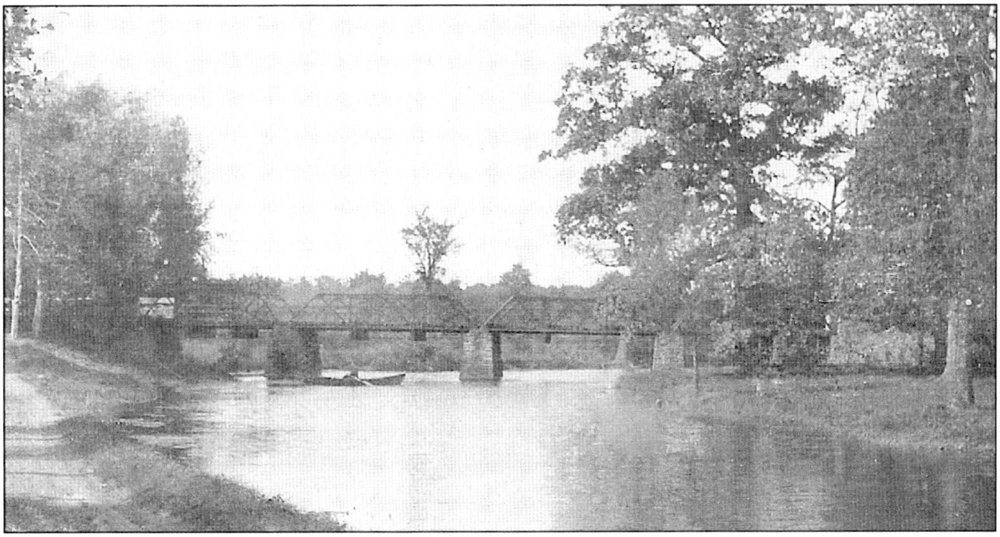

When the Quakertown Traction Company began to construct the trolley line to Richlandtown, a steel bridge was erected to carry the trolley tracks over the Tohickon Creek. The bridge provided a picturesque backdrop for boaters and swimmers at nearby Tohickon Grove. In 1898, the trolley line ended in Richland Township, just south of the Richlandtown borough line. (RLC.)

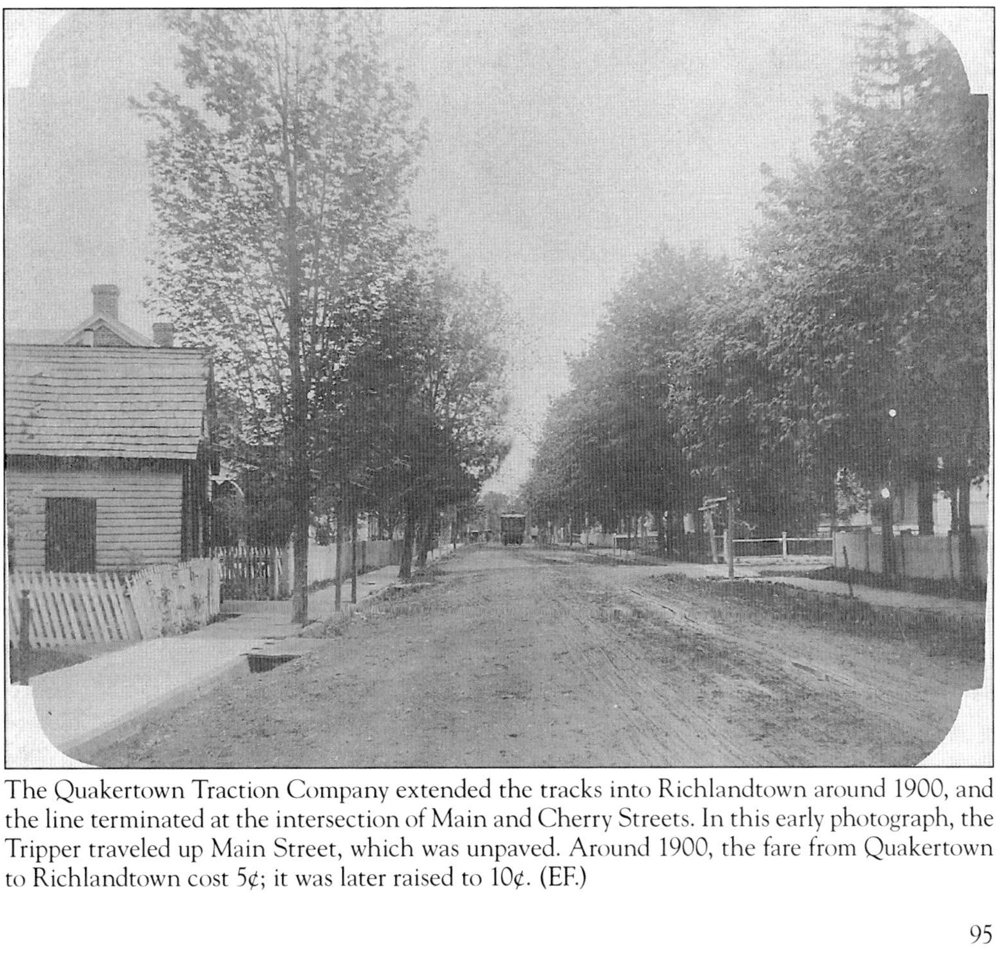

The Quakertown Traction Company extended the tracks into Richlandtown around 1900, and the line terminated at the intersection of Main and Cherry Streets. In this early photograph, the Tripper traveled up Main Street, which was unpaved. Around 1900, the fare from Quakertown to Richlandtown cost 5¢; it was later raised to 10¢. (EF.)

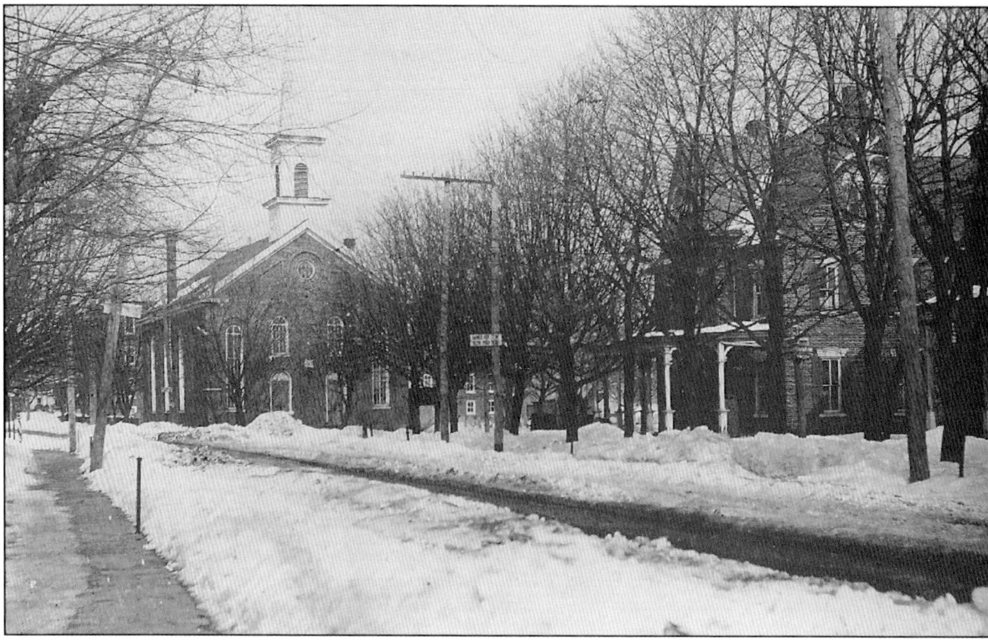

A heavy blanket of snow covers most of Main Street in Richlandtown in this photograph taken about 1920. The plowed section of the road is the right-of-way utilized by the Quakertown Traction Company for the Tripper. The heavy copper wire from which the trolley draws its power is visible above the tracks. (MM.)

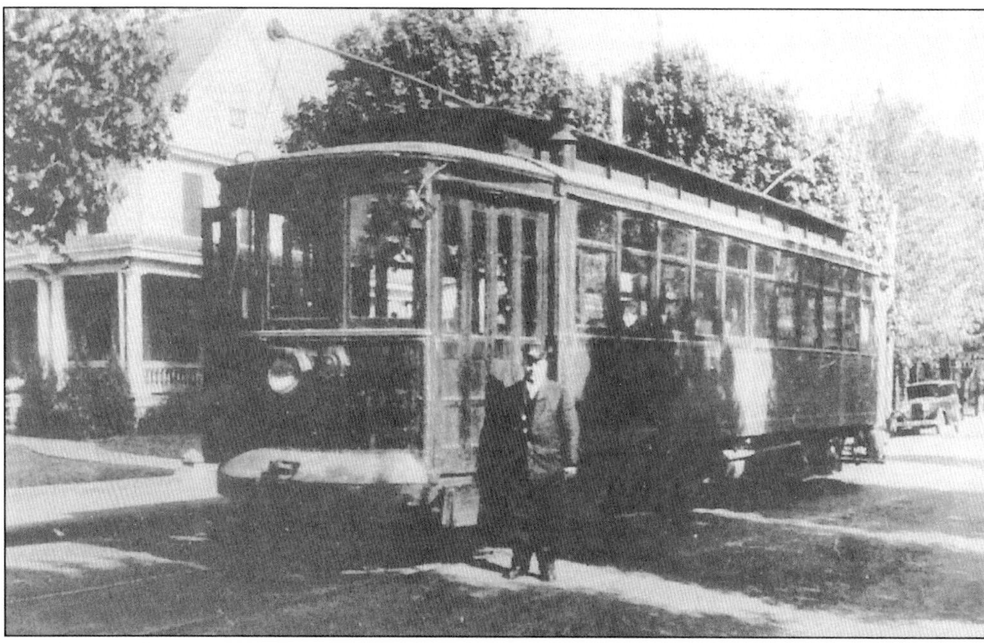

Conductor John S. Bean poses in front of the Tripper on Main Street in Richlandtown. He was employed by the Lehigh Valley Traction Company for 43 years, serving as a motorman on the Tripper and the Liberty Bell trolleys that ran through Richland. In this picture, the pole has just been reversed, and the trolley is ready to head south back to Quakertown. (RB.)

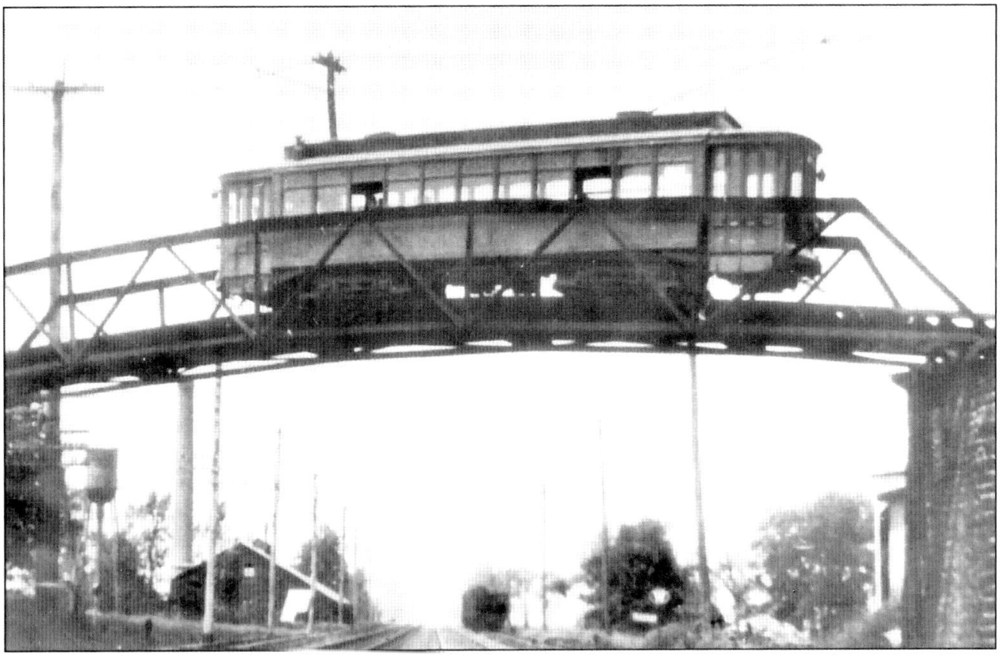

The trolley route from Quakertown to Richlandtown necessitated crossing the North Penn Railroad. This was accomplished by building a bridge over the rail line just a few hundred yards north of the Quakertown station. The last trolley to cross this bridge left Quakertown at 11:00 p.m. on May 31, 1929. The metal span of the bridge was removed in 1935; one stone pier remains. (TM.)

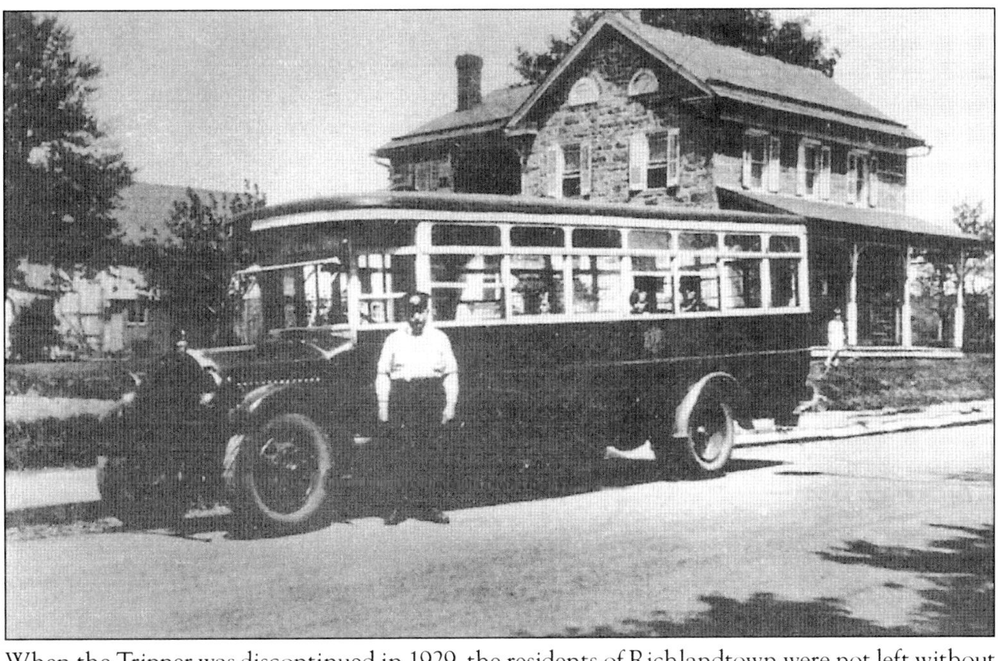

When the Tripper was discontinued in 1929, the residents of Richlandtown were not left without public transportation. Pictured above is an early public bus in Richlandtown. Service was instituted from Richlandtown by the Levy Bus Company, which operated a route from Richlandtown to Trumbauersville by way of Quakertown. Bus service continued until 1973. (RB.)

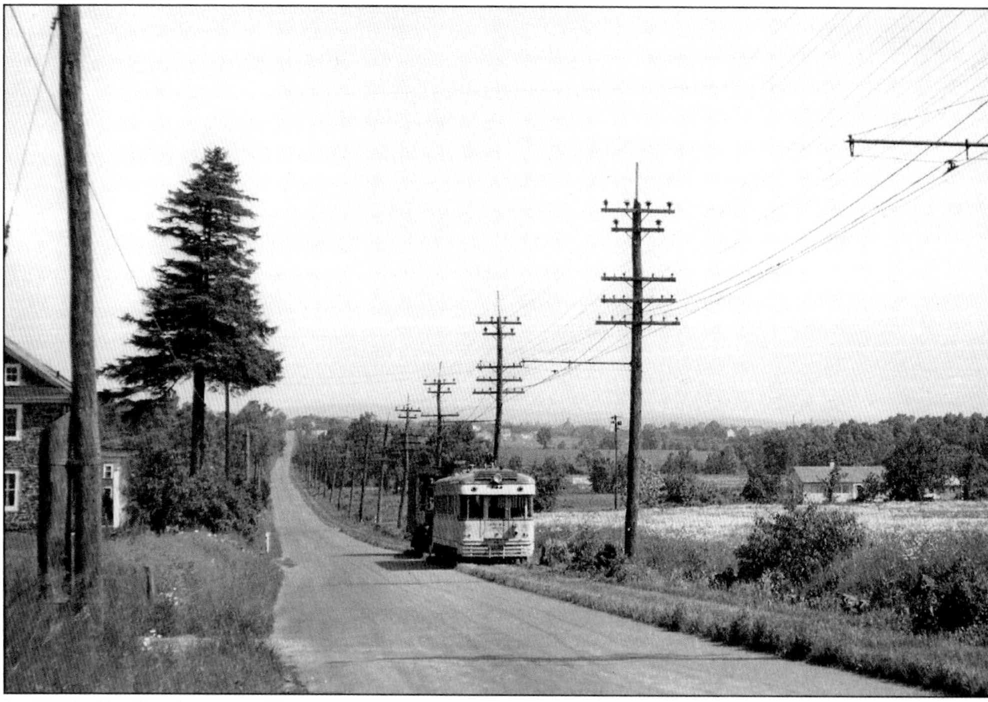

In 1900, the Quakertown Traction Company (QTC) extended its line to Perkasie, running tracks parallel to Old Bethlehem Pike. A few years later, the entire trackage of the QTC was leased to the Lehigh Valley Transit Company, which ran trolleys from Allentown to Philadelphia. The route was styled the Liberty Bell Limited. In the above photograph, a Liberty Bell car travels along Old Bethlehem Pike. (LKW.)

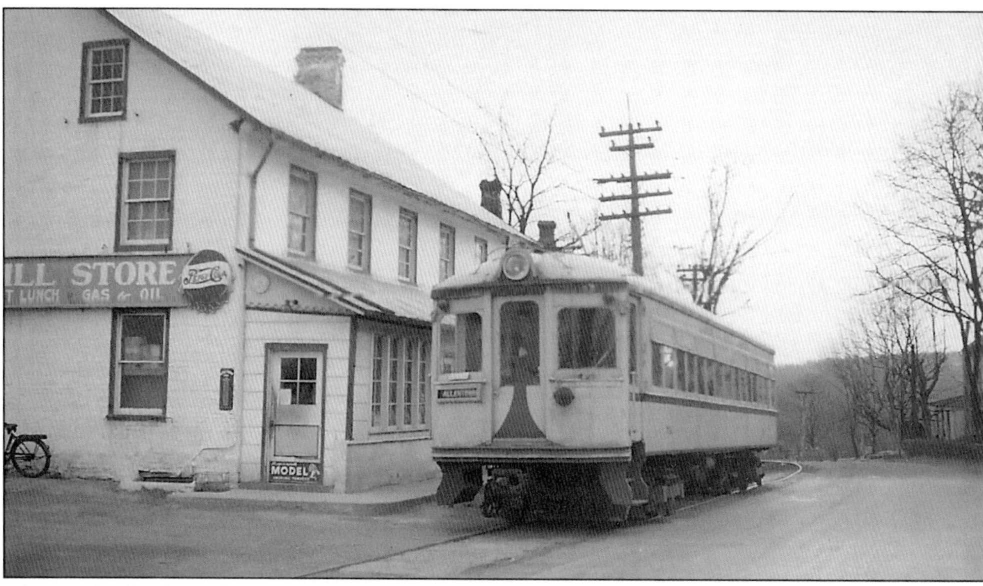

The tracks for the Liberty Bell trolley were laid along the east side of Bethlehem Pike for most of the route through Richland Township. The first stop from the south was Rich Hill. The rail line then continued north to Quakertown. The shoulder along the east side of Bethlehem Pike where the tracks were removed is the only reminder of the trolley line. (LKW.)

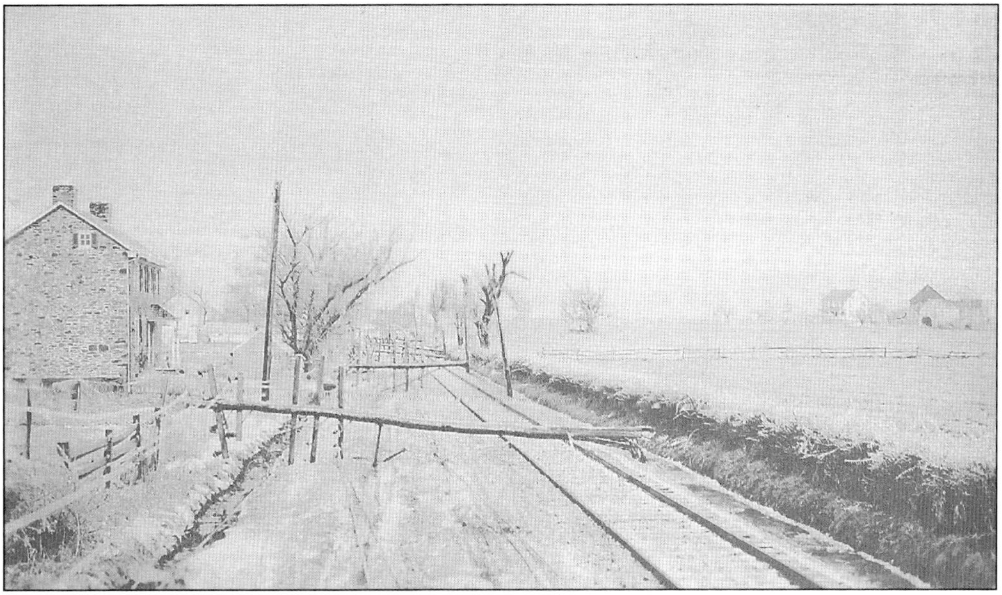

An ice storm created havoc for the Lehigh Valley Transit Company, as seen in this photograph dated December 6, 1914. The poles that carried electricity to the trolleys were snapped close to the ground, closing this section of Bethlehem Pike south of Tollgate Road. The Penrose farm is on the left, while the homestead of Jacob Stonebach is on the right in the distance. (TM.)

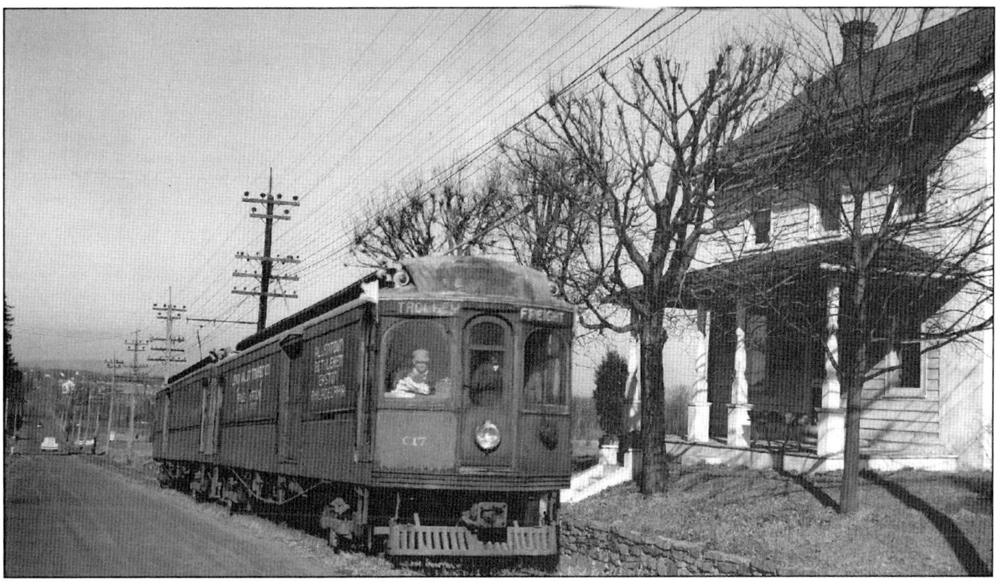

In addition to passengers, the Lehigh Valley Transit Company provided freight service between Allentown and Philadelphia along the Liberty Bell Route. In this photograph, two southbound freight cars travel along Old Bethlehem Pike in the late 1940s. The freight trolleys were painted red, while the passenger trolleys were cream-colored. (LKW.)

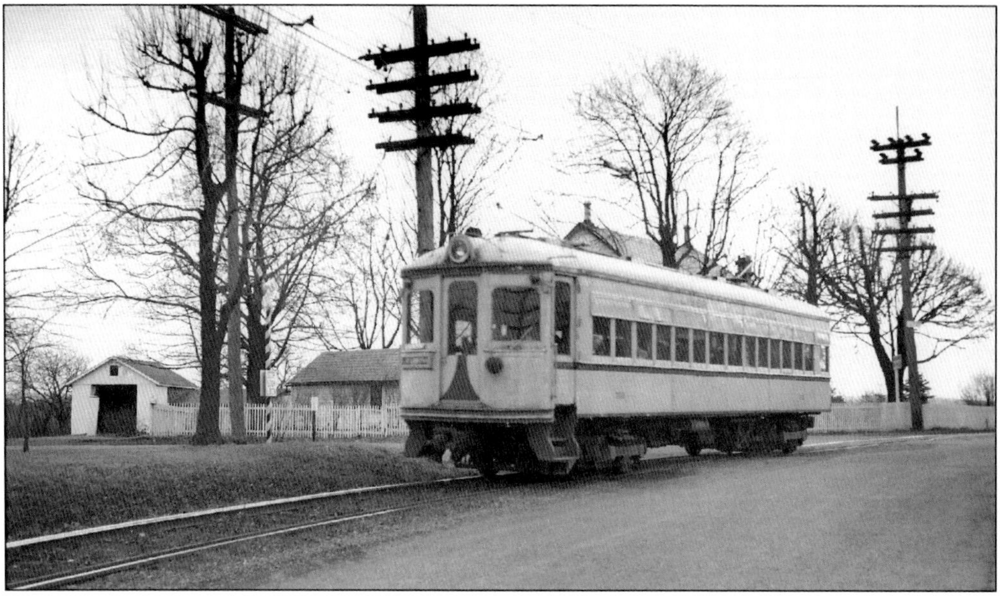

A passenger trolley of the Liberty Bell Limited travels north on the Old Bethlehem Pike in this photograph from the 1940s. A passenger could board the trolley at several places along the route, and the trip from Rich Hill to Quakertown took about 14 minutes. A morning commute from Quakertown to Allentown took less than 45 minutes. (LKW.)

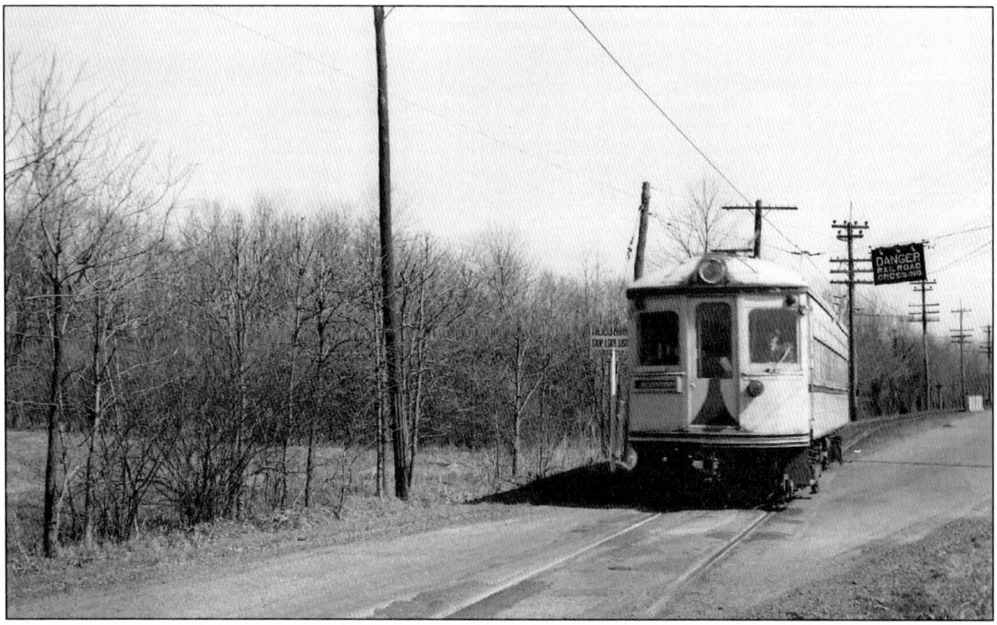

For most of the route through Richland Township, the trolley tracks were on the east side of Bethlehem Pike. Near where the Genesis Retirement Home is now, the trolley tracks crossed diagonally to the west side. As there was no signal for traffic on Bethlehem Pike, this was a dangerous crossing where accidents occurred. (LKW.)

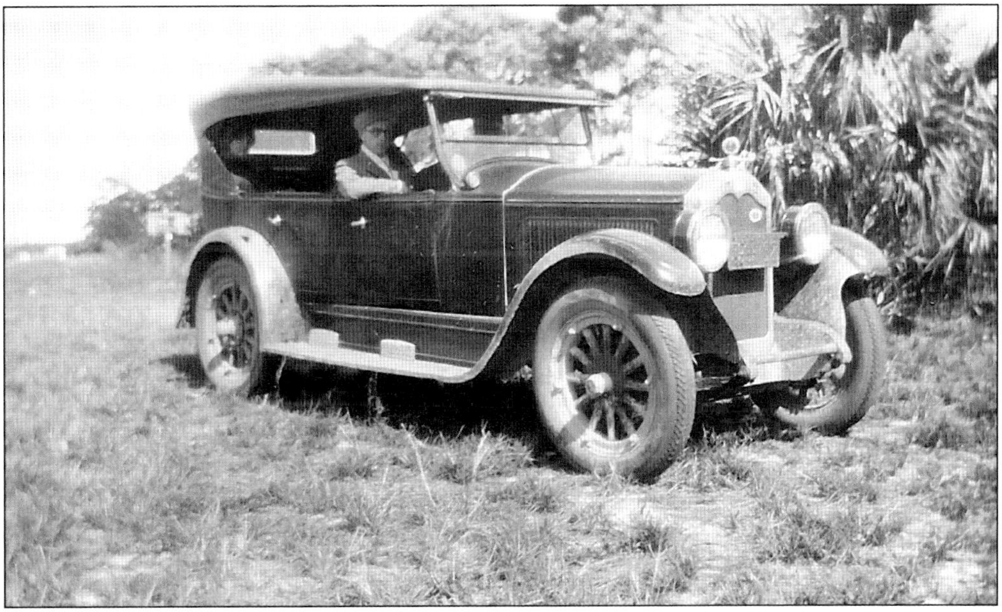

The Ritter family owned this automobile, which they used to travel to Florida in the 1920s. At the time, long-distance travel by car was an adventure. Cars were not built for bad weather, and not all roads were paved. The route system was also primitive, as there were no national standards for marking roadways or placing signage. (CH.)

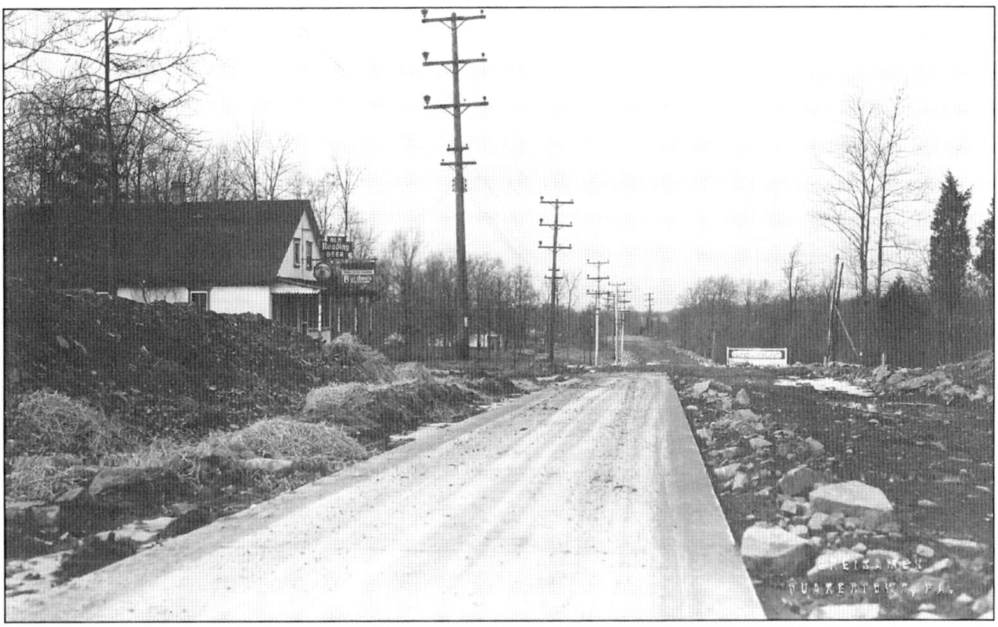

Route 309 was under construction in the mid-1930s as part of the public works programs of the Franklin Roosevelt administration to put people to work during the Great Depression. On the left is the original Meyers' Restaurant near Shelly. One lane of the highway appears to be completed; the other lane is full of rubble. (GM.)

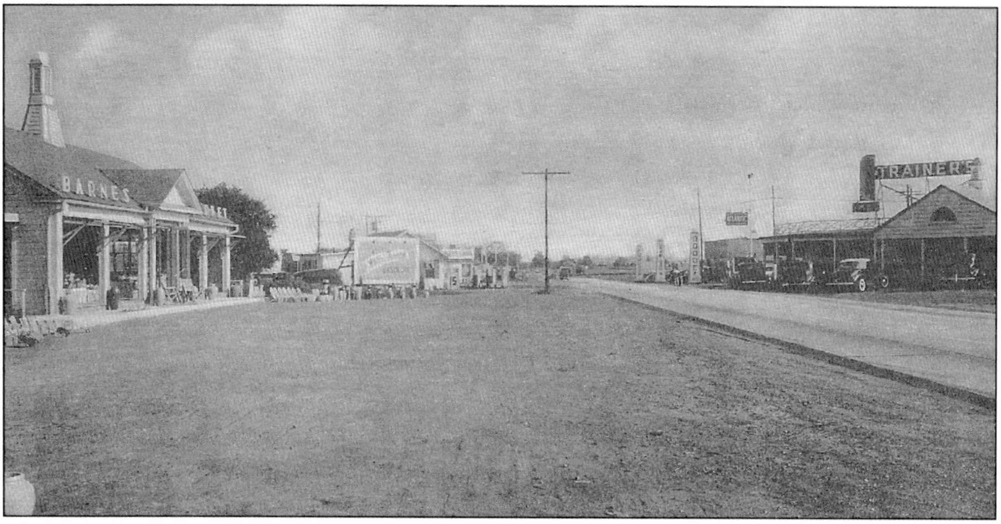

This picture of Route 309 looking south probably dates from the 1940s. Trainer's Restaurant, which opened in 1932, is on the right. Trainer's was known far beyond the area for its excellent food. The building on the left was Barne's Market, which became Smitty's Drive-In in the 1950s. (TM.)

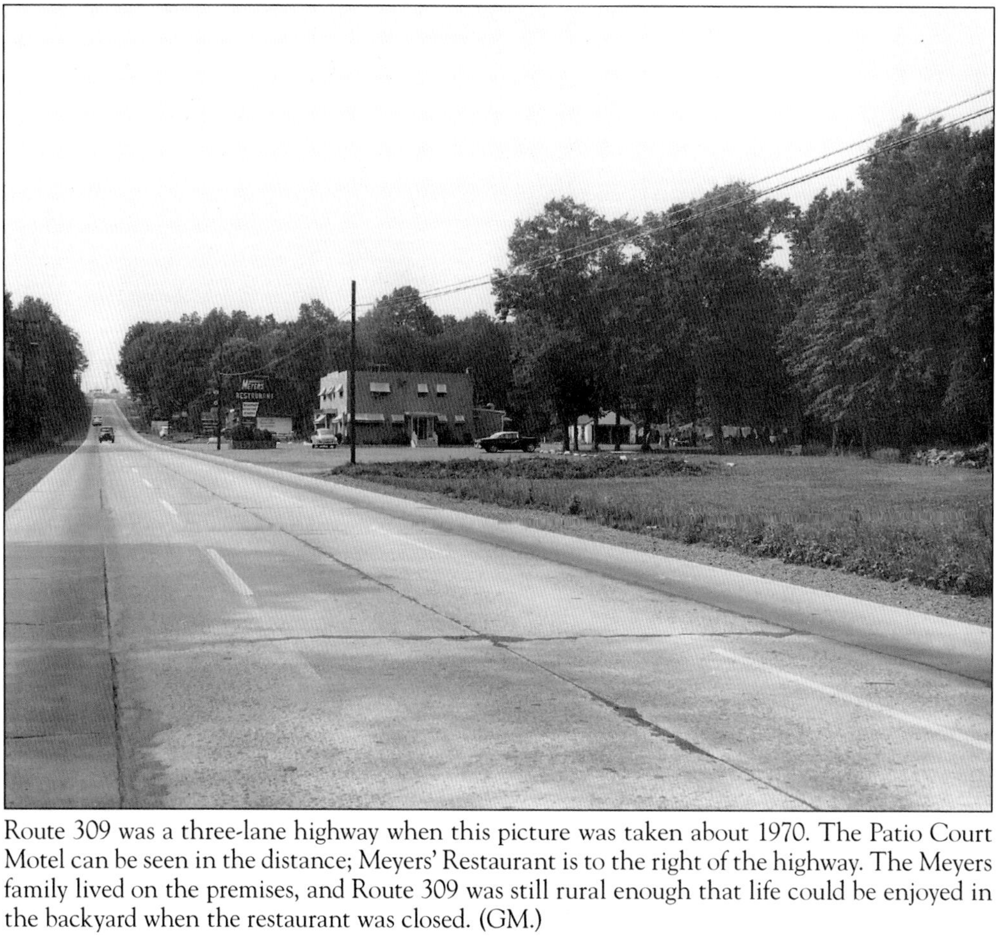

Route 309 was a three-lane highway when this picture was taken about 1970. The Patio Court Motel can be seen in the distance; Meyers' Restaurant is to the right of the highway. The Meyers family lived on the premises, and Route 309 was still rural enough that life could be enjoyed in the backyard when the restaurant was closed. (GM.)

Seven

Rural Life

During the 1700s, substantial numbers of ethnic Germans came to Upper Bucks County and established their homes and farms in Richland Township. During the next century, the descendants of these German settlers predominated in the rural areas, while the Quakers tended to remain in the villages such as Quakertown. The ethnic Germans were often called Pennsylvania Dutch.

To a large extent, farms in the 19th century were largely self-contained communities. Much of the food was produced on the farm. Grains were raised to feed the livestock and as cash crops. Dairy products were sold to creameries, and eggs and produce were marketed to the townspeople in the villages.

By the 20th century, farming became more of a business. Labor saving machinery made crop production more efficient. Many farms became electrified during the 1930s, and tractors replaced horses for field work. Some farmers kept their teams of horses until the 1950s for specialized work in gardens.

Although a woman's place was considered to be in the home taking care of the family needs, women were also expected to tend the garden and earn egg money with a flock of chickens. Men did the barn and field work. Children were supposed to help their elders.

After World War II, Richland Township became more urbanized. Single homes were built along the existing secondary roads. By the 1960s, zoning was adopted to regulate the locations of residential, commercial, and industrial developments. By the beginning of the 21st century, Richland Township had become in many ways a suburb. There are virtually no working farms, but enough farmland is still under cultivation by large-scale farmers that Richland maintains something of its rural character despite a large increase in population. Glimpses of a way of life from not long ago can be found in the photographs that follow.

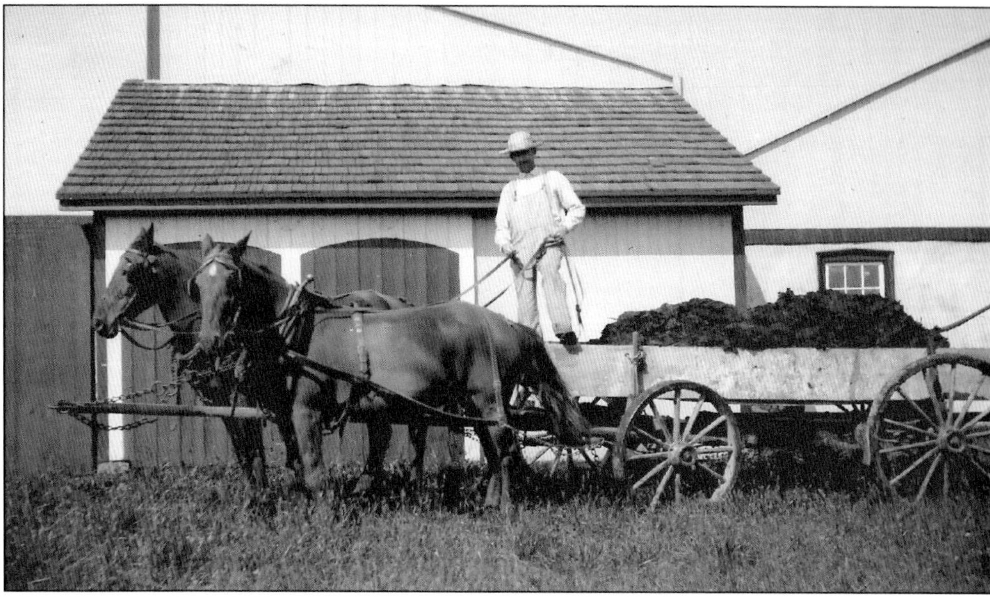

This photograph was taken about 1914 of Frank Smith, who was the hired man on the Fellman Farm on Paletown Road. Manure from the animals in the barn had to be loaded by hand on a wagon and taken to the fields where it would be spread to fertilize the crops. (FFIM.)

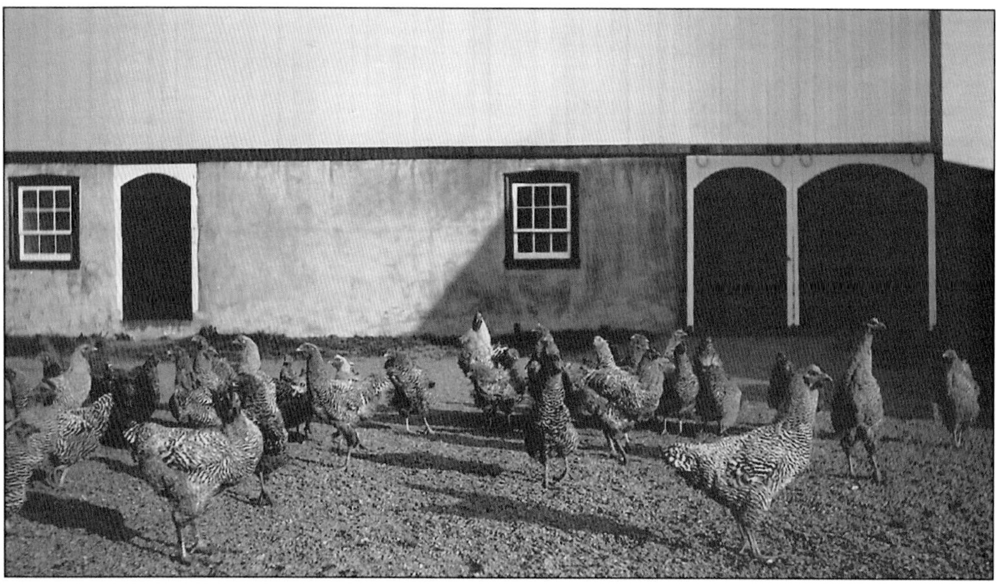

This photograph from 1914 shows a flock of the variety of chickens called Barred Rocks. The breed is supposed to have originated in New England near Plymouth Rock. The chickens were an all-purpose stock, producing eggs and meat. Surplus eggs were sold for cash to customers from town. Flocks had free range during the summer and spent the colder months inside. (FFIM.)

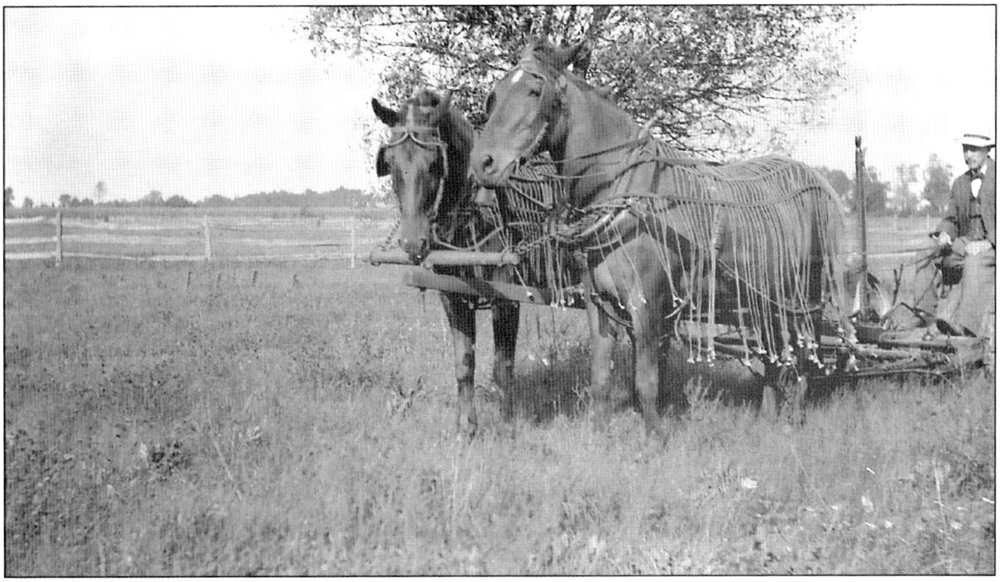

Harvey Fellman mows hay with a horse-drawn sickle bar mower in 1914. Richland Township farms with dairy cattle, sheep, and horses needed large quantities of hay, which was stored in barns or outside haystacks (below). Although the sickle-bar mower was a labor-saving device, making hay was hard work. Grass or clover was cut in the field when it was large enough and left to dry in the sun. After it had dried, the hay was raked onto rows and taken by horse-drawn wagon to the barn or haystack. If the weather was good during the summer, a farmer might get as many as three cuttings. (Both, FFIM.)

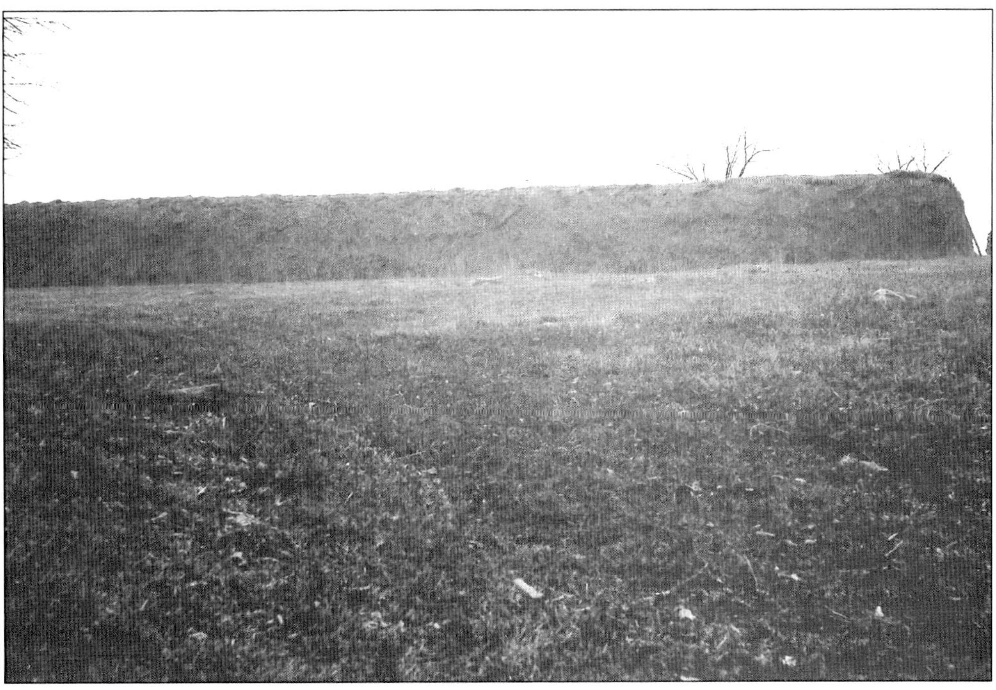

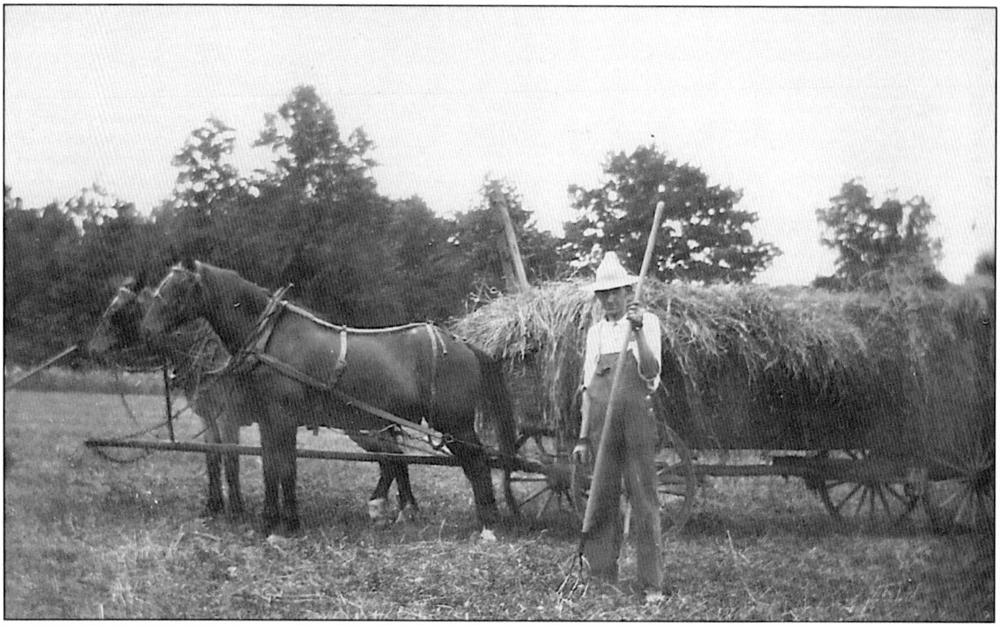

The Ritter family utilized a wagon and a team of horses to make hay well into the 20th century. The fields were of grass, clover, or alfalfa. When the plants were large enough, the family would cut the fields with a sickle-bar mower that was pulled by a horse. Depending upon the weather, the cut hay was left to dry for a day or so. The Ritters did not bale the hay. Using pitchforks, loose hay was raked up and tossed into the wagon. As the wagon filled, it became more difficult to pitch the hay into it. In the photograph below, the hay is nearly twice the height of the man. (Both, CH.)

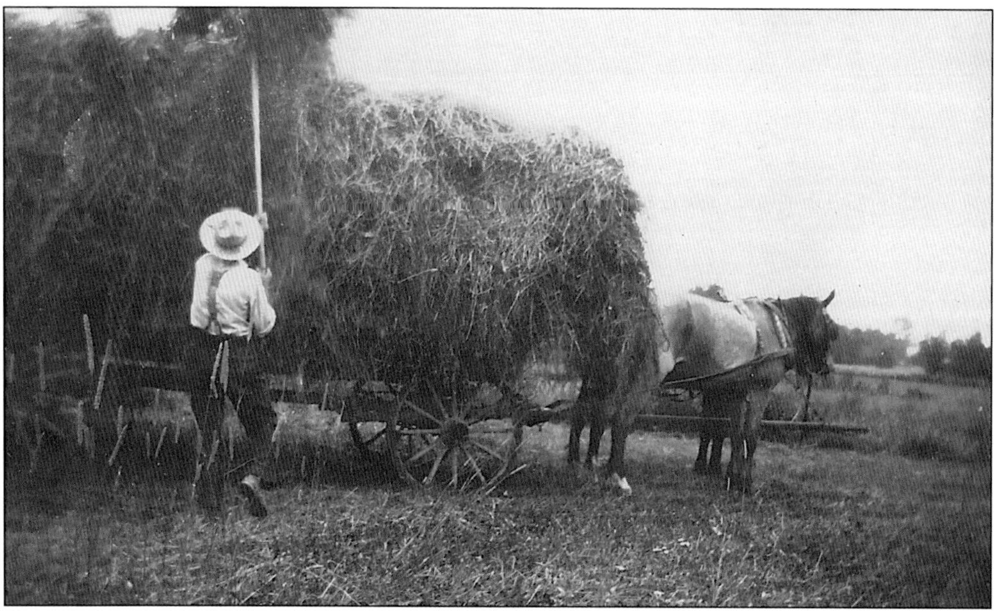

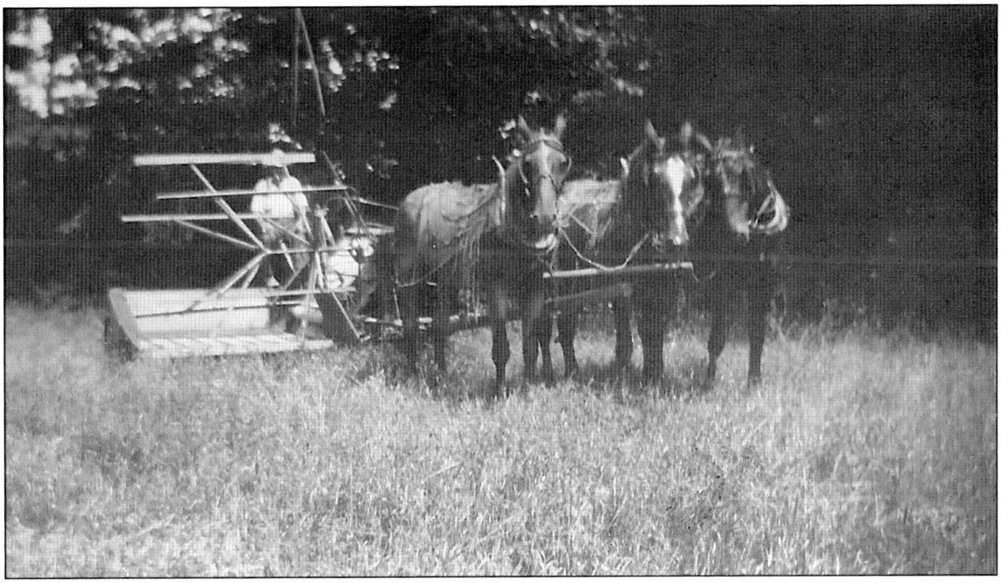

A binder cut the stalks of grain, such as wheat, rye, or oats, and bound them into bundles. Sheaves were taken to a stationary threshing machine, into which the bundles were fed in order to separate the grain from the stalks. Later the two operations of cutting the grain and threshing it were combined into one operation with a machine called a combine. (CH.)

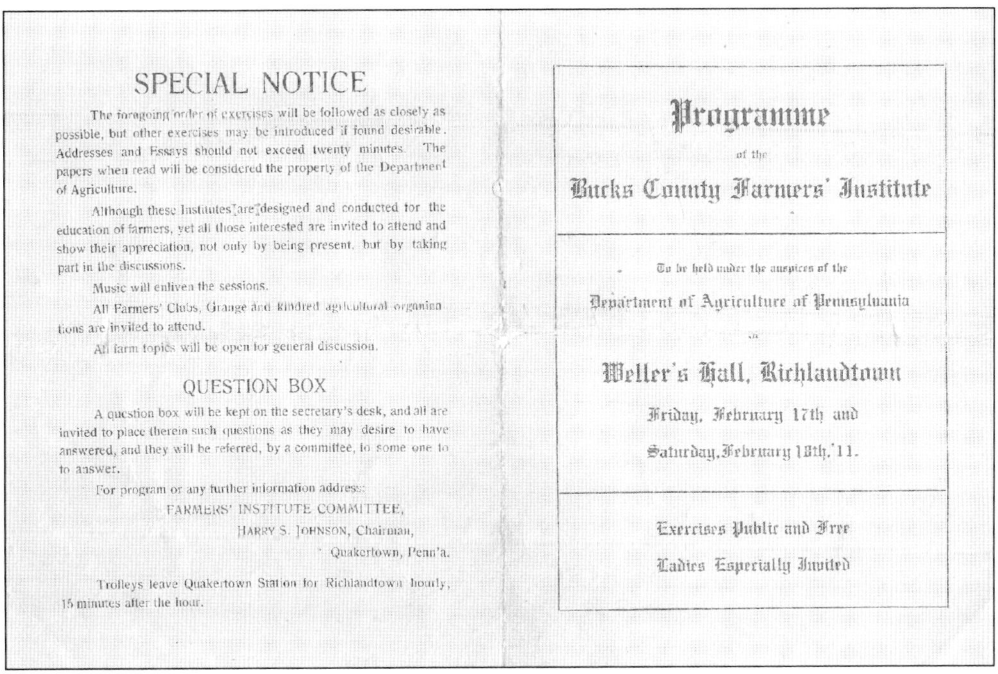

SPECIAL NOTICE

The foregoing order of exercises will be followed as closely as possible, but other exercises may be introduced if found desirable. Addresses and Essays should not exceed twenty minutes. The papers when read will be considered the property of the Department of Agriculture.

Although these Institutes are designed and conducted for the education of farmers, yet all those interested are invited to attend and show their appreciation, not only by being present, but by taking part in the discussions.

Music will enliven the sessions.

All Farmers' Clubs, Grange and kindred agricultural organizations are invited to attend.

All farm topics will be open for general discussion.

QUESTION BOX

A question box will be kept on the secretary's desk, and all are invited to place therein such questions as they may desire to have answered, and they will be referred, by a committee, to some one to to answer.

For program or any further information address:

FARMERS' INSTITUTE COMMITTEE,
HARRY S. JOHNSON, Chairman,
Quakertown, Penn'a.

Trolleys leave Quakertown Station for Richlandtown hourly, 15 minutes after the hour.

Programme
of the
Bucks County Farmers' Institute

To be held under the auspices of the
Department of Agriculture of Pennsylvania
in
Weller's Hall, Richlandtown
Friday, February 17th and
Saturday, February 18th, '11.

Exercises Public and Free
Ladies Especially Invited

The Pennsylvania Department of Agriculture sponsored an institute for farmers to help them improve their farming practices at Weller's Hall, Richlandtown, on February 17 and 18, 1911. The program included music and entertainment, but the objective was improving farming practices. Topics included "How and When to Use Lime," "Best Use of Barnyard Manures," "Educating the Poultry Keeper," and "Corn Selection and Culture." (RHS.)

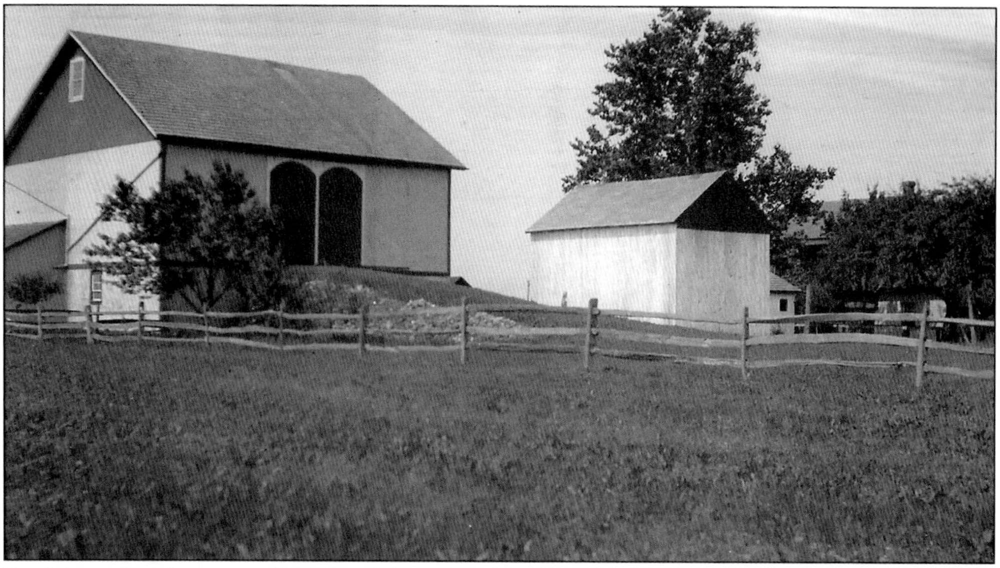

Bank barns dot the farms of Richland Township. This handsome bank barn was located in Paletown on the Fellman farm. Banks barns have two levels that are accessible to wagons at ground level. Sometimes the barn was built into a hillside. The Fellman barn had a built up ramp of earth and stone that gave access to the second floor. (FFIM.)

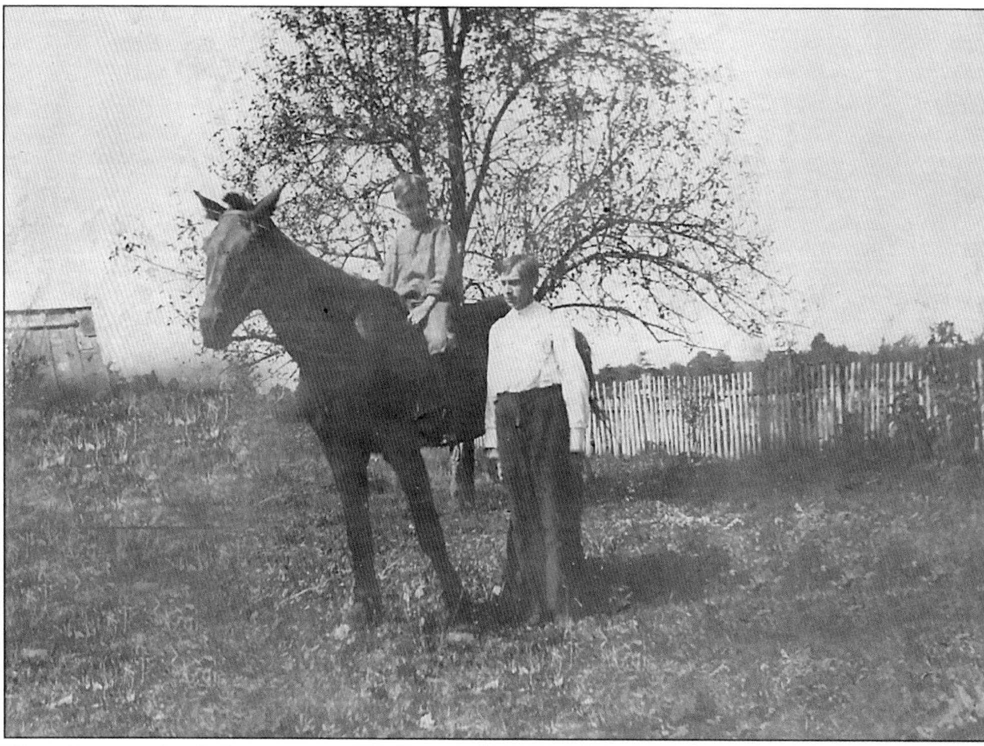

This photograph of a horse named Doll was taken on a farm in Richland Township early in the 20th century. Horses were valuable as work animals and as a means of transportation before the automobile became prevalent. Because there were so many animals that ran loose, fences like that in the photograph were intended to keep them out of a yard or garden. (KFDH.)

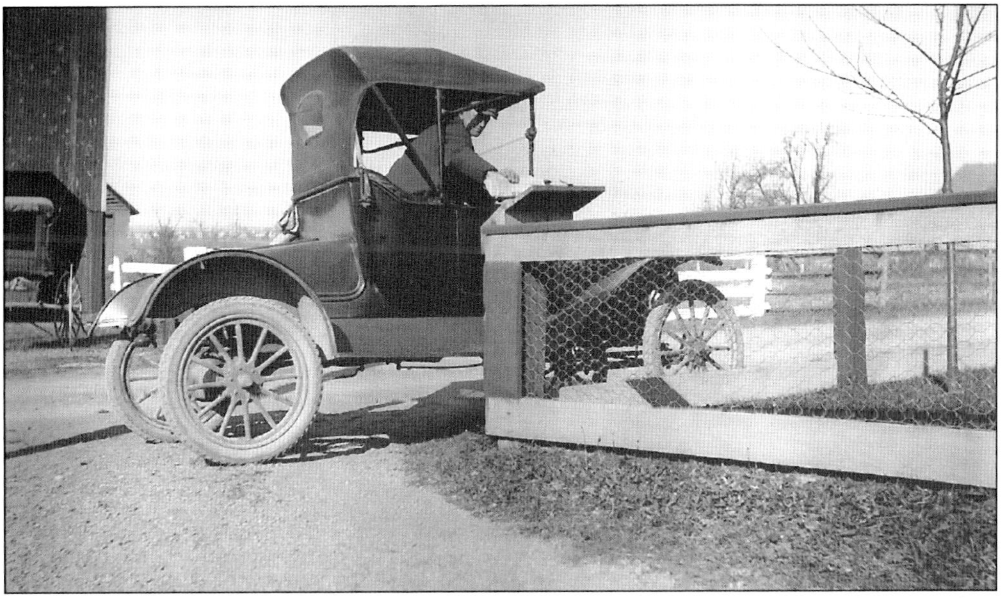

After Rural Free Delivery allowed country people to have daily mail service at home, pickup post offices in villages such as Rich Hill were closed. All of the mail to rural addresses from the Quakertown Post Office was delivered on three rural routes. This photograph shows the mail carrier delivering mail to the Fellman residence about 1914. (FFIM.)

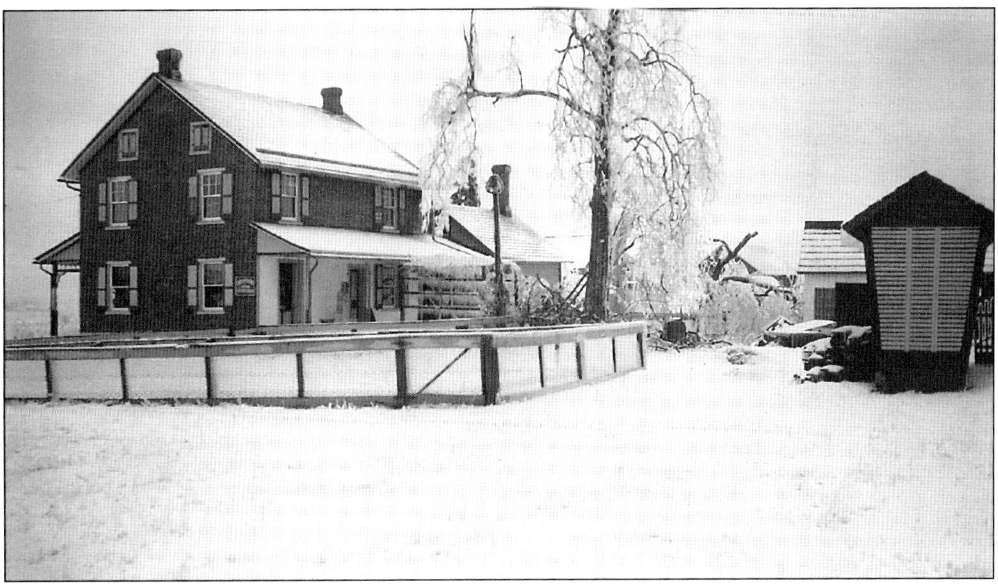

In her description of the results of an ice and sleet storm, photographer Flora Fellman wrote in 1914, "After that sleet storm, the branches of that big tree were broken off. That broke down the new fence on both sides of the gate. We had to go out of the side gate to get to the barn. It looks like a woods." (FFIM.)

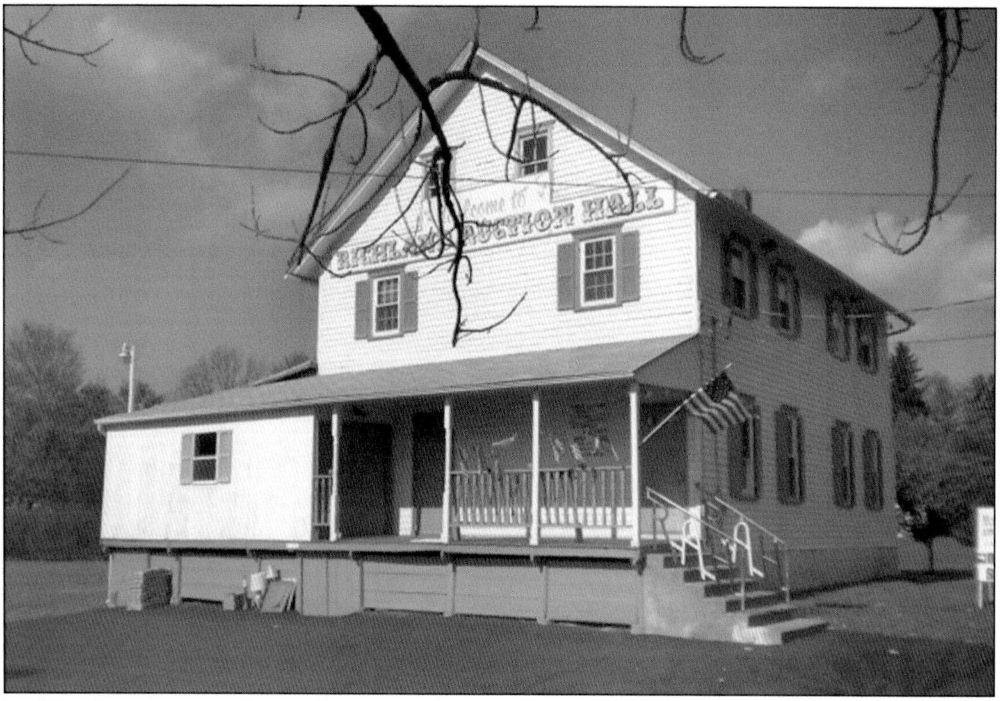

Richland Grange, on the Richlandtown Pike, was a branch of a national fraternal society of rural people originally known as the Order of Patrons of Husbandry and more commonly as the Grange. Local farmers formed Richland Grange in 1902 as a cooperative to purchase food and farm supplies. It became the township's social center for farmers. When farming declined in the 1970s, Richland Grange disbanded, and the building became an auction house. (KF.)

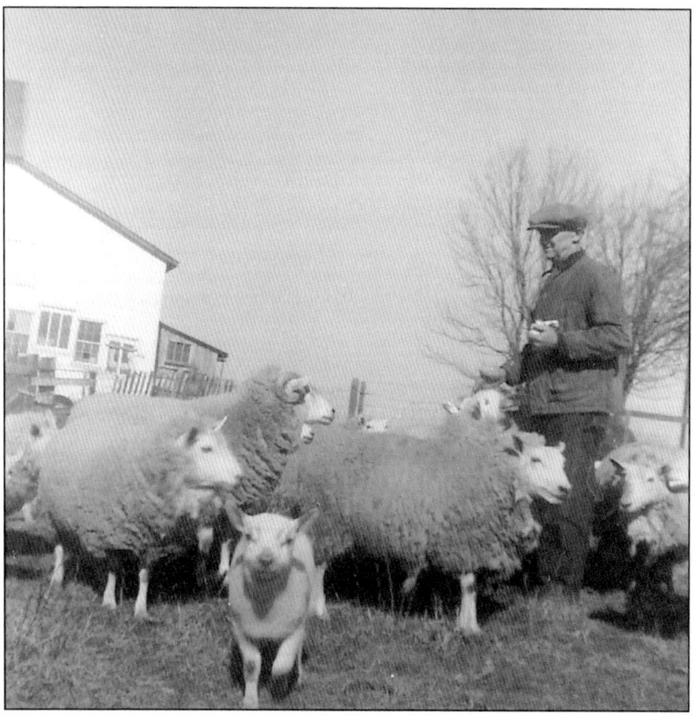

As most farmers raised the animals that would be used for meat, mutton was a change from the typical diet of beef and pork. The sheep hides could be tanned with the wool on to provide an extra layer of warmth in the winter. Before the invention of lawn mowers, sheep in the yard would keep the weeds and grass trimmed. (KFDH.)

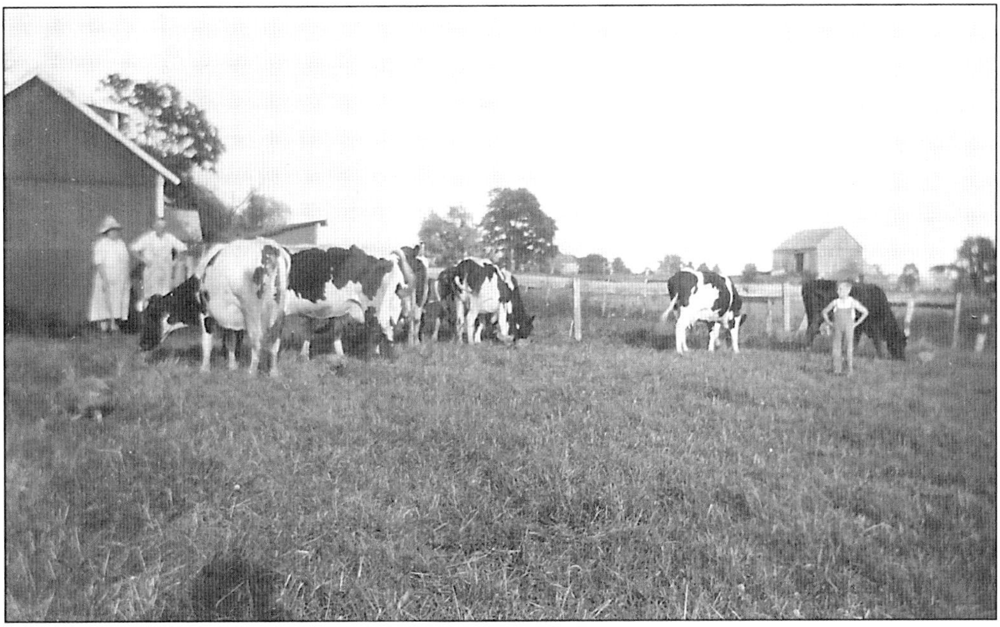

This herd of Holstein milk cattle is enjoying the lush grass in the pasture of the Ritter farm. Holstein cattle are black and white and produce the most milk of any of the common breeds. Dairy products were a major source of income on Richland Township farms in the 1930s, when this photograph was taken. The cattle were milked by hand, and the raw milk was taken in large cans to a creamery, such as the one in Richlandtown. After farms were electrified by the 1940s, farmers had refrigerators in their milk houses, and the milk was picked up at the farm and taken to large dairies. This marked the end of small local creameries. (Both, CH.)

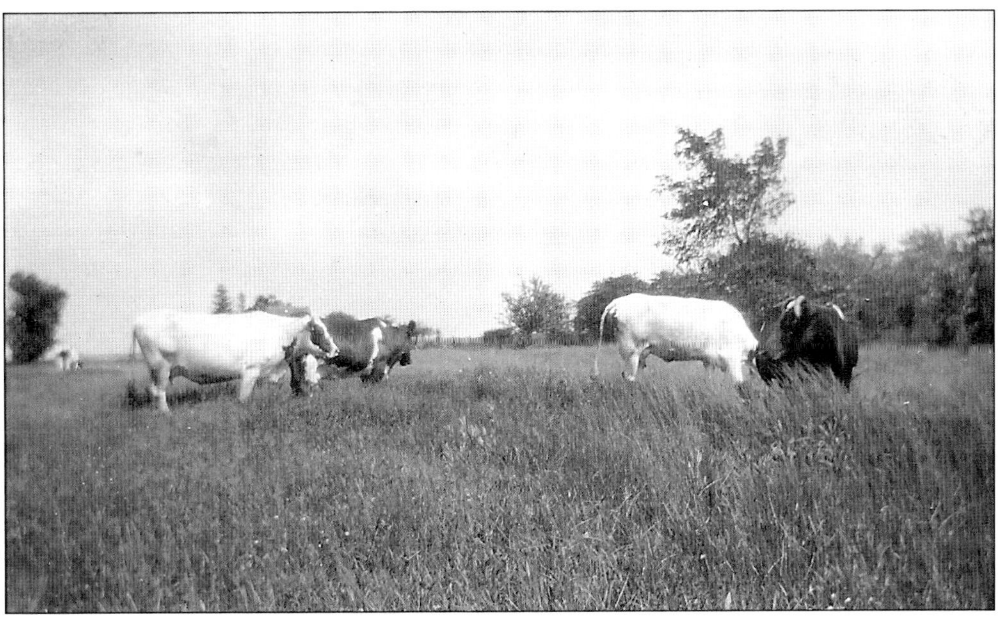

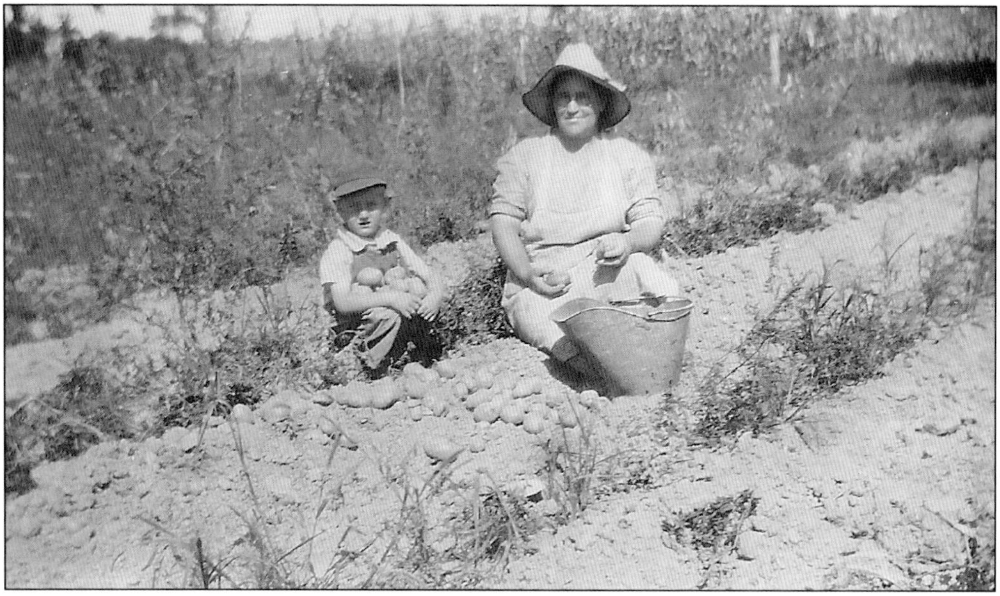

Hannah Ritter and a young helper picked up potatoes that have been plowed up in the fall at the end of a growing season. Seed potatoes were cut so that each section had eyes from which the young potato plants sprouted after planting. Potatoes were a good crop for the family garden. After being harvested, they kept well in the basement or a root cellar. (CH.)

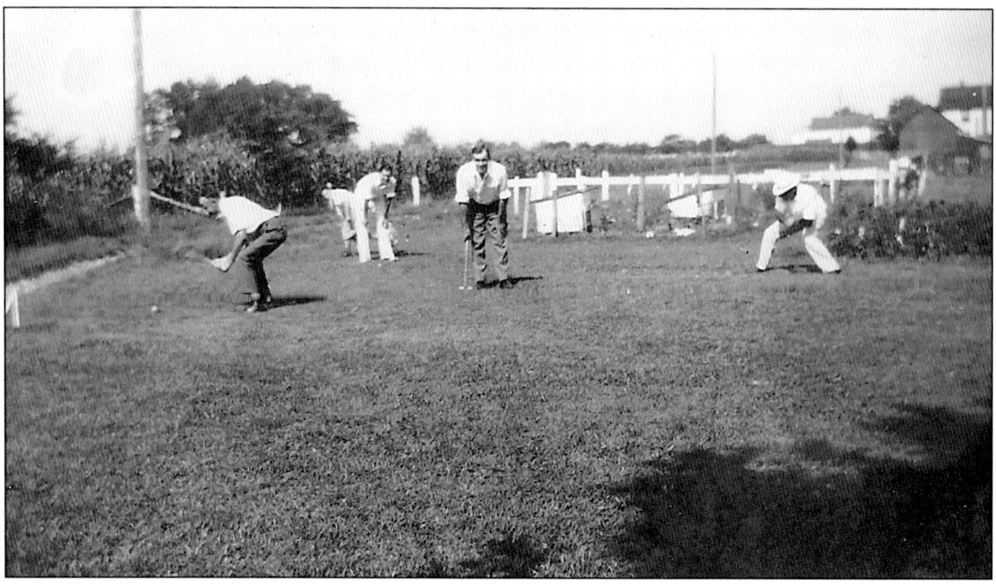

A favorite way to spend a quiet Sunday afternoon in the summer was to play croquet. Each player had a wooden mallet, matched in color to a wooden ball about the size of a softball. The object was to complete a course by driving the ball through wickets. If one player's ball hit another, the opponent's ball could be driven off the course. (CH.)

Eight

Landmarks

Some important landmarks in Richlandtown and Richland Township have been shown in previous chapters. This section provides additional images that are important in the history of Richland Township.

The main occupation of rural Richland Township was farming. Many farm families took great pride in their well-kept homes, barns, and other outbuildings. Unfortunately, some fine old homes and barns have been the victims of the housing developments of the last 40 years. The best existing examples of rural architecture are along the more rural highways, such as Rocky Ridge and Rich Hill Roads in Lower Richland, and Mine, Dickert, Cherry, and California Roads in the northeastern section of the township.

Route 309 north of Quakertown had three fine restaurants. Trainer's Restaurant was arguably the best known. It began during the Depression as a truck stop at the intersection where the Bethlehem Pike and Route 309 converged. Trainer's was esteemed for seafood dinners. Meyers' Restaurant was further north on 309 next to Kaufman School. It was sold to the Benetz family, who also achieved a fine reputation for their dinners. The Meyers family relocated their restaurant to the east side of 309. Among the specialties for which it was locally famous were apple dumplings and the salad bar. There are now many restaurants along the same strip of Route 309, but none have the personality of those three from the golden age from about 1950 to 1975.

Tohickon Creek was the major waterway in the township. It is said that shad were still caught in the Tohickon when Richland was first settled by the Quakers. The creek provided power for mills and ice for icehouses, and a dam further downstream allowed swimming and boating at Tohickon Grove. During the first half of the 20th century, it was probably the best-known recreation spot in the township.

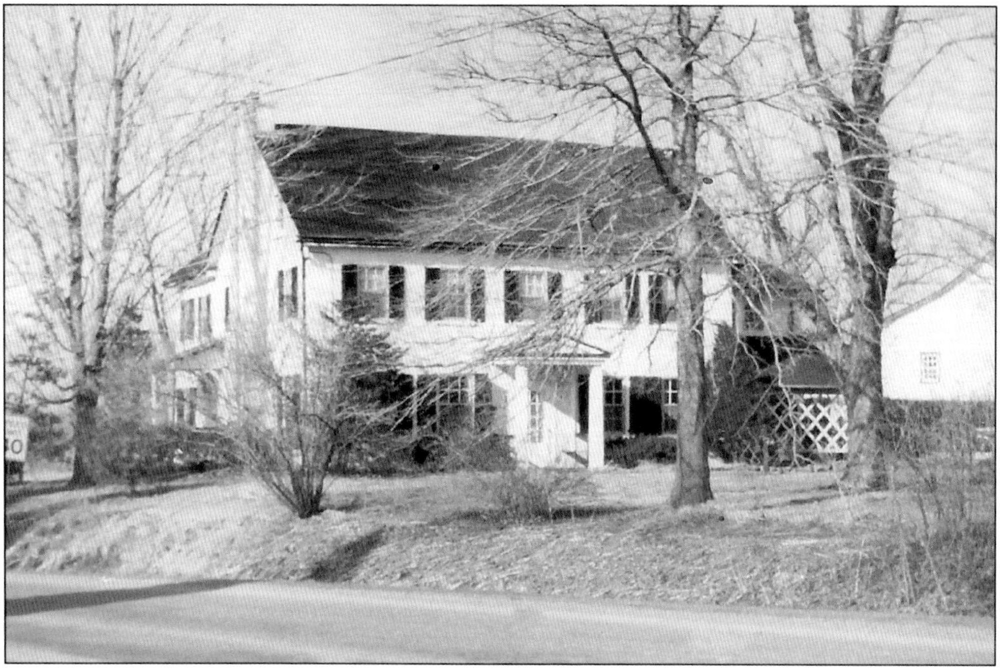

Located on Old Bethlehem Pike, this stone house sits on the site of the first Richland Friend's meetinghouse. By 1798, the house was occupied by William Penrose, who was a weaver by trade and owned much of the surrounding acreage. William Penrose died in 1808, but his wife, Mary, lived here until 1843. The house passed out of the family in 1844. (CR.)

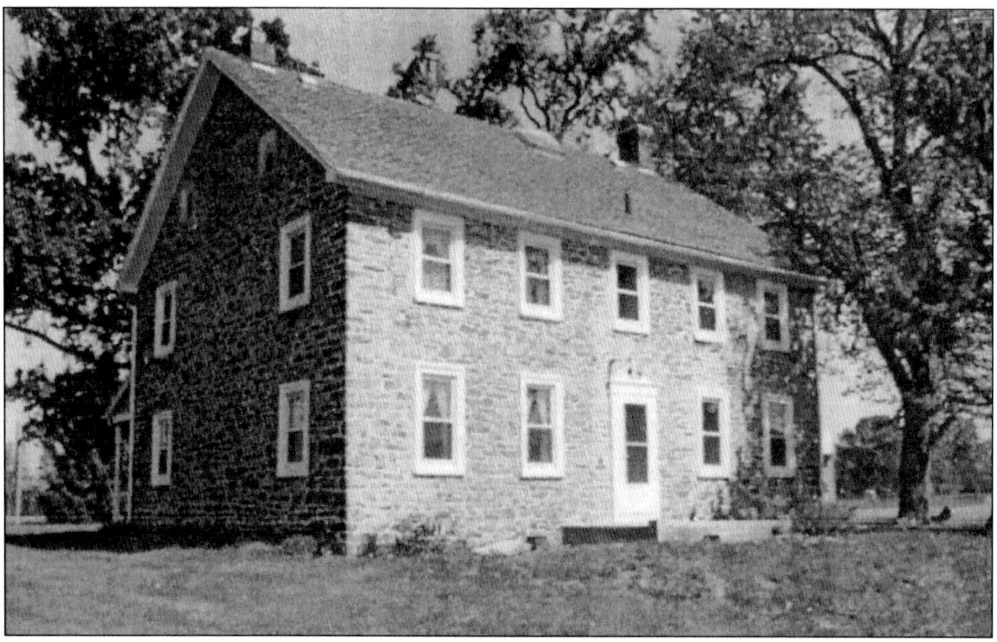

Randall Iden Jr. was born in Bristol Township in 1736 and moved to Richland about 1740. As an adult, he purchased a large tract of 158 acres, upon which he erected the above stone home in 1799. Randall Iden died here in 1812, and the home passed to his son Jesse, who owned the premises for 20 years. (RT.)

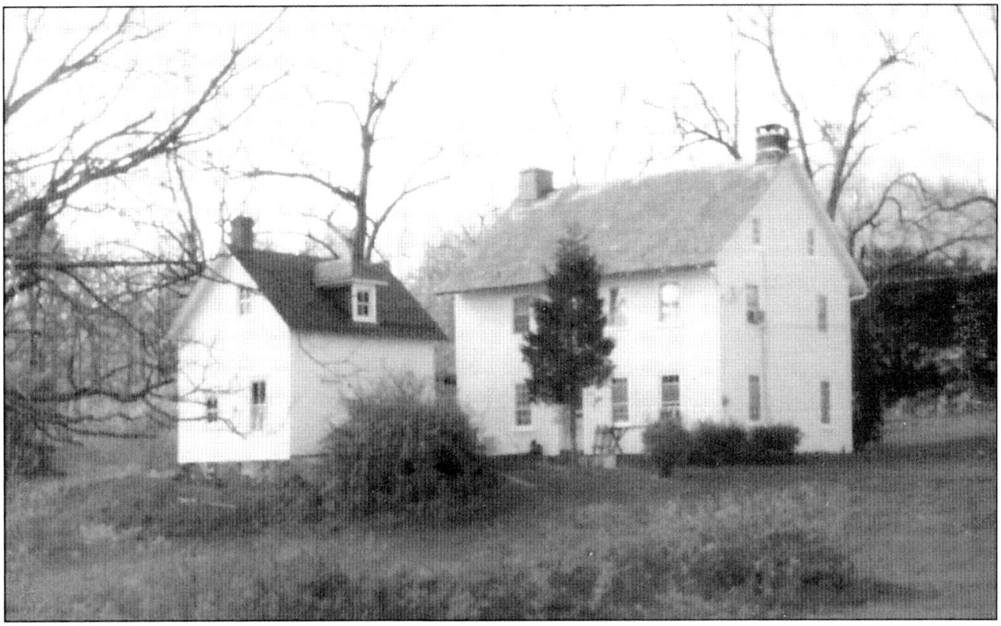

This house stands on property once owned by Leonard Hinkle, an early settler in Richland Township. At the time of the 1798 "window tax," Leonard Hinkle owned 140 acres and lived in a log home. The property was purchased by Jacob Benner in 1822, and the Benner family retained the place until 1883. (CR.)

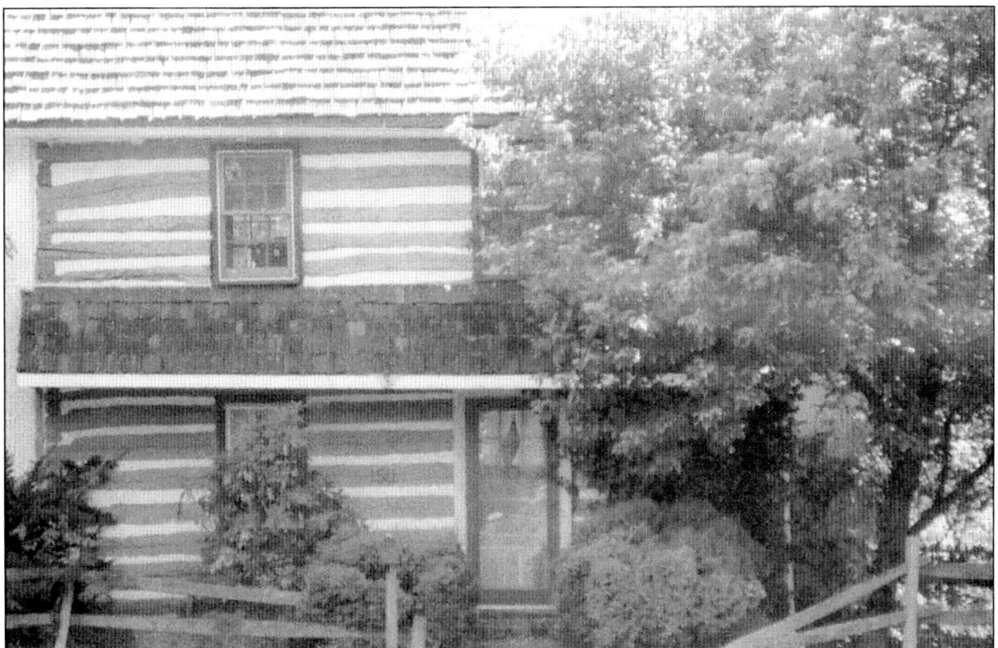

The earliest settlers in Richland constructed homes made of logs. As these pioneers accumulated wealth, they added wings or built new homes from native stone. This log home, built about 1800, still stands on Reservoir Road. It was purchased by Michael Martin before 1850, and he lived here until his death in 1890. (RT.)

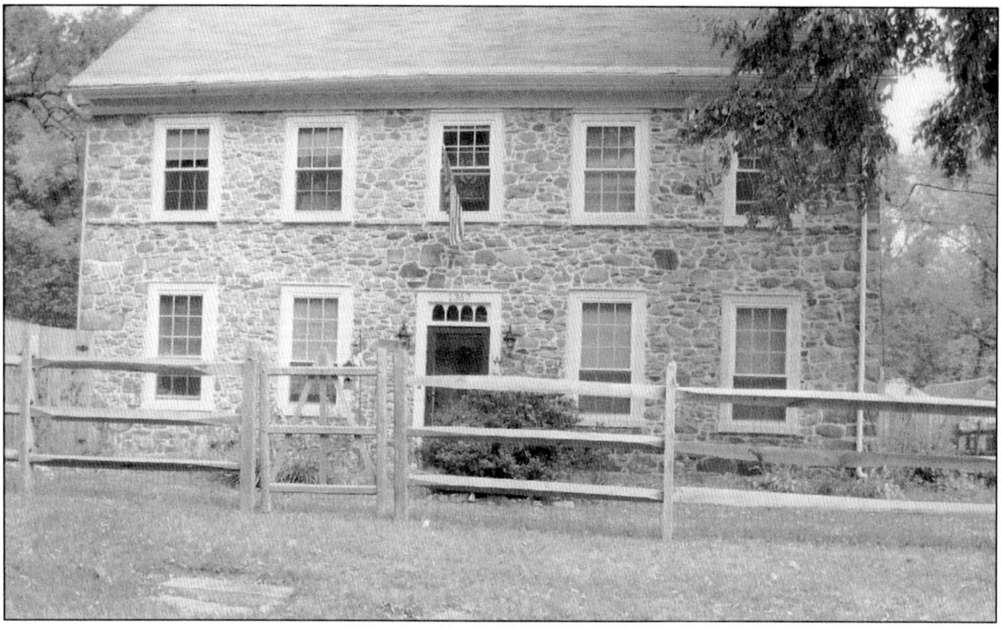

John Michael Matts settled in Richland in 1800, where he worked as a tanner and currier. His son John was born about 1786 and lived in this house above Richlandtown. John Matts was a farmer and a colonel in the 59th Regiment of the Pennsylvania militia. Elected to the Pennsylvania House of Representatives in 1824, he served four years. John Matts died in 1875, when he was 89 years of age. (RT.)

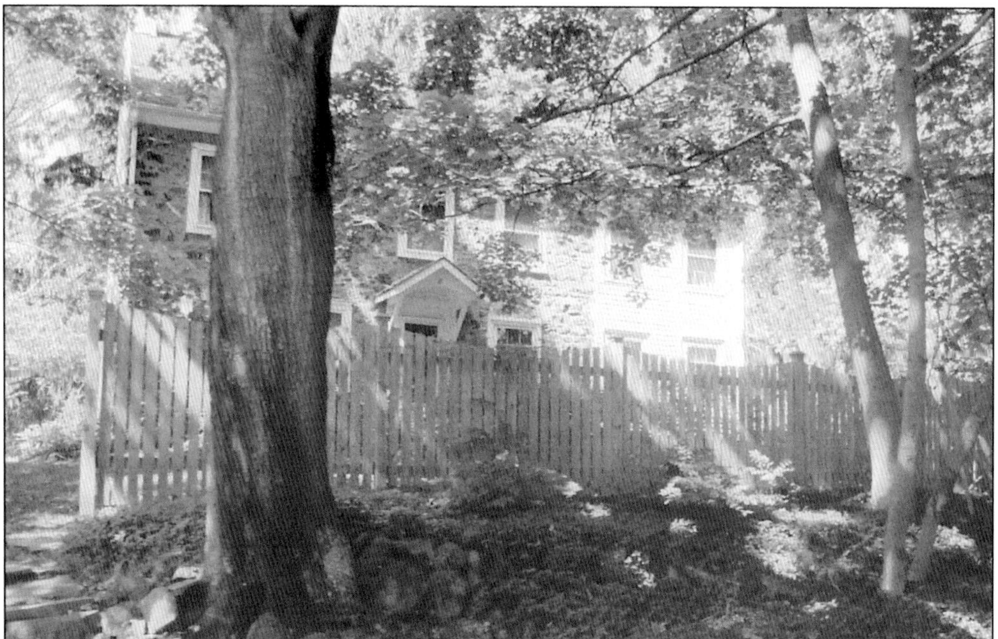

Michael and Margaretha Rudolph were early settlers in Richland Township. They owned land adjacent to the Springfield Township line and worshipped at St. John's in Richlandtown. This home remained in the Rudolph family for over a century, passing from Michael Rudolph to his son Michael, who then passed it to his son John Rudolph. (RT.)

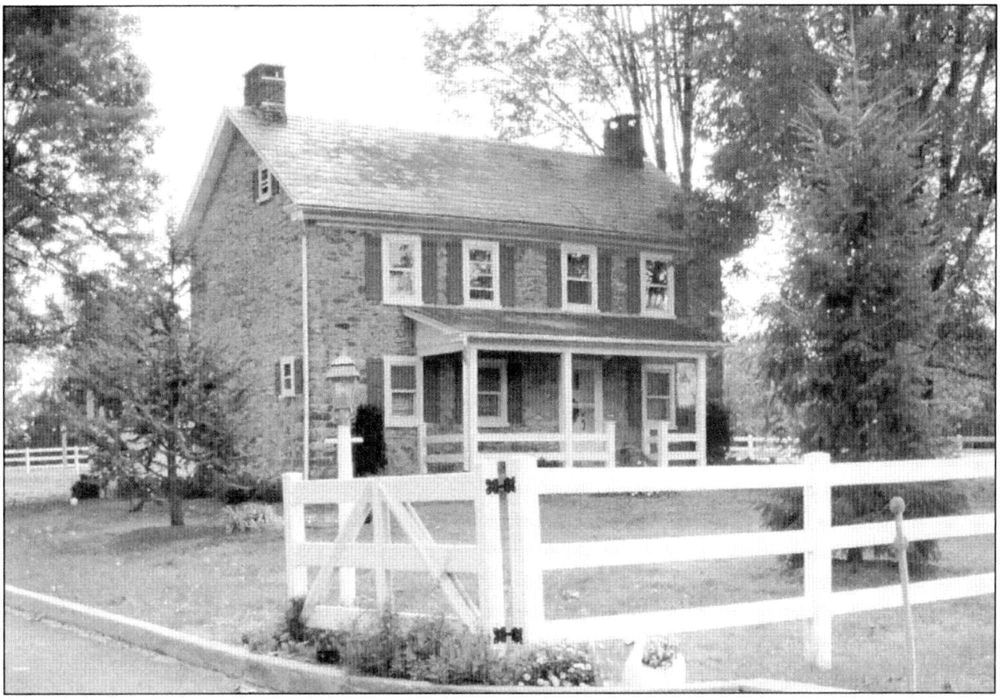

This handsome stone home was owned by the Sterner family at the end of the 19th century. The house dates from the early 1800s and is a typical residence from that period—stone construction, two-and-a-half stories, with chimneys at both ends. The Sterner homestead comprised 32 acres. (RT.)

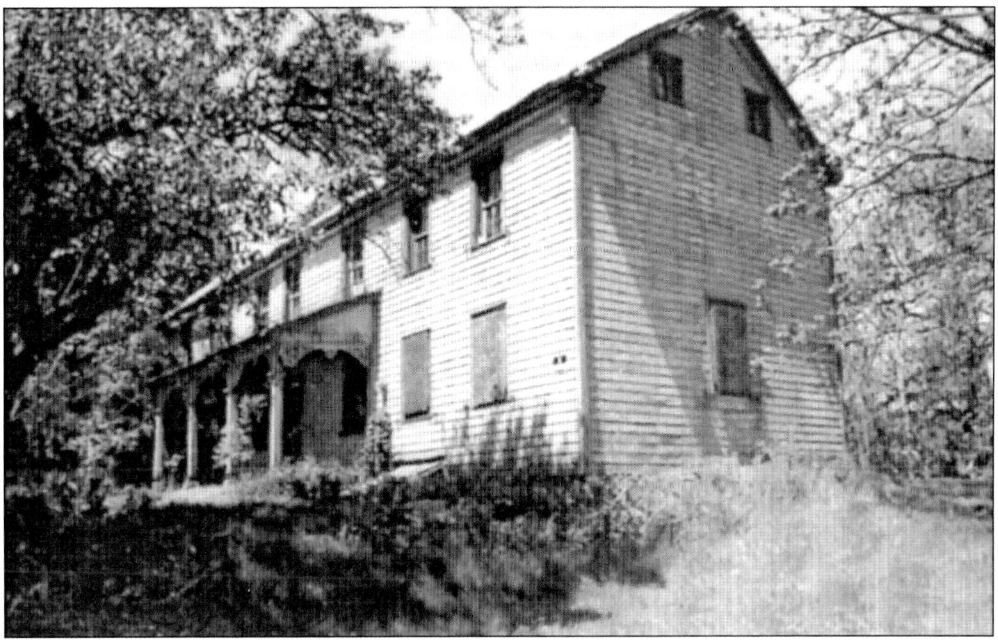

A 56-acre tract along Reservoir Road was purchased by James Mawson in 1874. He was born in Yorkshire, England, and came to the United States in 1847. Mawson worked in Philadelphia for some time but relocated to Richland in the 1870s. Mawson and his brother Benjamin manufactured ladies all-wool shawls in this building throughout the 1870s and 1880s. (RT.)

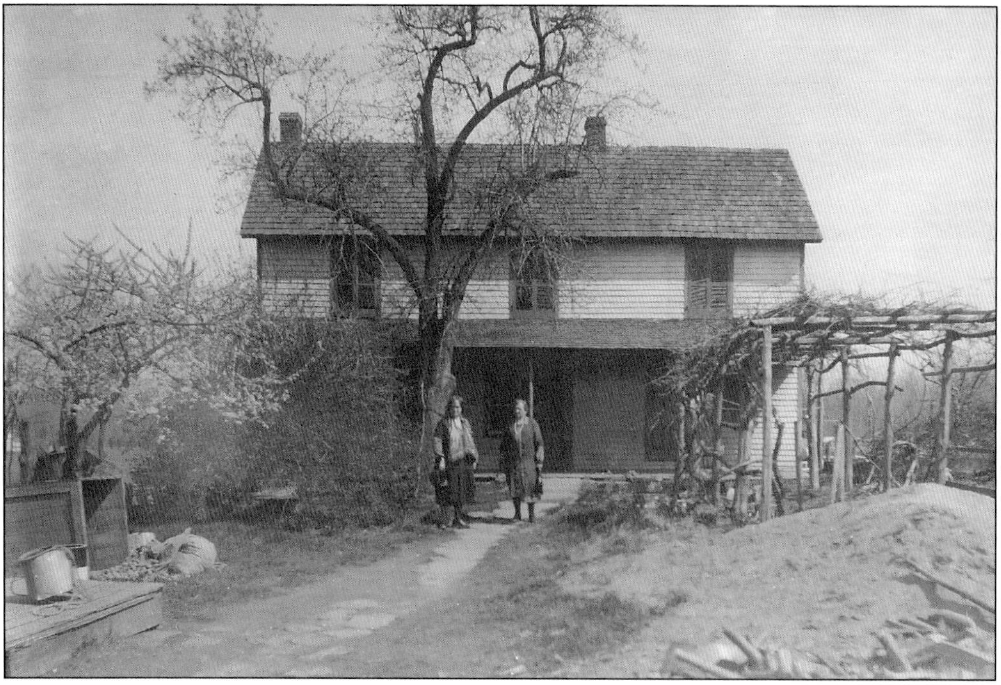

Elizabeth Heller Freed and her sister Ella Amanda Heller Schaffer pose in front of the Freed home in Richland Township. Like many Richland Township farms, this farm boasted several fruit trees and Concord grape vines supported by an arbor. A pile of potatoes rests to the left of the dirt path. (CR.)

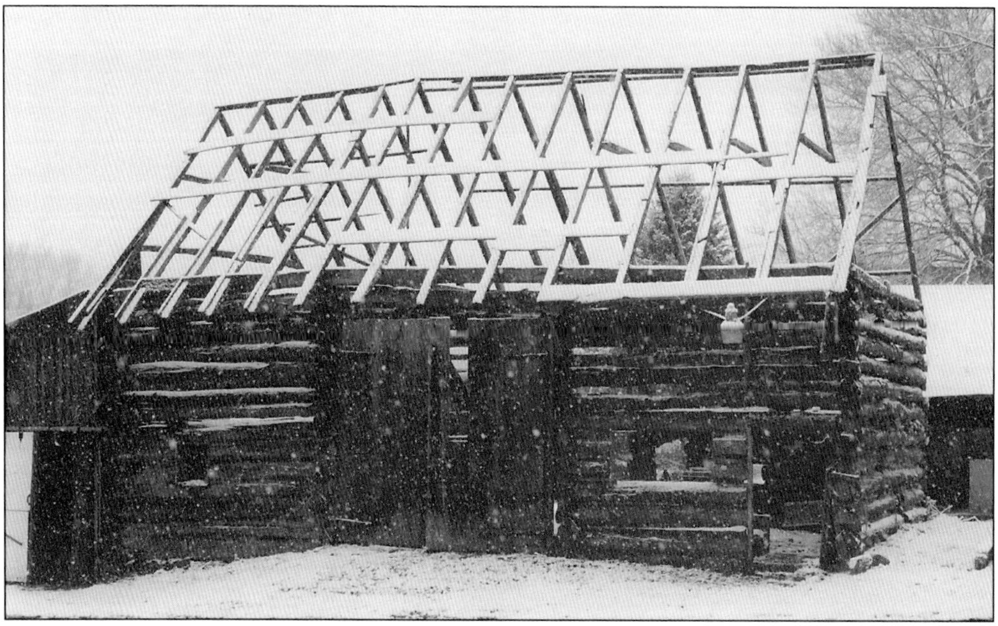

This log barn was built by Barnet Heller. His farm was located on Rock Hill Road in the lower part of Richland Township. Born in Germany, he came to Pennsylvania as a young man and later fought in the American Revolution. He died in 1809, at 78 years of age. The 200-year-old barn was dismantled and reerected in neighboring Milford Township. (CR.)

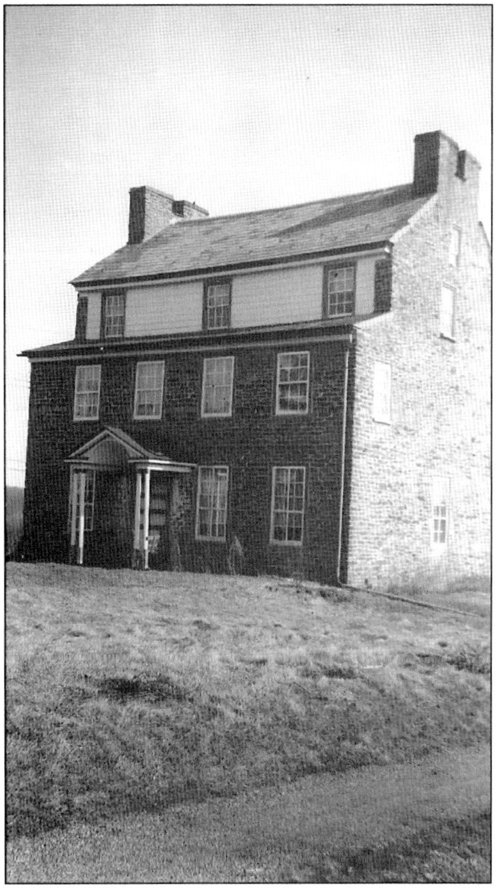

This handsome and unusual house along Tollgate Road was the victim of its proximity to Route 309. Located at the southwest corner of the two roads, it was razed in the 1960s to make way for a gas station. During the 19th century, the farm belonged to Aaron Ball. He was born in Richland in 1827 and lived in Quakertown. Ball married Rebecca Strawn, who was also a native of Richland. The barn on the homestead (below) had been the shop for the Ball family of cabinetmakers. They also constructed coffins. Like many casket makers in the 19th century, they worked as undertakers as well. (Both, CR.)

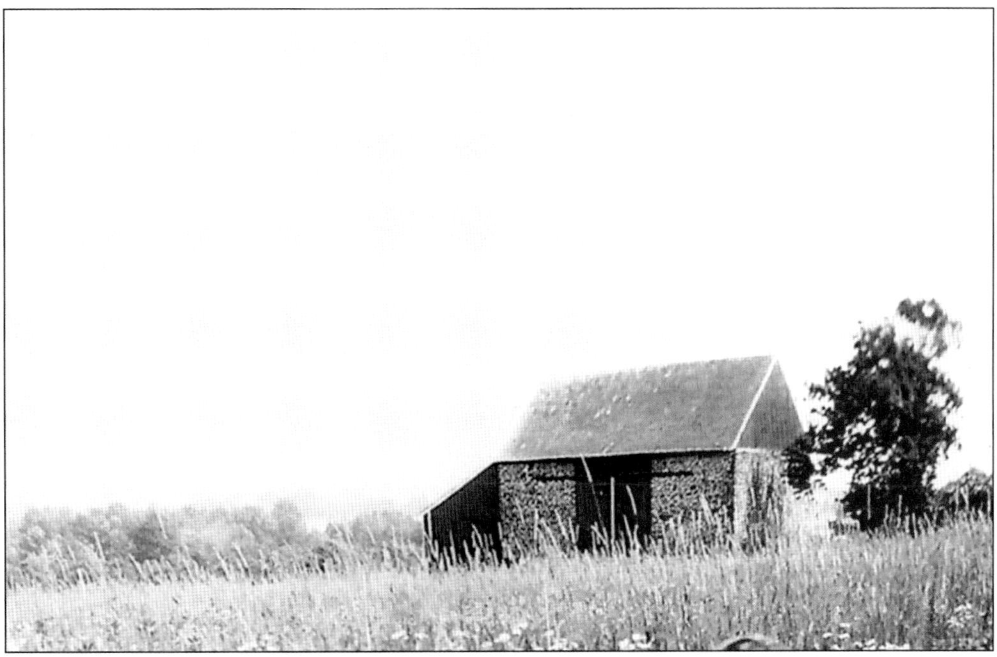

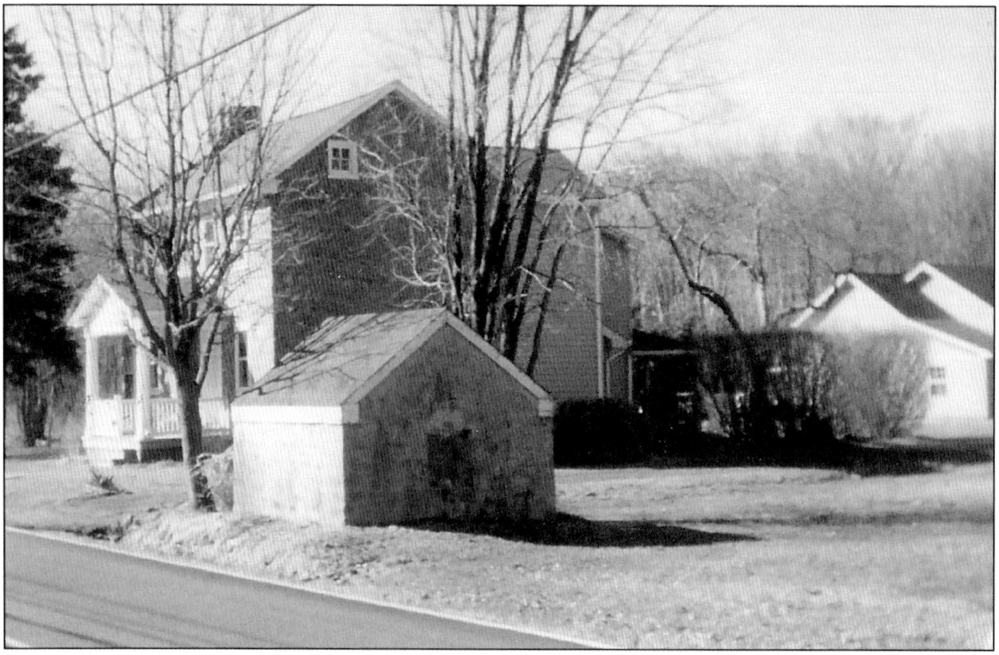

This home along Old Bethlehem Pike dates from the early 1800s. The springhouse, located near the road, is from the same era. Before the era of the refrigerator, springhouses were used to preserve food. Built over the source of the spring, the constant running water and thick stone walls helped maintain a consistent, cool temperature. (CR.)

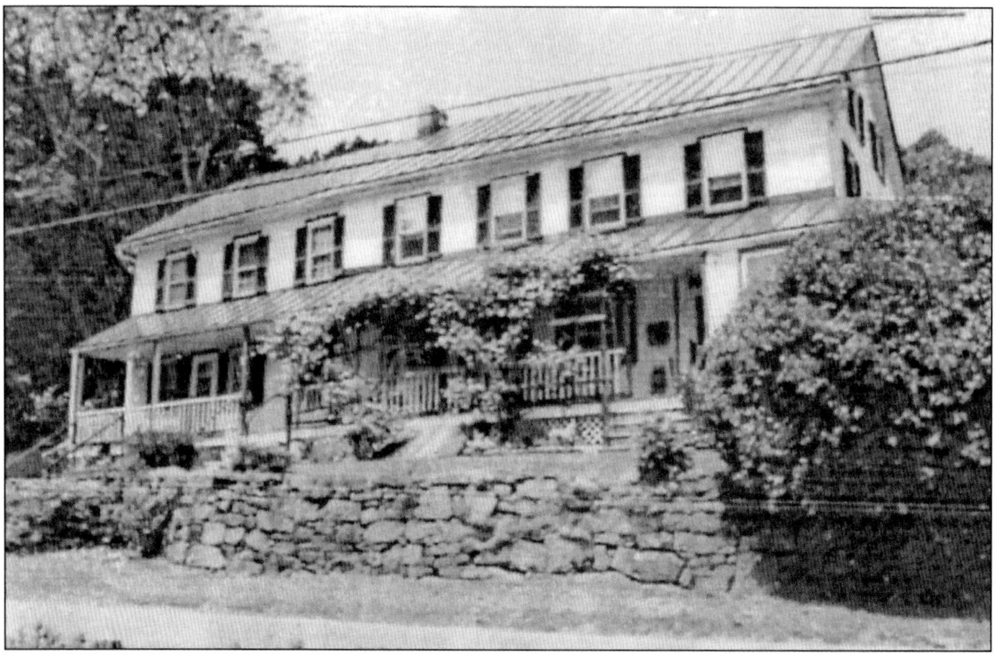

This large residence is located in the upper part of the township, not too far from the village of California. Originally it was a frame house over which stucco was applied in the middle of the 19th century. The house almost doubled in size in 1880 when owner John Dietrich added three bays to the western side of the house. (RT.)

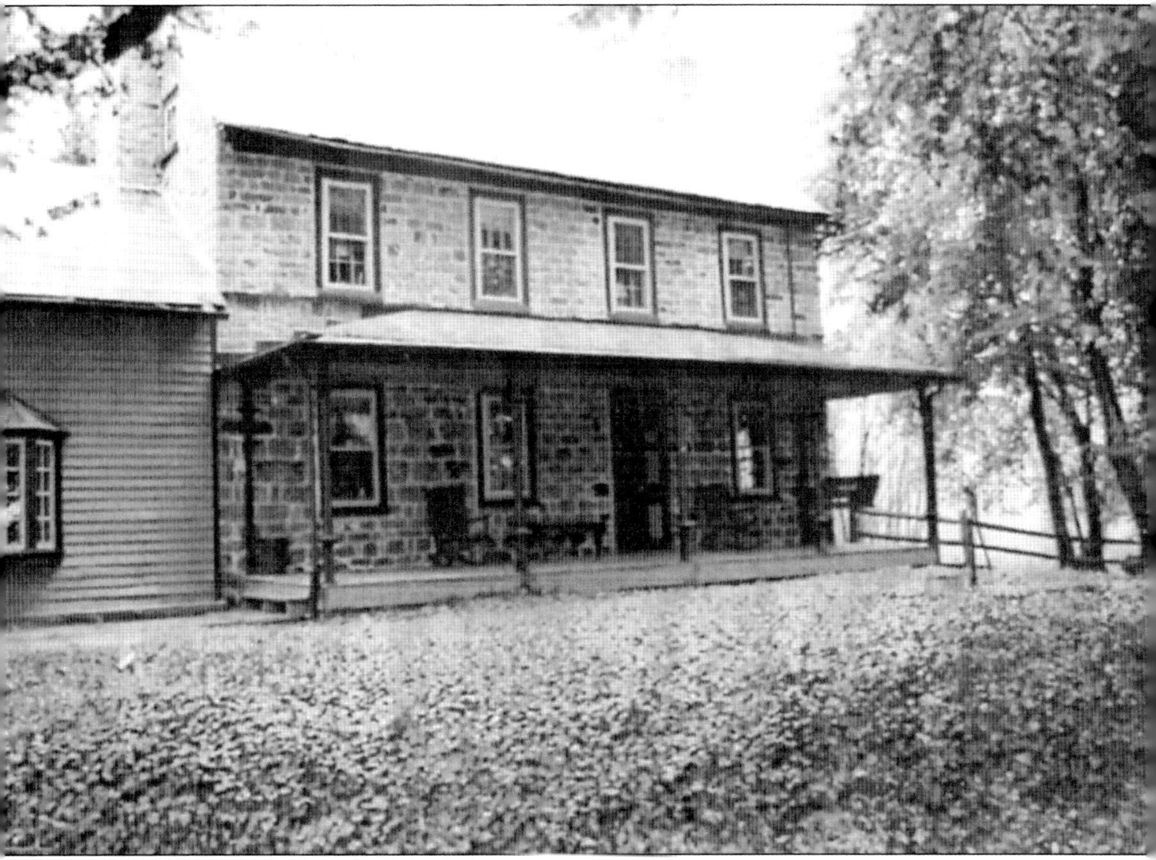

This home near Richlandtown was once the residence of Charles Albert Fechter, a noted actor. Fechter was born in London in 1824, and studied art, theater, and culture in Paris. He made his debut in the Théâtre-Français in 1844 and acted on the French stage until 1860, when he debuted in London. Fechter was wildly successful in England and came to the United States in 1870. He worked at several theaters in New York and Boston and was paid at the rate of $10,000 per year. A quarrel with his employer brought a turn of fortune. In 1874, Fechter set out to form his own theater company on Broadway. At the time, he became acquainted with Lizzie Price, whom he later married. They purchased the above farm, where Fechter intended to retire. He returned to the stage in New York in 1877 but was not successful. He died on the farm on August 5, 1879, and was buried in Philadelphia. (RT.)

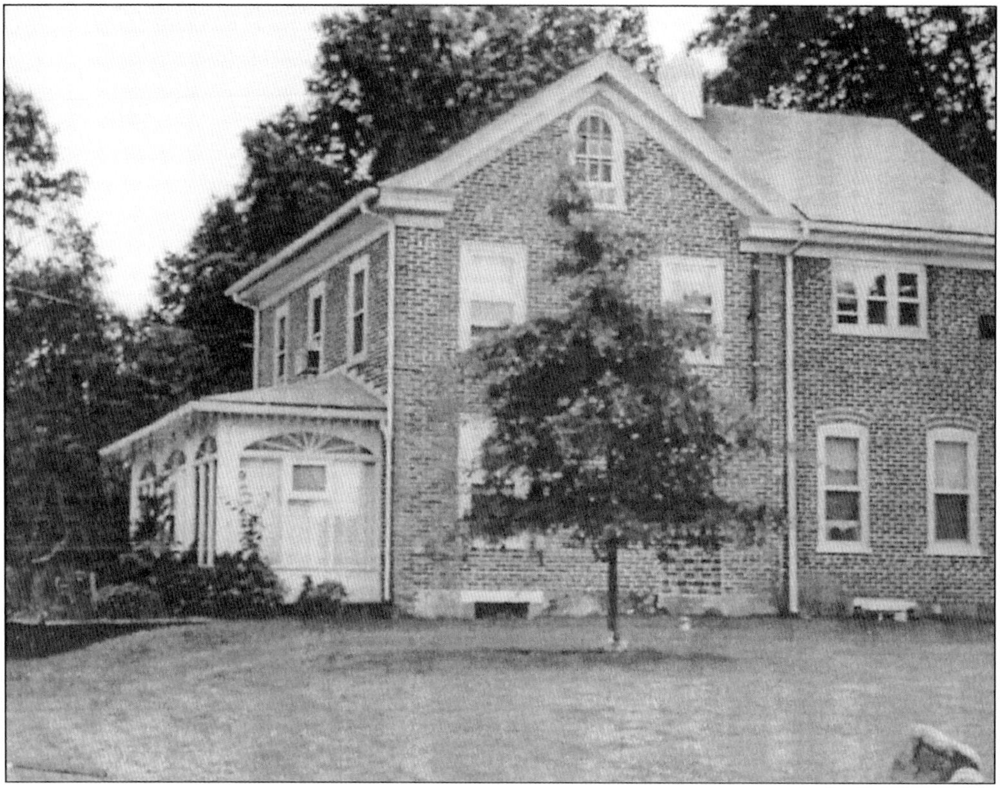

Eli Strawn farmed 96 acres on the Bethlehem Pike, where he built this brick home. Strawn was born in 1822 and married Margaret Penrose. The farm was part of a large tract that belonged to the Penrose family. Later the house passed to Milton Johnson, a dealer of farm implements. (RT.)

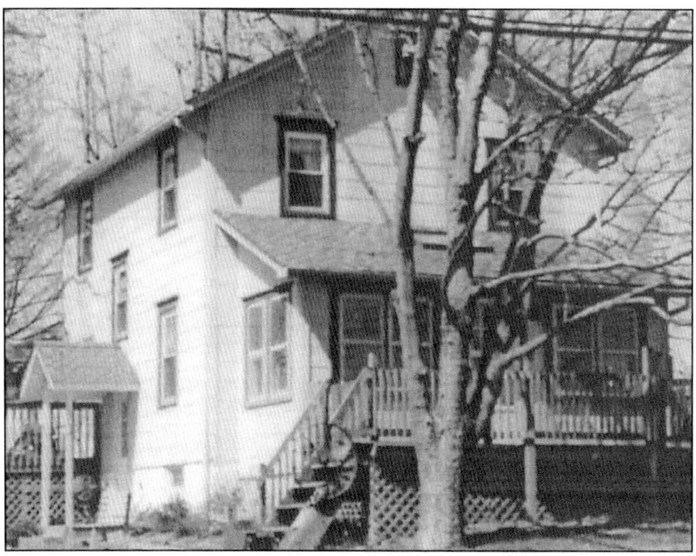

In the 1850s, local residents joined in forming the Quakertown and Sellersville Turnpike Company, which maintained 5 miles of the Bethlehem Pike between the two towns. A tollgate and tollhouse were constructed at the junction of the pike and the road to Trumbauersville. The tollhouse, left, still stands, and the road to Trumbauersville retains the name Tollgate Road. (RT.)

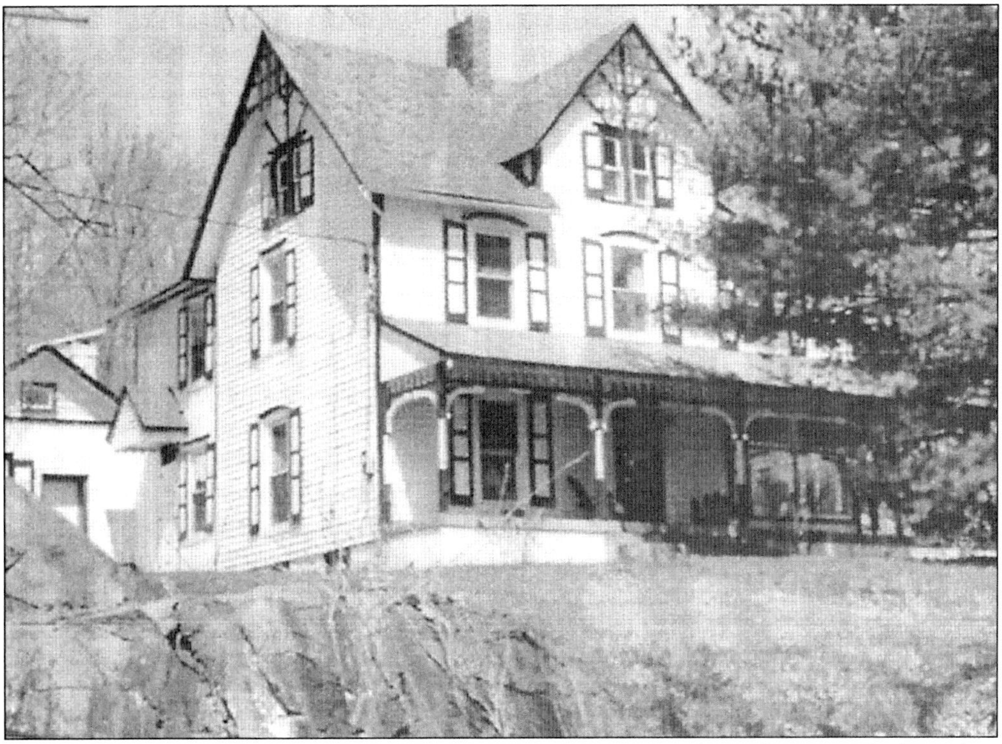

The Felt homestead was a 52-acre farm in the lower part of the township, adjacent to the boundary line with Rockhill. The house is of typical style for a farmhouse that was built in the latter part of the 19th century. The home is sheathed in white clapboard siding and trimmed in green. The windows have shutters, and the porch has fancy scrollwork. (RT.)

The Johnson homestead was on the south side of Pumping Station Road and comprised 150 acres. Hampton Watson Johnson was born on the homestead in 1832 and lived in this house. Johnson was president of the Richlandtown Turnpike Company and a director of the Line Lexington Mutual Fire Insurance Company. He served as a school director for 15 years. (RT.)

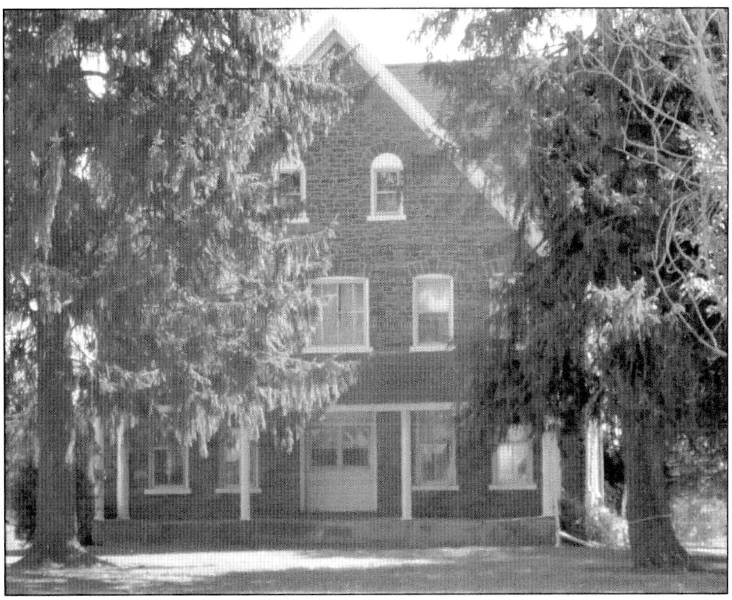

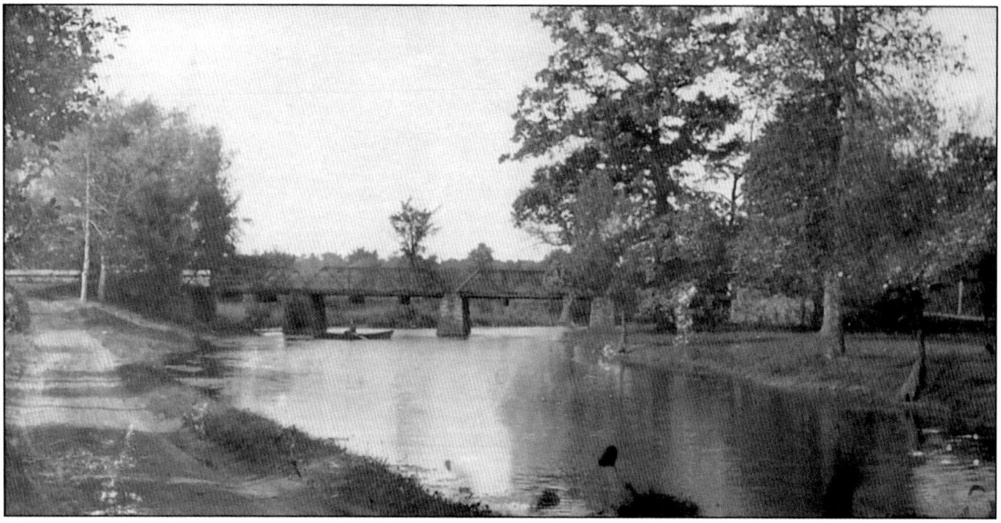

Tohickon Grove, located on the Tohickon Creek between Quakertown and Richlandtown, was a favorite recreation spot. The above image shows the bridge that carried the Tripper across the Tohickon. John Eichner owned and operated the place, which offered picnicking, swimming, and boating. In a later photograph (below), several rowboats are tied to the bank awaiting renters. In the winter, ice-skating was a popular pastime at the grove. The popularity of the grove as a recreation spot waned after World War II, and the area closed. (Both, TM.)

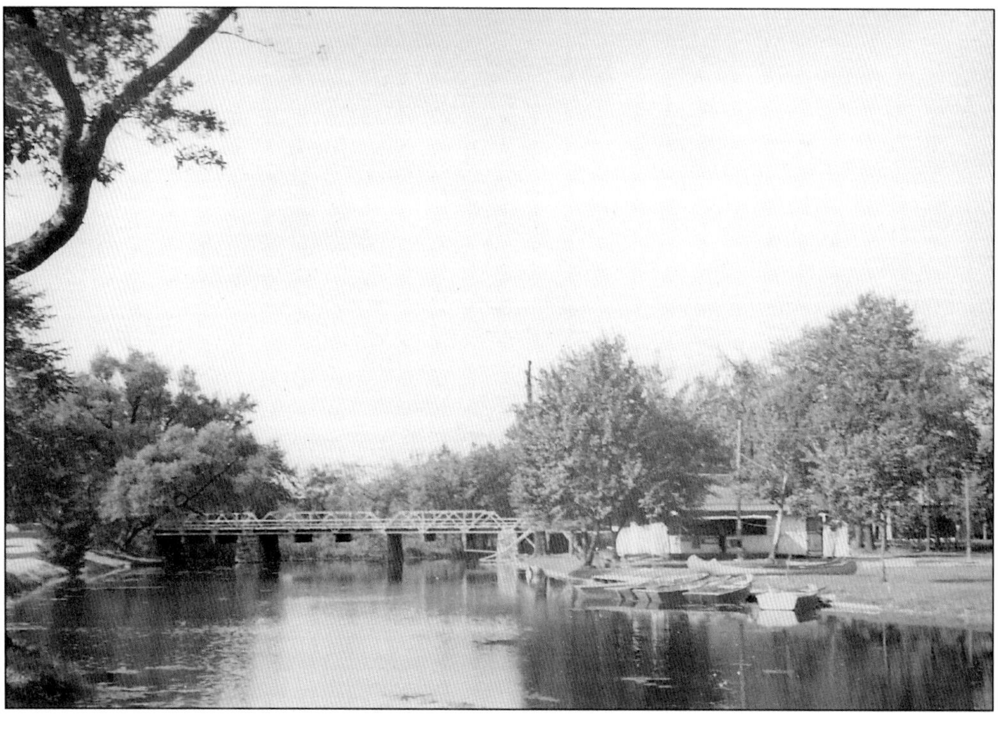

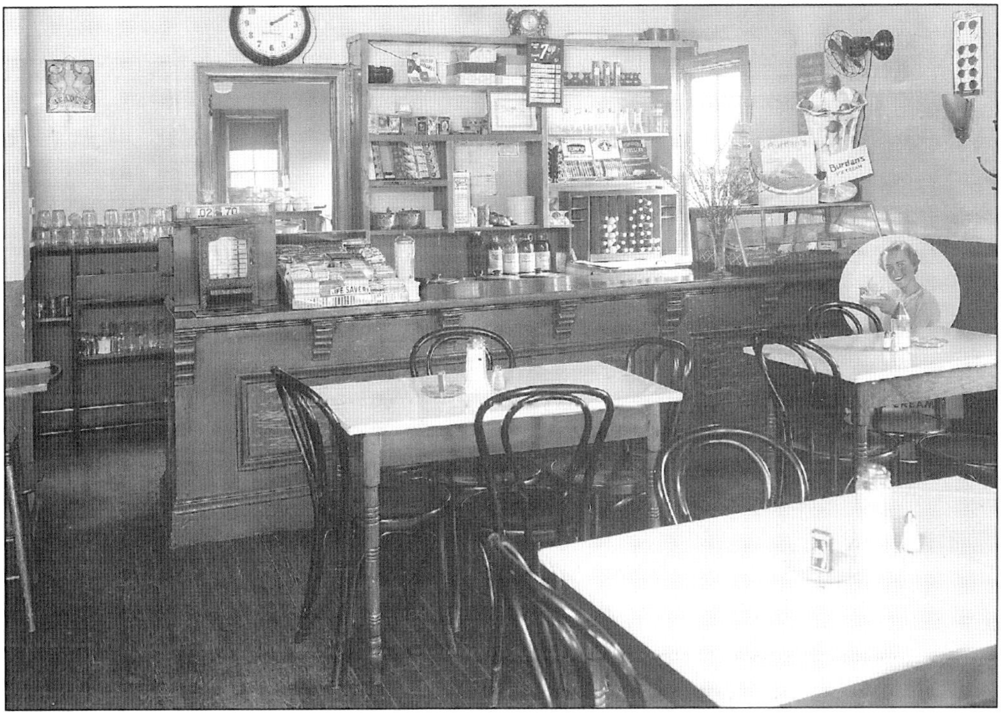

Joseph Meyers was the proprietor of the original Meyers' Restaurant, near Shelly, when this photograph of the interior was taken in the 1930s. The counter displays a tempting array of food and drink, such as Burdan's ice cream, candies, and chewing gum. (GM.)

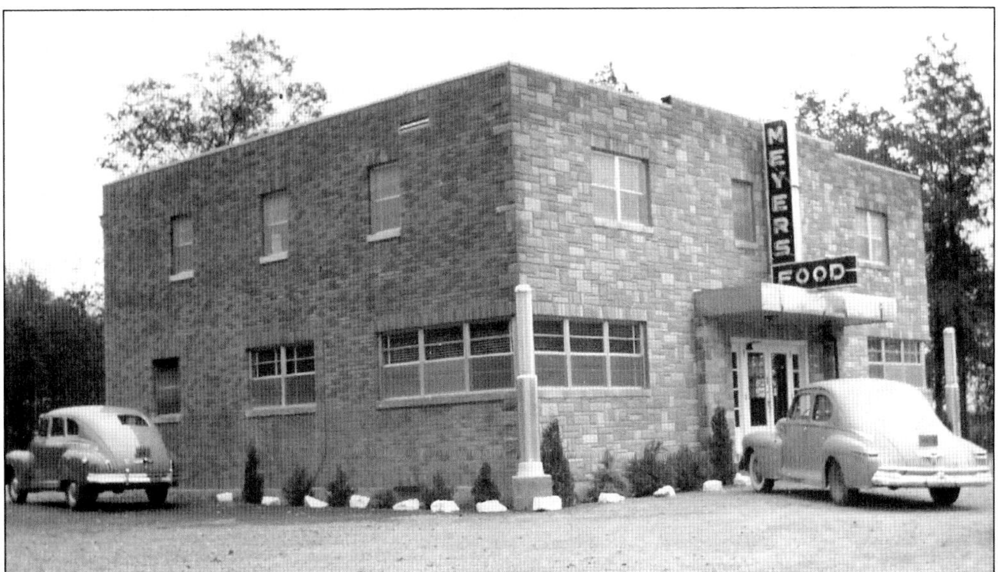

Meyers' Restaurant relocated to new premises on 309, just north of Quakertown, around 1951. A souvenir postcard described the place as "a moderately priced family restaurant with pleasant surroundings." Young members of the families that dined there could win a pin that described them as a "member of the clean plate club" if they ate all of their meal. (GM.)

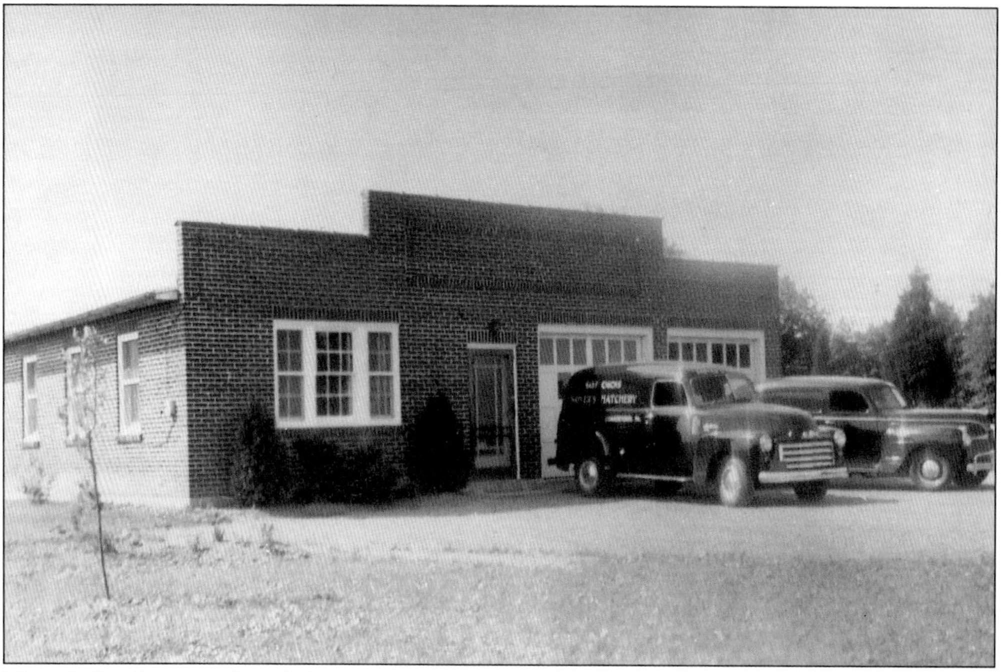

Moyer's Hatchery was founded at its present site on Paletown Road by Ernest Moyer in 1946. The hatchery employs about 30 workers. During the period soon after World War II, its major market was local poultry farms, but the hatchery has adapted to new markets throughout the United States and Canada. There is an emerging interest among local residents in maintaining a small flock of hens for personal use. (IM.)

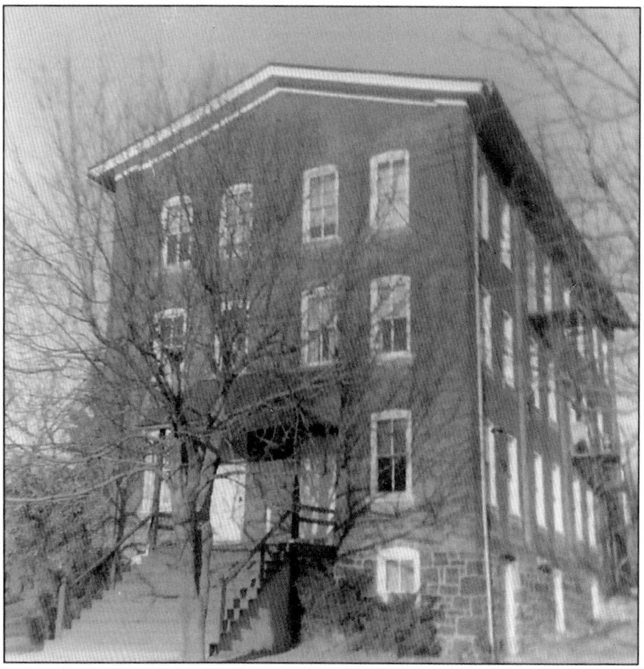

This brick factory, located in Shelly, was typical of the multiple-floor buildings where cigars were manufactured, from the Civil War to the Depression. By the 1930s, cigarettes had replaced cigars as the smoke of choice, and the factories closed. This factory served the congregation of Salem Mennonite Church until it was demolished to make way for the present church building about 1970. (SB.)

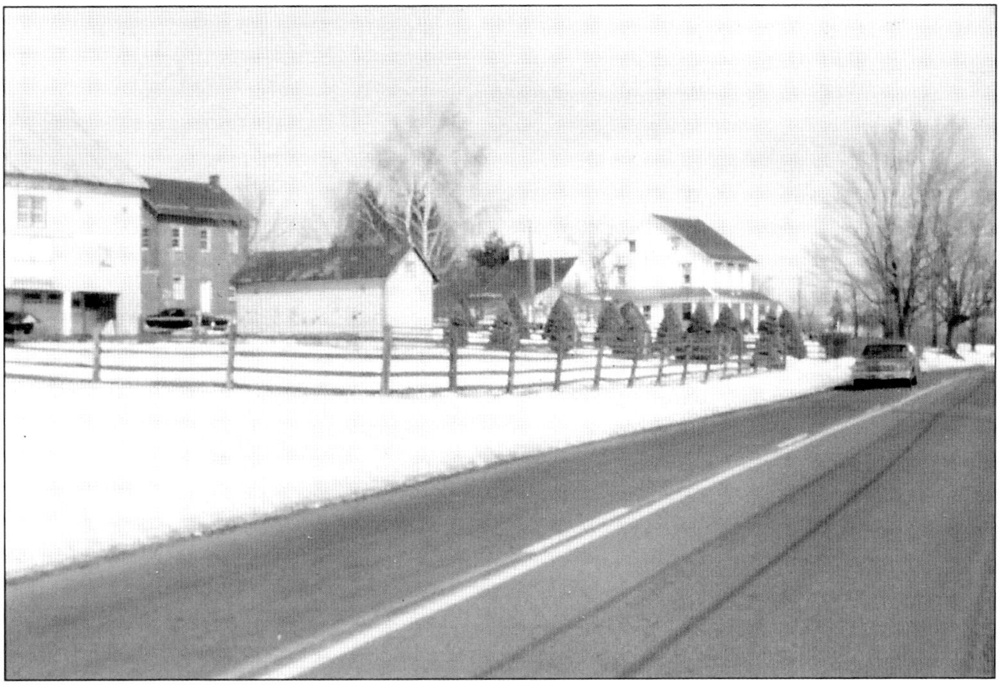

For many years, the Suelke farm was the prominent landmark at the junction of Tollgate Road and Old Bethlehem Pike. The farm had a handsome house, several outbuildings, and a gigantic barn that dominated the property. The farm buildings were razed to make way for housing and a shopping center. (CR.)

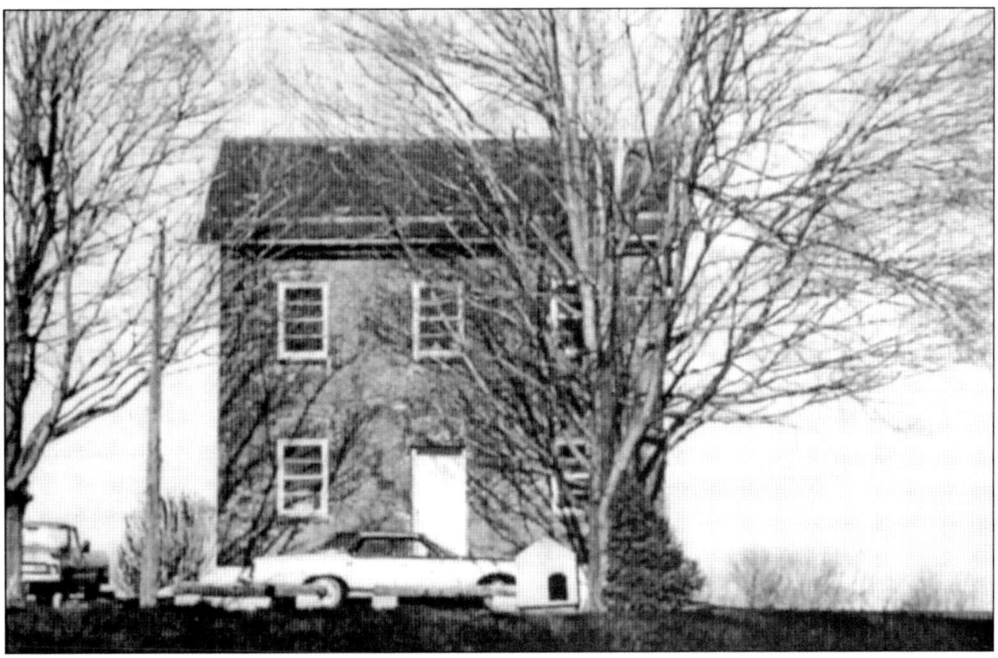

This two-story brick structure was located on the Suelke farm between the family home and the large barn. It was utilized for processing tobacco and manufacturing cigars. Demand for cigars was high in the early 1900s, and many farmers could augment their income by rolling cigars. (CR.)

Consistent with our mission to preserve history on a local level, this book was printed in South Carolina on American-made paper and manufactured entirely in the United States. Products carrying the accredited Forest Stewardship Council (FSC) label are printed on 100 percent FSC-certified paper.

MADE IN THE USA